Other Publications by Sunday A. Aigbe

Theory of Social Involvement: A Case Study in
the Anthropology of Religion, State and Society
(Hardcover 1993, eBook, paperback 2015)

A Template for Life: The Beauty and Expectations of John 3:16
(Hardcover, eBook, paperback 2014)

THEORY *of* PRODUCTIVITY

DISCOVERING AND PUTTING TO
WORK THE IDEAS AND VALUES OF
AMERICAN CULTURE

SUNDAY A. AIGBE

WESTBOW®
PRESS
A DIVISION OF THOMAS NELSON
& ZONDERVAN

WestBow Press books may be ordered through booksellers or by contacting:

WestBow Press
A Division of Thomas Nelson & Zondervan
1663 Liberty Drive
Bloomington, IN 47403
www.westbowpress.com
1 (866) 928-1240

ISBN: 978-1-4908-7576-7 (sc)
ISBN: 978-1-4908-7577-4 (hc)
ISBN: 978-1-4908-7575-0 (e)

Library of Congress Control Number: 2015905677

Print information available on the last page.

WestBow Press rev. date: 04/15/2015

We hold these truths to be self-evident, that all men are created equal, that they are endowed by their Creator with certain unalienable Rights, that among these are Life, Liberty and the pursuit of Happiness.
The Declaration of Independence

We the People of the United States, in Order to form a more perfect Union, establish Justice, insure domestic Tranquility, provide for the common defence, promote the general Welfare, and secure the Blessings of Liberty to ourselves and our Posterity, do ordain and establish this Constitution for the United States of America.
The Constitution of the United States

TABLE OF CONTENTS

LIST OF APPENDICES

CHAPTER 1

LIFE, LIBERTY, HAPPINESS, AND PROPERTY

Admittedly, America has a burgeoning economy. According to the Census Bureau, the Bureau of Labor Statistics, the Bureau of Economic Analysis, and World Bank, America's population was estimated at 320 million in 2014, or 4 percent of the world's population. Yet, in the same year, the country registered a Gross Domestic Product (GDP) of $17.7 trillion or 22 percent of world's GDP. In 2013, the country recorded military spending of $640 billion, or 37 percent of world's military spending for national security and peace and humanitarian missions around the world. During the last 5 years, there have been, on average, 150 million private-sector jobs in the economy, plus another estimated 5 million jobs in the federal government; there are also well over 130 million housing units in the continental United States, to mention a few stats. (See Appendices 1, 6,and 22).

The argument that America is only 4 percent of the world's population but consumes 20 percent of the world's energy is tenuous at best. The argument fails to take into account the amount of energy consumption and the associated costs that go into the production of goods and services that benefit other nations in the form of export commodities, foreign services, and peace and humanitarian missions. Actually, the argument (weak as it is) only reinforces the point that America is a very active and benevolent economy—a beacon of hope to all nations. Thus, America is not only the land of the free and the home of the brave, but also a very active and wealthy nation. It is a country of endless possibilities—that is, provided a person is willing to start from the bottom and work his or her way up the economic ladder. (The opportunities for upward mobility are discussed in more detail later in this book.)

As a great nation, the United States of America is very productive. America is productive partly because it is a nation of immigrants, a historical constant dating back to the pre-Columbian era in the 1490s. Immigration is as American as apple pie, then and now. In the past decades, millions of foreigners entered the United States every year for purposes ranging from casual visits to tourism, education, employment, sports, business, diplomatic relations, and permanent residency. Of these, over 1 million skilled professionals and unskilled workers come to stay as legal, permanent residents. Behind these numbers is the understanding that the immigrants have something to contribute to and gain from American society.

However, studies have shown that the longer it takes an immigrant to adapt to American culture, the less likely that the immigrant will maximize his or her potential to become productive in America. An often overlooked question is, "With dwindling resources, what does it take today for an immigrant to become a productive member of society within a reasonable period of time?" This author is a living example that migration can make a difference for the immigrant as well as for the receiving country. Understanding immigrants, meeting them where they are, and introducing them to American ways of life are critical first steps for the success of immigrants as productive members of American society and for the renewal that each generation of immigrants brings to bear on American culture.

But suppose that we ask, "Why do so many people want to come to America rather than other places?" The number of responses to this question would probably be as high as the number of immigrants who come to America each year. No one person will give a response or responses that will do justice to all of the reasons that so many people want to live in America. However, there is consensus among immigration scholars that the reasons for migration fall into two broad theoretical frameworks—the push factors and the pull factors. According to the push-factors theory, people migrate because of conditions in their home countries—unemployment, human-rights abuses, political persecution, lack of economic opportunities, low-paying jobs, corrupt and inefficient businesses, youth violence, poor living standards, and lack of infrastructures, to name a few. Although these factors explain why people migrate, they do not sufficiently account for why people make America the destination of choice.

According to the pull-factors theory, people migrate to a destination where they can make a better living. That is, the presence of employment opportunities and a relatively better standard of living in a country entices people to want to go to that country. Although this theory partly explains why certain people migrate to America, it still leaves much to be desired. After all, many countries offer great amenities, and people do migrate to those countries—but not to the extent that they migrate to America. Given the choice, most immigrants would rather migrate to America.

Suffice it to say here that the literature on immigration agrees that the bulk of immigrants come to America in search of a better future for themselves and their posterity. The better future includes a decent life, freedom, human rights, hopes and dreams, and better living conditions. They seek a city where they can provide food, clothing, and shelter for themselves and their families, and where they are not afraid but rather encouraged to pursue these goals. At the core of these hopes and dreams is the immediate need for economic opportunity, jobs, and business. Additionally, immigrants want the peace of mind from living in a functioning and stable society, where virtues are rewarded and vices have consequences.

Put differently, people are eternally searching for what the cultural geniuses and European philosophers of the 17th and 18th centuries expressed in their writings—namely, life, liberty, happiness, and property. Yes, people stream to America because of its commitment to the inalienable human rights that the founders of this nation variably articulated in the Declaration of Independence: life, liberty, and the pursuit of happiness. These fundamental rights and their evolving expressions in all aspects of the American society personify the genius of American culture.

The purpose of this book is to explore the genius (ideas and values) of American culture and to identify ways that young and middle-class Americans—as well as immigrants—can put this genius to work in order to be productive. The book draws on my research and experience as a student, educator, researcher, author, entrepreneur, and human-services employee in the public and private sectors in identifying key lessons learned along the way in my sojourn in Africa and in the United States. The approach is a symbiotic analysis of research data and my experiences as a participant/observer of American culture in the last 33 years. The goal is to provide young and middle-class Americans and immigrants with the evidence-based knowledge and skills needed to become productive members of the American society (or any society, for that matter) within a reasonable period of time. We begin by exploring what it means to be a productive person in a culture of productivity, followed by an examination of the habits that are characteristic of productive people (Chapter 2).

In the next three chapters, we will examine the economic factors that make America so productive: jobs as the basic mechanism for productivity, and a prescribed way of making an honest living (Chapter 3); and business as a mechanism for doubling down on productivity en route to wealth creation (Chapters 4 and 5). Together, these elements—people, jobs, and business—form the mechanisms of productivity of American culture, or the means of production of the economy.

What is it that makes America tick? The short answer is a lot. The long answers are the subjects of the next four chapters: the quest for a more perfect Union (Chapter 6); appreciation for diversity in a big tent called America (Chapter 7); the desire and effort for a fair law and order for all (Chapter 8); and the acceptance of life (and productivity) as good but not always easy and fair (Chapter 9). Together these themes form the hardware of American culture.

The remainder of the book explores the software that makes the culture run smoothly: the motivating power of gratitude (Chapter 10); the soothing role of apology (Chapter 11); and the pursuit of health and happiness with cautious optimism (Chapter 12). These intangible elements exemplify the ties that bind and the values that lubricate the people and the machineries of American culture.

The book concludes with a reflection on the observation that, as a nation of laws, America is a nation of rights, rules, responsibilities, and rewards. Together, these principles or civic duties account in large part for a civilized citizenry, civil society, and the wealth of a nation (Chapter 13).

CHAPTER 2

LEARNING THE ROPES: THREE HABITS OF PRODUCTIVE PEOPLE

The goal of this chapter is to lay the foundations for constructing a theory of productivity and for analyzing the elements thereof. All books make assumptions; this book is no exception. Thus, the first two sections of this chapter provide a brief cultural context for understanding my sojourn experiences in Africa and in America, and how the cultural context and subsequent experiences shape the symbiotic approach adopted in this book.

Growing Up in Africa

I was honored to live in many different places in Africa when I was growing up and during my school years. As an adult, I have also lived in many different places in America the past 30 years. All of the places have one thing in common—fascination with my name or names. My christened name is Sunday. The name was given to me at birth by the missionaries who brought Christianity and modern ways to my village in Africa.

Prior to the coming of Western countries, almost everyone in my part of Africa had two names—one name from their father's side and the other name from their mother's side of the extended family. With the coming of the missionaries, a person would basically have two or three names—one from the missionaries or colonial officers and teachers, a second name from the father's side, and a third name from the mother's side of the extended family. The name from the mother's side would become optional and was seldom used. The name from the father's side was referred to as the vernacular name and was usually the middle name. The missionary name was referred to as the first name. It was usually the name everyone would call that person, partly because it was easier for the Westerners to pronounce and remember.

In keeping with tradition, vernacular or middle names are carefully constructed to reflect the circumstances leading to or surrounding the birth of a child. Some names are a reflection of the past, while others focus on the present or the future, or a little bit of the past, present, and future. But they are meant to have meaning, a purpose, and a message. So there was great expectation regarding what name my father would give me that would summarize the drama of my birth and the fire accident that resulted in my loss of right hand. Would the name articulate the family history and experience while at the same time not assign blame? What name would reflect my parents' hopes and dreams for me and especially my mother, who had gone through a lot in her life and now in the young and innocent life of her healthy and bouncing baby boy?

After all of the cooking had been completed, the guests welcomed and seated, and the meals set, came the climax of the occasion—the announcing of the name. My father, following meticulously prescribed rituals, announced my name in well over 44 syllables. Transliteration: Life goes on! Life goes on! Life goes on! The short version of it is Agbonasebhasele. Can you say that? Okay, just call me Sunday.

My father was a great farmer, an herbalist, and a divination specialist. I followed my father time and again to the forests to collect herbs, and then watched him prepare the herbs and treat people with them. He used the herbs to treat and cure people of all kinds of ailments, including mental health issues, infertility, and stomach ulcers.

The healed patients expressed gratitude to my father with all sorts of gifts, food, money, chicken, and goats, to name just a few. My father sold these gratuities to pay the fees and buy books and uniforms for my siblings and me so that we could go to school. He also harvested and sold kola nuts and cocoa nuts to supplement his income from herbal practice. He used the proceeds to defray the costs of our education. The women and extended family members also chimed in with their share of labor and proceeds from petty trading in agricultural produce such as cassavas, coco yams, yams, plantains, vegetables, and fruit. For our part, we would do odd jobs, such as pulling weeds on farms and hunting rabbits and snails for sale to come up with additional money to make up for the needed money for school. That is how we got through grade schools in those days.

Although my parents were not literate by Western education standards, they were very hardworking, industrious, economical, perceptive, and eternally loving. They made sure that we went to school so that we could have good education. My parents provided my siblings and me with a dose of spirituality and moral upbringing. They made sure that we went to church every Sunday, especially my mother, who rarely missed Sunday worship. Above all, they made sure that we were always safe and healthy.

My childhood was full of fun, love, and frugalities. My siblings and I would go to the farm to help with manual labor. We would bring fruits, vegetables, and other produce home for happy meals in the evening. There were many obstacles to overcome when I was growing up, from my disabilities to my obsession for safety and security. I always found a way or a resource to solve a problem and, looking back, I always wondered how I managed to put the situation behind me or get something good out of a hopeless situation. I then realized that, no matter the opportunities and challenges, life always goes on. My journeys to college in Africa and then graduate school in America are cases in point.

Going (or Coming) to America

Yes, I had a loving upbringing under the watchful eyes of my parents, extended family members, villagers, teachers, and missionaries and preachers. Life was fun, with opportunities, but also full of challenges and youthful restlessness. The restlessness grew out of my ambition for knowledge, opportunity, and a better life—a life that was defined not so much in terms of material acquisition (although there is nothing wrong with that), but rather by ambition for a better life that could be defined in terms of purpose and meaning in life here on earth. My ambition for meaning and purpose in life further fueled my restlessness, which reinforced my ambition. The result of the quest was constant exploration and travel that took me many places. I had never seen some of the places and people before and never saw them again. There were a few places and people that made an impact on me. I returned to these places for a closer look, and then moved on. In essence, the quest for opportunities and the overcoming of challenges during my youthful life can be defined by three C's – Community, Country, and Continent.

My teenage years in the community revolved around a wide variety of peer activities in and around the cluster of villages that constituted the town of Ekpoma. We would go hunting and took pride in our kill. During the festival months, we went places from one village to another with masquerade dance. We would split the proceeds and have money for school items, daily provisions, and offering in church. Another source of revenue was doing menial jobs such as helping to do weeding for the villagers for modest pay. That is, after we returned from helping our parents with farm work. We competed to see who would do the most weeding and hence make the most money. We learned to economize and manage money because we had no idea where and when the next job or money was going to come from.

There were also the opportunities to go to school and work with the missionaries. I was lucky to have been born when Western medicine had made inroads in Africa. I was vaccinated and inoculated against many diseases that had claimed so many lives when I was growing up. The missionary grade school in my village afforded me the opportunity to learn how to read and write very early in life, laying the foundation for my interest in reading and study, almost to the point of obsession. We realized the importance of education, both as a way to survive the harsh reality of life in Africa in the 1950s and 1960s, but also as a key to a better future for us, our parents, and posterity.

Then there were the positive outcomes of going to school. A teenager was the envy of the village if he or she could serve as a record-keeper in family meetings or as an interpreter for missionaries, preachers and Western businesspeople. It was a great honor to be able to read and speak English. Such a person was next in line to White people in cleanliness, godliness, education, job opportunity, and possibly going to post-secondary school or even college. The motivations and incentives were so great that school was almost a magnet for my generation.

Another game in town was church. The only school in my village was missionary school. Although a person did not have to go a particular missionary church in order to go to that church's school, students were highly encouraged to go to church of some sort. But there were only two churches in my immediate village and several churches in the surrounding villages. I have been told that I was a bit stubborn and so grew up in at least two villages—that of my parents and the village of my maternal ground parents. So I actually attended two different elementary schools and several different churches. I had two different sets of school bags (similar to backpacks). The experience might partly explain why I like exploration and going places. From the very beginning, I have loved and admired diversity and still do till this day.

There were many challenges along the way. There was never enough of anything, so I had to constantly compete for parental attention, financial resources, food, shelter and even a spot to sleep on in a crowded room. People were always coming and going from one village or another, many seeking help for resources from my parents, even though our limited resources were not enough for my siblings and me in the first place. I learned early on in life that no matter your condition, there is always a person who is worse off and in more dire need than you. My parents were very generous and would never turn anyone away.

Thus, at the community level, I navigated villages and jungles. I was well indoctrinated in Esan tribal culture and values. At the country level, I navigated cities and tribes. I became knowledgeable about Nigerian culture and values. At the continental level, I navigated countries and major regions. I was exposed to a wide variety of African cultures, traditions, customs, housing structures, community landscapes, religious worships, taboos, and prohibitions. One variable that was constant in all of these explorations, encounters, and experiences was the American factor. By the time I graduated with a Bachelor's degree, I had spent more time with American missionaries and businesspeople in school, at church, business, and social settings than I had spent with any other social group, including my parents. In fact, I knew quite a lot about America—second only to my knowledge of African culture, traditions, and values. Or so I thought until I landed in the United States, one year after my undergraduate work in Togo.

It was cold a day when I landed in America at O'Hare International Airport in Chicago, by way of Europe. I do not recall whether it was late fall or early winter. I do recall that it was cold at the airport. But the wonders of the airport, the lights, the conveyor belts, the escalators, the elevators, and the restrooms, to name just a few, blew my mind and the cold away. I felt as if I was in some kind of heaven. With the jet lag, loss of sleep, dreaming about going to overseas, and the hard work preparing for the trip, I lost track of time. Then I took a short flight to Springfield, Missouri, where I would make my home for the next two years, first to get a prosthesis for my right hand and, later, to enroll in graduate studies.

I recall that it snowed in Springfield upon my arrival. I had seen a little bit of snow in Europe but had never seen this amount of snow before—snow, snow, snow everywhere! I recall wondering what had happened to the houses and asked if that amount of snow was usual or unusual. I finally crashed at the hotel. When I woke up a day or two later, the sun was shining and the snow had melted considerably. I stepped outside to nearby convenience stores and other places around the block, and was not disappointed. It was just what I had expected. After all, I had been reading *Time* magazine, *Christianity Today*, *US News and World Report*, and other monthly and weekly magazines from cover to cover for several years now.

To my amazement, Springfield was filled with schools and churches, department stores, hotels, grocery stores, hospitals, and clinics, especially, compared to where I had come from. Yet people would say that Springfield was a small city, adding "You ain't seen nothin' yet." And I would smile and say to myself: "America, here I come!"

My first impression of Americans in America wasn't without its surprises, though. What surprised me the most, at least initially, was how nice and how polite the Americans were. I had met and studied under the tutelage of Americans. I always thought they were taught to be nice to us and that they worked hard to show examples of what was expected of us. I was very impressed to observe that they always said thank you for big and for little things, such as opening the door or pulling a chair back for them to sit down. They always said "I'm sorry" and sincerely apologized for little things such as bumping into a person in the hallway.

Although I was raised to be appreciative and to admit when I was wrong, most of the time we just took expressing gratitude or offering an apology for granted. In fact, in many instances it would be considered a sign of weakness. So it was a culture shock to me to actually observe the value that Americans place on such habits as apology and appreciation. Thus began a journey of lessons learned and many more lessons that followed over the years.

Put differently, I was already "into" America before coming to America. It was a journey of 5,000 miles that began with one little step in an African village or villages. There were many hills along the way. Each hill presented another hill to climb. Each hill brought its sets of challenges and opportunities. My determination, in one word, was "Try." My journey of three C's, which spanned communities, countries, and continents, was guided by a set of principles that can be summed up in the following iteration:

> My best I'll always try
> If I try I know I'll succeed
> If I fail, I'll know I tried!

Throughout the trial and error, and successes and failures along the way, I would always remind myself that at the end of the day life would always go on. And life has always gone on, especially in learning the habits that are characteristic of productive Americans. These habits are the subject matter of the reminder of this chapter.

Learning the Ropes

My first few years in America were mostly devoted to learning the ropes—that is, learning about the people and culture of America. Those few critical years made a fundamental difference in my ability to navigate myriad social and cultural systems while attempting to decode a body of spoken and unspoken languages. An understanding of these verbal and nonverbal clues was critical to understanding American people and culture. Years later, during my graduate studies and postgraduate research, I discovered that my experience was not unique.

One observation that most immigrants agree on is that America is indeed a rich and wealthy nation, compared to countries that immigrants are coming from. One indicator of America's rich culture is the huge number of people, called the Middle Class, who are productive and, in effect, successful Americans by any measure—education, employment, family, property, leisure, and standard of living. An extension of this observation is that these people have certain habits that appear to be inherent in their personality and permeate their lifestyles and aspirations. In the following sections of this chapter, we will identify and explore these habits that are characteristic of productive people in America.

The 3 W's of Productive People

Upon my arrival in the United States, in keeping with my habits, I read a lot of books about being productive in America. I had a million conversations almost anywhere with anyone who would pay attention to me regarding what it takes to be successful in America. One of the first lessons I learned was the connection between employment and productivity in America. I learned that it is not enough to go to school and get a job if a person wants to experience upward mobility in his or her career. For a person to enhance his or her social economic status, the person needs to adopt a lifestyle that is consistent in principles and practice. That is, a person must consistently do the following five things:

Work hard
Save money
Live in an older, less expensive home
Drive a used car
Be frugal

Over time, I attended lectures, seminars, and church programs—some designed for immigrants, others open to the general public. I would later be introduced to and read many books on productivity. One of these books, "The Seven Habits of Highly Effective People" by Stephen R. Covey, stood out. The book identified and discussed the following seven habits of highly effective people:

> Habit 1: Be Proactive
> Habit 2: Begin with the end in mind
> Habit 3: Put first things first
> Habit 4: Think win/win
> Habit 5: Seek first to understand, then to be understood
> Habit 6: Synergize
> Habit 7: Sharpen the saw

The lessons learned from these interactive experiences and readings served me well over the years by helping me to rediscover the values of self-reliance, human interconnectedness, and continuous improvement/learning I learned in Africa.

Overall, my first impression was that what you know was very important. Productive Americans and immigrants alike appeared to know a lot of things as evidenced by the sheer volume of "expert" knowledge in the area in which they were productive. It became apparent over time that what a person knows can only take him or her so far. I would soon be introduced to the adage "It's not *what* you know, but *who* you know." Consider the following networking quotes:

> The way of the world is meeting people through other people. Robert Kerrigan

It's not what you know but who you know that makes the difference. Anonymous

It isn't just what you know, and it isn't just who you know. It's actually who you know, who knows you, and what you do for a living. Bob Burg

More business decisions occur over lunch and dinner than at any other time, yet no MBA courses are given on the subject. Peter Drucker

Informal conversation is probably the oldest mechanism by which opinions on products and brands are developed, expressed, and spread. Johan Arndt

It's all about people. It's about networking and being nice to people and not burning any bridges. Mike Davidson

Position yourself as a center of influence—the one who knows the movers and shakers. People will respond to that, and you'll soon become what you project. Bob Burg

The successful networkers I know, the ones receiving tons of referrals and feeling truly happy about themselves, continually put the other person's needs ahead of their own. Bob Burg

Sometimes It's Not What You Know But Who You Know That Matters. Terry Frerker

I suppose these people and many others make these assertions based on their experiences. From my observations, there is an element of truth in the statement that "it's not just what you know, but who you know" in order to be successful these days. But the statement is only half true. It implies the supremacy of who you know over what you know. I suppose there are those who would probably reverse the order based on their experience and assert the supremacy of what you know over who you know. Again, based on my observations, the truth is "who you know" is just as important as "what you know," and vice versa. Furthermore, I have learned both in Africa and America that "where you know" is equally as important as who you know and what you know.

From the foregoing and from the literature on the habits of successful people, it appears that productive people in America and in most countries for that matter share many of the same habits. These habits tend to fall into the three domains of what we might call, for lack of better terms, the 3 W's of productive people. As noted above, the 3 W's are What, Who, and Where. That is, productive people share the following three habits:

> What you know
> Who you know
> Where you know

Put another way, productive people exhibit a lifestyle that articulates the following three variables:

> They know something
> They know people
> They know places

In effect, to be productive in America, you need to know something, people, and places. Productive people are aware of the power of knowledge, people, and space to be productive. Education and networking are just about as important to productive people as where they are educated and who they network with in order to position themselves for productivity and to stay competitive.

Productive People Know Something

In Africa I learned from both the Americans and Africans that education is a critical key to leading a productive life. When I arrived in the United States, this lesson was reinforced by the value that Americans place on education. This is evident from the access to free universal education for all citizens and immigrants from Kindergarten through the 12th grade. Many graduate and continue on to a two- or four-year college/ university. Others pursue professional studies and/or graduate education beyond the four-year college. The number of grade schools, colleges, and universities, as well vocational schools, in America is mind boggling, compared to other nations.

According to the US Department of Education, National Center for Education Statistics (http://nces.ed.gov), in 2012, a total of 4.7 million degrees and certificates were awarded to graduates in various disciplines, from Art History to Physics to Zoology. In 2014, a total of 21 million Americans were enrolled in or attending 4,726 degree-granting private and public colleges and universities in America, plus another unspecified number of enrollment in 2,527 non-degree, post-secondary and adult continuing education institutions. A total of 55 million Americans were enrolled in or attending 129,189 public and private elementary and secondary schools in 13,576 schools districts across America.

All these institutions of learning provide both knowledge and the skills for learning in preparation for careers in the public, private, or nonprofit sectors. The faculty and students have a common goal—productivity. Educators have as their overarching goal the contributions that graduates will make to society. With a decent education, the graduates are, in effect, positioned to make a decent living through employment and business opportunities. Productive people are aware of these trends and take advantage of the opportunities offered by these institutions.

A fundamental habit of productive people is their insatiable quest for knowledge as a source of power. They know what they know and also know what they don't know. They are very aware that knowledge is power. They acquire knowledge about a discipline, a career, or a business, not for the sake of knowledge about that discipline as an end, but through formal education and vocational training as a means to an end—productivity and success in their chosen field or line of business.

Knowledge is Power

There is general consensus that knowledge is power, especially when that knowledge is put to use through entrepreneurship, employment, business, invention, and research and development. What you know is empowering. With knowledge, you have a variety of options related to the career you want to pursue, where you want to pursue that career, and when. To get an education is, in this regard, to empower yourself. To empower yourself is to chart a course for productivity and, in effect, success.

One measure of what you know is education. The role of education in developing the mind and body and eventually in cultivating a productive personality has been well recognized from time immemorial. Consider the following remarks from the Quotations Page (www.quotationspage.com):

> You don't need fancy highbrow traditions or money to really learn. You just need people with the desire to better themselves. **Adam Cooper and Bill Collage**, *Accepted, 2006*

> A well-informed mind is the best security against the contagion of folly and of vice. The vacant mind is ever on the watch for relief, and ready to plunge into error, to escape from the languor of idleness. **Ann Radcliffe (1764 – 1823)**, *The Mysteries of Udolpho, 1764*

> Education is the best provision for old age. **Aristotle (384 BC – 322 BC)**, *from Diogenes Laertius, Lives of Eminent Philosophers*

> It is the mark of an educated mind to be able to entertain a thought without accepting it. **Aristotle (384 BC – 322 BC)**

> Education is what survives when what has been learned has been forgotten. **B. F. Skinner (1904 – 1990)**, *New Scientist, May 21, 1964*

> The strength of the United States is not the gold at Fort Knox or the weapons of mass destruction that we have, but the sum total of the education

and the character of our people. **Claiborne Pell (1918 –)**

Everyone has a right to a university degree in America, even if it's in Hamburger Technology. **Clive James**

The foundation of every state is the education of its youth. **Diogenes Laertius**

Education begins a gentleman, conversation completes him. **Dr. Thomas Fuller (1654 – 1734)**, *Gnomologia, 1732*

Only the educated are free. **Epictetus (55 AD – 135 AD)**, *Discourses*

Education has for its object the formation of character. **Herbert Spencer (1820 – 1903)**

Next in importance to freedom and justice is popular education, without which neither freedom nor justice can be permanently maintained. **James A. Garfield (1831 – 1881)**, *July 12, 1880*

That's what college is for—getting as many bad decisions as possible out of the way before you're forced into the real world. I keep a checklist of 'em on the wall in my room. **Jeph Jacques**, *Questionable Content, 01-04-07*

Education, as a good indicator of what you know, comes in many ways—some formal, others informal. Formal education consists of a course of study that leads to a certificate, diploma, degree, or a license. Grade schools, colleges, and universities fall into this category. Informal schools consist of vocational and technical schools that teach specific skills for specific vocations, such as Cosmetics, Medical Transcribing, and Laboratory Technicians, to name a few. Additionally, there are apprentice programs that are designed for learning by doing. These are on-the-job training and are usually offered by and in private shops, such as auto mechanics, barbers, and florists.

The Commencement Concept

The concept of graduation as a commencement is unique to the American educational experiment. In many countries, the completion of a course of study, especially in formal education, culminates in graduation. Formal education in this context is perceived of as a long journey that has come to an end. In effect, graduation is celebrated as a coronation. The unintended message is that the arduous work is over. The educated person can now relax and enjoy the fruits of his or her labor.

For Americans and the American system of education, graduation is seen as both an end and a beginning. Graduation is an end to a prescribed course of study leading to a diploma, certificate, or degree, or a combination thereof. The diploma is validation that the student has successfully completed all the required and recommended courses in the degree program and has met any and all applicable requirements. Graduation is seen as a celebration of this important accomplishment. However, graduation is generally called a commencement because it also signifies a new beginning. It is the beginning of the actual work of your career—of getting a job and becoming a productive member of society.

The diploma and the transcript are a license to get a job in your chosen field of endeavor. For some disciplines, such as law, you'll still have to study and pass an examination to get a license to practice, following graduation from the law school. In medicine, a residency is required upon graduation from medical school. No additional requirements are required in most disciplines (Sociology, Anthropology, History, Chemistry, Mathematics, etc.) to enter the workforce after graduation.

Tangible and Intangible Gains

An important aspect of education that is critical to a person's productivity in America is that it bestows on a person both tangible and intangible gains. These gains pave the way to personal successes. Over time, these personal successes lead to productivity at the individual and society levels. Intellectual property is one example of intangible gains from education. The knowledge and skills that a person acquires through education will eternally serve him well as a gift that keeps on giving.

Generally, higher education as tangible gains translates to open doors to many opportunities with higher earnings. The higher your level of education, the higher the likelihood that you will find a job that pays a higher salary. The more money you make from employment, the higher the likelihood that you can afford to pay higher rent or a higher mortgage to be able to live in a stable and decent community. Over time, the equity on your home can be a source of income or capital for even more opportunities, such as further education, starting a business, and providing a decent education for posterity.

Good as the foregoing outcomes sound, productivity starts with what you know. Productive people know something. They possess knowledge of something that they do very well as a hobby or a career. Admittedly, education is only one variable relative to what it takes to be productive. Productive people also know other people in order to translate what they know into production machinery.

Productive People Know People

Productive people know something, but they also are aware of who they know. They value the relationships they have with other people. Productive people are generally people persons. They love networking and meeting people. They make great connections and network a significant amount. They know the power of knowing people and tap into that power and use it to their advantage.

One important byproduct of education and the quest for knowledge is the capacity to put a person in touch with many people from all different walks of life. Formal education in America, in particular, opens doors to meeting people from different countries, cultures, disciplines, and foci. Productive people recognize that people are their powerbase. They usually begin building this powerbase from their years in school. They keep friends from previous schools and make new ones from their current school. They stay in touch with friends and see them as potential employees, employers, and/or customers sometime along the way in the future. This wisdom is captured in the following observations:

> For success, and especially to obtain employment, one's knowledge and skills are less

useful and less important than one's network of personal contacts. **1951**, G. P. Bush and L. H. Hattery, "Federal Recruitment of Junior Engineers," *Science*, vol. 114, no. 2966, p. 456.

Eighty-four students referred to political influence as a disadvantage of federal employment with such remarks as, "There are too many political connections necessary ... **it's not what you know but who you know**—in spite of apparent merit systems." **1993**, Heidi Gruber, "Cross film earns recognition in Hollywood," *Ellensburg Daily Record*, 25 Aug. (retrieved 19 June 2009)

"In Hollywood, **it's not what you know but who you know**," said Cross, who added that the awards ceremony was the perfect place to make connections. **2008**, Natasha Davies, *Webc@m Girl*, ISBN 9780973584042, p. 53

Productive people know that to get a job they'll need people for a reference or as an employer. They know that to start, build, and sustain a business, they'll need people as investors and as customers. They see networking as an important element in their quest for success in their endeavor. Networking is good indicator of the depth and scope of who they know. Networking can be formal or informal; but networking must retain element of quality interaction to make a difference.

Formal and Informal Networking

Knowing people involves meeting them in many different places under many different circumstances. The motivations for networking are different for different people. And there are many different types of networking, which fall into the following two broad categories of networking—unstructured networking and structured networking. Unstructured networking, also called informal networking, consists of social events and meetings that are loosely organized. Participants do not necessarily have a common interest. These meetings range from running into a person in an elevator, hallway, or restroom to acquaintances at training, fundraisers, or town hall meetings. Some of these acquaintances are short in duration, but usually long enough to strike up a friendship or exchange contact information. A series of unstructured meetings can often lead to common interests and lasting friendships. The key is to learn and share something new about each other at each impromptu meeting or networking event.

Structured networking, also called formal networking, consists of formal connections through associations, business organizations, and schools, to name just a few. This type of networking is more enduring in nature and produces lasting personal friendships or business associates. The key here is to build trust and mutual respect for each other over time. The reward can be direct (e.g., land a job with him or her) or indirect (e.g., referral to a hiring opportunity).

Quality Networking: Who You Know Who Knows You

Productive people know that who they know is only one part of the networking equation. Quality networking is a two-way street. Productive people are fully aware of this observation. They invest time and effort into the networking "business" with a view to giving others something of value as well as gaining something from them.

In effect, if networking is to be productive, it is not enough to just know people, their names, and contact information. Who you know is important. But even more important is: Who you know who knows you. Although it is important to know people through networking, productive people actually take it a step further to make sure that the people they know, know who they are. This means that you need to introduce yourself to the people you meet, give them your business card, inform them of your business or career interests, and let them know the skills that you possess. Over time in network meetings, you do need to let the people know about your accomplishments and how you or your business can benefit them or their business. In the same vein, make a concerted effort to know their accomplishments, their backgrounds, and how their personal and business accomplishments can benefit you, your career, and/or your business.

Networking and Social Media

In the past decade, the use of information technology (IT) tools to network as a way of "meeting" people has proliferated. For the Millennial, IT gadgets such as mass communication channels (cable, direct TV), social media (e-mails, texting, Twitter, Facebook, YouTube, Tumbler, Wikipedia, LinkedIn), and Internet browsers (Google, Yahoo, AOL) are networking tools of choice. Although it appears that these modern technologies are here, it not clear whether or not they actually serve any useful purpose in quality networking by contributing to the cultivation of productive habits. What is clear is that the tools are useful to search for long-lost friends, business associates, and relatives, or to provide a way to stay in touch with them.

Productive People Know Places

As said previously, it is not enough to know something through education or to develop your profession or business through the people you know by means of networking. The very place where you know what you know and who you know is critical to being a productive person. Where you know assumes the power of being on the road again going places. As a legendary American musician once stated, it is always a good thing to be on the road again. This is especially necessary when the circumstances and conditions of the present location are neither productive nor welcoming of your presence and what you have to offer.

Mobile Society – On the Road Again

As another legendary American musician put it, you've got to know when to walk and when to run. This explains, in part, why many have observed that America is a mobile society. Its people are always on the move. It is not unusual for people to be born in one state; go to school, take a job, start/raise a family in other states; and finally retire in an entirely different state. At the same time, there are many Americans who are born, raised, go to school, work, and retire in the same state or even a locale. That's the beauty of American culture—the freedom to dream big and to pursue those dreams wherever those dreams may take you.

What is important to keep in mind here is that productive Americans tend to live in environments that support the very habits that nurture productivity. They live in communities, municipalities and counties, or states that provide them with a good education and a welcoming opportunity to network and meet other people. The theme song of the popular American sitcom Cheers put it best, saying that people want to go where everybody knows your name and they're glad you came. So Americans tend to congregate the same way that birds of a feather flock together. Although this fosters homogeneity in America, it also nurtures diversity, since people are free to seek likeminded people not only along ethnic lines but also according to social, economic, business, and religious interests. The overarching criteria are that productive people seek, build, and sustain nurturing communities, which, in turn, reinforces their productiveness.

The American Social Experiment and Individual Productivity

Another essential dimension of going places is that productive people tend to go to places that promote the habits of education and networking. They go to such places as school campuses, libraries, community centers, and places of worship. Most productive people (with a decent education, job, family, home, property, modest car) tend to value and frequent places like the library, worship centers (church, synagogue, temple), school campus (high school, college, university), and community centers (recreational facilities, senior facilities, etc.). Even when they go on vacation, they are naturally attracted to these places.

Evidently, these places have a lot to offer with respect to what you know and who you know. For the most part, you can't go wrong with or in these places. The majority of people who frequent these places tend also to be productive people. Birds of a feather do indeed flock together, although not always.

To understand the important roles of these institutions in America, one needs to understand one of the great ideas of the American social experiment, namely, the Constitutional guarantee of free association. People are free to gather and to associate with whomever for whatever legitimate purpose. People are free to form all sorts of organizations to pursue shared interests. The organization could be in the form of a professional association, a public speaking club, a church, a business chamber, or an educational coalition, to name just a few.

Some of these organizations are formal (Toastmasters, American Bar Association), while others are less formal (a neighborhood watch, a community garage sale), with many others in between. Smaller and/or seasonal organizations across the United States number in the millions. Many are registered with Internal Revenue Service (IRS) as nonprofit organization, while others just meet to serve an ad hoc purpose but are not registered with IRS. Whether large or small, they all nevertheless contribute to the dynamic nature of the American economy. They also serve as resources for individuals and a context for groups of individuals to thrive.

Although many of these organizations are large and can afford to build, acquire, or rent a facility for meetings and daily operations, others are just small groups or splinters groups that cannot afford a facility of their own. In some cases, the organization's purpose, goals, and operations do not require the use of an entire facility. In this case, public facilities such as libraries, schools/universities, community centers, and religious centers serve as locations where many of these organizations hold meetings, conduct business, and serve their constituencies.

Take, for example, the presence of schools, colleges and university across America. As stated earlier, according to the Department of Education (http://nces.ed.gov), there are 129,189 elementary and secondary schools in 13,567 districts in America. Of these, 98,328 are public schools and 30,688 are private schools. There are 4,726 degree-granting colleges and universities across America—1,623 public colleges and universities and 2,527 private colleges and universities. There are a total of 2,527 non-degree institutions. (See Appendices 3 and 4 for details.) Put differently, that is a total of 136,442 campuses with libraries, halls, stadiums, and recreational facilities available for students, staff and faculty meetings, lectures, sports activities, and networking opportunities. These campuses and facilities serve as venues for professional meetings, social events, and group networking opportunities for various organizations and individuals in the communities where the schools and universities are located. Major colleges and universities embody all of the desirable characteristics of productive people—education, networking, libraries, worship centers, parks, people, to name a few.

This means that many different events are taking place at these locations—especially large colleges and universities—at any given time. It also means that there is a tendency for a lot of people to gather, share, and network or just hang out at these locations anytime during the week and on weekends. Many small nonprofit organizations and professional associations post and distribute newspapers, magazines, fliers, and useful materials at these locations for general public consumption. These materials provide useful information for free. Productive people are aware of these resources. They frequent these locations to access free information and services and to meet people.

Social Space

One more dimension of American socialization is the use of social space for networking. Traditionally, Americans live at one end of a city and have friends on the other end. It is not unusual for a family to live on the east side of a city, go to church on the south side, and shop on the west side. The availability of a family car or public transportation makes it easy to network and socialize in social spaces and, in effect, expand one's circle of friends and business associates, which can enhance productivity. In the past decade, the use of social space has been enhanced and expanded through the use of virtual space. Social media, Internet Explorer, and all sorts of information technology gadgets have made it easier to stay in touch and even hold meetings with just about anyone anywhere. Whether these trends actually enhance networking and, in effect, productivity remains to be seen. The jury is still out as to whether they have any harmful or negative effects on users. Meanwhile, no productive person can afford to leave home without social media technology or to not have them if he or she is to stay productive.

Bottom Line

The role of what you know, who you know, and where you know in order to be productive and stay competitive can hardly be overemphasized. Productive people in America have an appetite for knowledge, networking, and going places.

They acquire formal or technical education in a discipline and continue to develop their skills and careers through continued education. They never stop learning. They engage themselves in quantity and quality networking, developing personal friendship and professional/business associates along the way. They go places that provide them with the opportunity to learn and meet people. They take advantage of places like libraries, worship and community centers, schools and universities in their communities and the resources that these places provide them. In fact, they make a concerted effort to live in communities with nurturing amenities that reinforce productive habits.

In sum, productive people know full well that:

> The adage "It's not what you know, but who you know" is only half true.

To be productive they must embrace three habits:

> Know something through education – What you know
>
> Know people through networking – Who you know who knows you
>
> Know places by going places – Where you know what and who you know

They frequent places that foster productivity:

> Libraries
> Community and religious centers
> School, college, and university campuses
> Other places

Productive people are also fully aware that the positive habits identified in this chapter are good to have, but habits do not put food on the table, clothes on one's back or shelter over one's head. To be productive, positive habits must translate to a quantifiable commodity, namely, work. It is work itself that contributes to productivity and, in effect, the economy. It is work that is rewarded with a salary and benefits package. It is the reward package that provides the individual with purchasing power, which, in turn, fuels the demand for goods and services and raw materials. The demand for goods and services ultimately leads to the creation of more jobs and "help wanted" ads. The interplay between these elements constitutes productivity—the subject of the next chapter.

CHAPTER 3

JOBS AND PRODUCTIVITY IN AMERICA

Productivity is critical to the existence and survival of all civilizations. It involves producing goods and providing services by the people's labor for the people's consumption. Productivity entails work that must be done. And in our modern economy, work entails jobs and positions that must be filled. The creation of jobs implies employment of people to do the work of these jobs. At the individual level, a person needs to work in order to be productive, to earn a living wage to provide food, clothing, and shelter for himself and his family. That is, he needs to get a job. For a modern economy to flourish and be productive, it must create jobs for its people. To do otherwise makes the economy to fizzle. America is not an exception to this observation. In fact, productivity is the substance of American culture. Creating the conditions for the creation of jobs for people and preparing people to work at jobs is a primary concern of the public sector.

Productivity is thus defined here as the capacity to develop civil capabilities from the natural environment and to convert those capabilities into cash or some means of transaction. A society is said to be productive when it invents a culture or way of life from its habitat for the benefits of its members. That is, the government fashions the environment to ensure maximum capabilities for the people. A productive person is an individual who nurtures and converts those capabilities into cash. Capabilities in this regard encompass, but are not limited to, the means of production, including human, natural, and material resources.

The government's understanding and acceptance of its role as described above dates back to colonial America and continues until this day. It follows that in order to understand America's greatness and the success of its people, a person needs to understand the nature and structure of productivity and jobs in America—the subject matter of this chapter. We begin by exploring the way a nation organizes its natural habitat into primary culture (economy) and how the elements of primary culture (infrastructures) interact with secondary cultures (multi-structures) to produce the essential ingredients of a vibrant economy. Next, we examine the systemic and dynamic nature of jobs in America. The chapter concludes with an analysis of other means of production on which individuals can capitalize in order to optimize their overall productivity.

The Culture and Structures of Productivity

Scientists have observed three elements that make life possible: heat, water, and air. These three elements have to be present for life to exist. The most vivid documentation of life on earth—the creation story—recognizes the reality of water and air. It wasn't until stars, including the sun, emerged onto the scene to give off heat that life as we know it was possible. Even in that primordial era, it was necessary to structure the natural habitats to favor life and thus began the existence of human intelligence as we know it. Over eons of years, the universe has expanded and countless natural habitats have emerged—some hospitable to life, others not quite as favorable to human existence and civilization.

As the human population grows, giving rise to foragers, hunters and gatherers, horticulture, sedentary communities, mobile societies, nation states, modern states, and a whole civilization, there has always been need to structure the natural habits to support each stage of the social and cultural evolutions. Whether or not a civilization will evolve to the next phase depends in large part on the level of efficiency and effectiveness in altering their natural habitat to nurture and sustain the social evolutionary trajectory. Put another way, a civilization's survival depends by and large on its ability to organize the natural habitats for efficient and effective productivity at two levels—namely, at the existential structuring level (primary culture) and at the level of subsistence multi-structuring (secondary culture).

Primary Culture and Infrastructures

First, a society must organize its natural habitat in order to survive. The group must structure the environment in such a way that it protects itself from itself. That is, the group must seek the most efficient and effective use of natural resources to build and not to destroy itself. They must also use natural resources to defend against external hostilities, be this natural disasters, other societies, or nonhuman agents such as wildlife and microorganisms. The overall structuring of the environment is existential in nature. Anthropologists have observed this existential structuring as a society's primary culture, also commonly recognized as infrastructures. These infrastructures (safety and security, law and order, water systems, transportation systems, and energy systems) usually set the stage for members of a society to pursue individual/family interests in connection with productivity. In modern states, the primary culture or infrastructures are usually structured by the governments in the interest of the public or for the public good.

Within the United States, society rests on three major sectors, also called metaphorically the three legs upon which society rests. These sectors are the public sector, the private sector, and the nonprofit sector. The public sector consists mainly of government institutions; the private sector consists primarily of business operations; and the nonprofit sector consists largely of social, humanitarian, and philanthropy institutions. Although the private and nonprofit sectors fall within the multi-structures or secondary cultures, the public sector falls within the primary culture or infrastructures. Each of these sectors creates jobs and people are hired to fill those jobs and carry out their respective responsibilities for the overall functioning of society. From this perspective, we can posit that jobs are the predominant determinant means of productivity in America and in any civilized society for that matter. To fully appreciate this assertion, we need to take a closer look at the way these sectors are structured.

As stated previously, the public sector as the primary culture is responsible for the infrastructures and all of the jobs associated with the infrastructures, as listed above. The public sector is structured into four tiers: the federal, the state, the county, and the city or municipalities. Each layer generally has three branches: the executive, the legislative, and the judiciary. Each of the tiers has functions and missions assigned to it, as does each branch within the tier. These functions and missions are broken down into tasks and work that has to be done. The tasks are functions that translate into jobs and, of course, into employment. For example, the federal government of the United States hires well over 5 million employees to perform the functions and missions of the federal government. Or consider that there are more than 3,000 counties in the United States. Each county has its own respective executive, legislative, and judicial branches to carry out the responsibilities of creating and maintaining a wide range of infrastructures for the overall functioning of that county. This easily translates into jobs, jobs, and more jobs. The same dynamics play out at the multi-structures domains, which consist of the private and the nonprofit sectors with respect to tasks, functions, and job creation.

Secondary Cultures and Multi-structures

The second level of social organization for the survival of the members of society takes its lead from the primary culture. That is, with the natural habitat secured and protected, the members can now go about pursuing their individual interests, be this the need to procreate or to meet basic human necessities such as food, shelter, and clothing. It is important to note that this secondary level of social organization, also called the secondary culture or multi-structures, takes its cues from the primary culture. The primary culture defines the broad rules, sets the parameters, and builds the framework, while at the secondary culture level members of society fill in the blanks, play by the rules, and pursue their own interests within the limits imposed by primary culture. Individuals can form groups, take jobs, start businesses, hire laborers, build homes, buy houses, start a family, and take vacations, to name just a few, as prescribed (or proscribed) by the primary culture. These activities are usually conducted in the form of products and services through the mechanisms of business and nonprofit organizations. That is, individuals or groups of individuals start businesses or nonprofits that manufacture products and provide services for consumption by members of society, including individuals, other businesses, and the governments. To perform and assemble the functions and means of manufacturing goods and providing services, these organizations create work to be completed. These works translate to jobs to be filled, hence employment.

In the previous chapter, we saw that the nonprofit sector plays an important role in American society. The organizations that fall into this category provide social functions that the business sector or the public sector would generally not perform. These organizations provide services or supply products to the vulnerable and the needy, such as the elderly, the poor, and the homeless. Businesses are in the business of making money and government institutions are in the business of the public good. But the government and business sectors recognize the importance of taking care of the vulnerable segments of society, hence grants and donations given by governments and businesses to nonprofit organizations. With a steady flow of funding from the public and private sectors as well as from other sources (e.g., donations and gifts from the general public, philanthropists), the nonprofit organizations are able to provide goods and services to a target population. These organizations carry out their missions and functions much like government and business organizations by breaking the functions down into tasks to be completed and work to be done. This exercise translates into creating jobs and hiring people to fill those jobs, also called positions. With the number of nonprofit organizations in the millions across the United States, this means jobs, jobs, and more jobs.

The private sector pertains to business and business operations in the United States whose influence goes far beyond the nation's borders. Business operations manufacture goods, deliver products, and provide services. There are small businesses, with 500 or fewer employees. Mid-size businesses have a few thousand employees, and large corporations hire tens of thousands of employees to work in the United States and around the globe. Overall, the private sector accounts for 75% of the national productivity output. More employees work in the private sector than in the government and nonprofit sectors combined. These employees work in factories to build homes; make cars; manufacture appliances such washers and dryers; deliver products to consumers; supply stores, offices, and hospitals with goods; and provide services to moviegoers and sports, to name just a few. There are those who play direct roles, such as machinists, engineers, teachers, actors, and actresses. There others who are play a multiplier role (such concierges and security guards at a stadium) by providing products and services that make the direct roles possible. This all translates to jobs, jobs, jobs, and more jobs in the private sector.

Jobs and Productivity

It is important to note that both the infrastructures (governments or public sector) and the multi-structures (nonprofit and private sectors) hire people to do whatever projects or business ventures they undertake. Put differently, the public, private, and nonprofit sectors are constantly creating jobs and employing people to fill those jobs in order to get the work done, be that doing police work, maintaining domestic peace, locking up criminals, making cars, building houses, treating patients, or delivering parcels, to name a few. The documentation and the coordination of the interplay between the services and products of the public and the private sectors form the basis of a civil society. The ability to sustain the interplay over time determines which societies will thrive and become developed nations and which ones will flounder and be underdeveloped.

Instruments and models such as Gross Domestic Product (GDP) and Income per Capita (IPC) have been developed by societies to measure the productivity of individuals and nations, as compared to other individuals and nations. This helps nations determine their level of productivity and, in effect, the rate at which they are depleting their natural resources. In recent decades, efforts have been made to measure the rate by which humans or societies are taxing the natural habitat and whether a societal impact on its environment can alter that environment beyond its ability to serve a hospitable habitat for society. For the purposes of this chapter, the very undertaking to measure human productivity itself means yet more jobs and employment, further adding to productivity. As economists have observed, no economy grows exponentially forever. At some point, the law of diminishing returns kicks in, during which time the environment is used up and can no longer produce or sustain the population, regardless of any additional investment and new policies.

Governments have a responsibility to ensure that policies are in place to guard against productive activities at the individual, business, and governmental levels that will undermine the quality of life. History is replete with societies that had great intentions but which faded over time because they failed to guard against human greed and an insatiable lifestyle that was unsustainable.

Jobs as the irreducible engine that drives productivity come in many forms and shapes. To be productive, a person needs to grasp the structure of jobs in America and how the structure affects employees.

Formal and Informal Jobs

All jobs fall into two broad categories—formal employment (payroll) and informal employment (non-payroll). Formal employment refers to jobs that are included in the payroll of an employer. This means the holder of that position is formally hired and the rules and regulations of employment apply to the position and the person holding that position, including benefits and tax deductions. This is important with respect to determining and documenting how long a person has held a job when it comes to credit rating or taking out a loan to buy a car or a home.

Informal employment refers to jobs that not on an employer's payroll. Informal jobs could be temporary or transient, such as a temp hire for data entry to clear backlog, babysitting so that a couple can attend a party or yoga sessions, or selling baseball tickets during a World Series, to give just a few examples. This does not mean that the position is not valid or that the paycheck has less value. After all, green is green and the color of money is the same for formal and informal jobs. Nor does it mean that tax deductions or paying taxes does not apply. As the saying goes, two things are certain in life in America: taxes and death. It means that these jobs are not counted with certainty or not documented as payroll positions when economic productions are being calculated by agencies charged with that responsibility. Since the job holder is not on payroll, he or she will most likely miss out on payroll-driven benefits. Documentation of informal work history for credit rating or loan purposes can be a challenging task. The burden of proving one's employment history falls on a borrower.

Career Ladder

Jobs are structured on a career ladder scale to encourage high performance. Most jobs start at the entry level, followed by the mid-level and management or executive levels. The assumption is that each level requires a set of skills, experience, efficiency, and effectiveness. This means productivity on the part of the employer. On the part of the employee, it means upward mobility. Ideally, the career ladder is a win-win scenario for all parties involved. It is incumbent upon the employee to understand the career ladder upon entry of duty (EOD) and to know what it would take to move up from one level to the next. A smart employee homes in on those required skills, accomplishments, and productivity indicators that further the missions and goals of the employers, realizing that they are key to upward mobility in the workplace. This may require retraining in a particular skill set or acquiring a whole new formal education and earning a degree. It may also require developing the habits that are characteristic of successful and productive people, as discussed in the previous chapter and throughout this book. In some situations, it may involve finding a niche in your workplace and developing a solution to meet the needs created by that niche.

Professionals, Skilled and Unskilled Workers

Another way that jobs are structured is through categories, based on the levels of education, experience, and skills involved in a particular job or vocation. Jobs that involve a high level of risk and liability tend to be professionalized. Professional jobs in medicine, engineering, aviation, for example, require a higher level of formal education and licensing. Individuals seeking employment in these professions are required to demonstrate a highly developed skill set before they can be employed to do that work. This would include such professions as doctors, engineers, lawyers, public health scientists, pilots. Professionals are entitled to maintain their titles by virtue of their credentials, regardless of whether or not they are currently working or hold a position in that industry. Appendices 20 and 21 list occupational requirements and pay grades in the healthcare industry and in the recreational entertainment industry, respectively.

Because of the risks, responsibilities, and liabilities associated with these professions, these individuals are highly paid, well respected in society, and have little difficulty in attaining upward mobility. Professional jobs rank very high on the social economic status (SES) scale, ranging from middle class to upper class. They are also valued, because their services and products involve life and death situations or a loss of freedom to the consumers. Not all professionals are highly paid, though. Those involved with the helping services, who serve in mostly in the nonprofit sector, such as clergy, social workers, teachers, and librarians, are not highly paid, partly because the level of risks, skills, and education associated with these professions is not as high as those of, say, lawyers, engineers, physicians, and those working in related fields.

Professional employment generally falls under the category of white collar jobs. These individuals work in the office or indoors, for the most part, and are well dressed in suits, ties, white uniforms, dress shoes, or a combination thereof. Although some skilled workers are classified as white collar jobs, most skilled workers tend to fall under blue collar jobs (different from unskilled workers who hold minimum wage jobs). (See Appendix 11 for a listing of white collar and blue collar occupations.)

Skilled workers tend to have received basic and secondary education but mostly technical education in their field of interest. They build skills over time and become an expert in their particular specialties. Many skilled workers are self-employed or run a small business with skilled employees to help do the job. And there are millions of them in America. Skilled workers include, but are not limited to, plumbers, electricians, drivers, some machinists, and certain mechanics, to give a few examples. They usually are required to be licensed, insured, and bonded for their protection and the protection of their customers, based on local, state, and/or federal regulations. Skilled workers are highly valued and in high demand across America. They maintain and keep American homes and other businesses humming, churning, and productive. The pay is decent and can propel a skilled worker into the middle class and to some extent into the upper class. However, the work is often difficult, requiring hard work, long hours, and little to no vacation time.

Unskilled workers tend to work in minimum wage jobs and are paid by the number of hours worked. Many unskilled jobs require a high school diploma or its equivalent, the general educational development (GED) test. Most unskilled employment requires no education. The employees are usually trained on the job. Some jobs require that an employee be proficient in English; other jobs have no English language requirement. These include clerks, cashiers, janitors, security gate keeper, housekeepers, and dry cleaning employees, to name a few.

These jobs generally provide entry level opportunities into the American workforce. From the point of view of the American experiment, no condition is expected to be permanent. A person is expected to start from somewhere and then work his or her way up. The rags-to-riches concept is alive and well in American movies and literature of all genres and is highly celebrated in the everyday American media. The key is working so hard to move up to the next level on the food chain. The secret is that the conditions are good enough to make a subsistent living but not good enough to make you want to remain there. The alternative is to have a plan and stick with it to move up. For example, while working at a minimum wage job in a fast food restaurant, a person can enroll in a community college or vocational technical school. Upon graduation, he or she can look for opportunities to hold a more lucrative, skilled job.

Assorted jobs are available at any given time in America. Some jobs are part time, while others are full time. Some positions are temporary in duration (e.g., earning quick cash during occasional special events or a holiday season); others are permanent, or a combination thereof. If none of these kinds of jobs exist, a person can actually create a job and become self employed. America is, by nature, entrepreneurial. This observation reflects the reality that almost all great American companies started with one or two persons who saw a need and had the creativity and courage to develop a solution to that need. In so doing, he or she had a job. By soliciting help from family and friends to help meet the demand of filling that need, he or she becomes an "employer." This was true years ago and is still true today, from General Electric to Google and Apple companies.

Higher Education and Earnings from Jobs

There is consensus in career development literature that post-secondary education plays a critical role in an individual's prosperity and upward mobility through employment earnings. Data from Bureau of Labor Statistics and other sources support these observations (http://chapterportal.saportal.org/public/ education_fast_facts.pdf, (http://www.bls.gov/news.release/ empsit.nr0.htm). On average, someone with an advanced degree earns $74,602/year. Someone with a Bachelor's degree earns $51,206/year, on average, compared to $27,915/year for someone who has a high school diploma. A high school dropout or someone with no secondary education earns approximately $18,734/year. Consider the following:

> In 2008, college graduates earned $55,700, compared to high school graduates, who earned $33,800.

> College graduates hold jobs with a benefit package that includes quality health care, savings money for retirement and likely to send children to college.

> In 2009 at the height of the Great Recession, the unemployment rate for college grads was 4.6%, compared an unemployment rate of 9.7% for high school graduates.

The Multiplier Effect

What is even more revealing is the multiplier effect of job creation. Knowledge of the multiplier effect adds to an understanding of and appreciation for the nature of productivity in America. Social scientists have long observed that jobs are gifts to the economy that keep on giving. Take, for example, the toilet. The invention of toilet led to the creation of jobs. As toilets became a permanent feature of American homes, more jobs were created to make more toilets. Over time, engineers designed the toilets to ensure proper mechanical functioning without the use of energy such as electricity. Toilets have to be shipped and marketed to the customers, hence the need for drivers, salespeople, accountants, etc. Then they have to be installed, once purchased, and repaired, if broken. This need created a category of jobs—namely, technicians and plumbers. Then came the need for toilet accessories – tissue, repair kits, hand washing soap, and air freshener, to name a few. That added multiple skilled and unskilled jobs to the invention, installation, and use of one item—the toilet.

According to a refinance real estate company, there are 98 toilets per 100 people in Washington, DC, for a total of 5,460,900 toilets in the area (*Washington Post Express*, October 23, 2014, p. 4). By comparison, Boulder, Colorado, has 102 toilets per 100 people. Based on the economies of scale, that translates to quite a bit of toilets across the United States and the jobs associated with manufacturing, installing, maintaining, and repairing the toilets every year.

Now think of the multiplier effect for the following domains: the stove in your kitchen, your dining room table, the bed in your bedroom, and the engine underneath the hood of the car in your garage. Imagine, for a moment, the number of direct and indirect professionals, technicians and unskilled workers at the entry, middle, and executive levels holding full-time, part-time, temporary, or permanent jobs involved in manufacturing, shipping, setting up, installing, maintaining, replacing, or repairing the item in each of the domains listed above. You are right if you imagine a web of jobs, jobs, and more jobs all over the map.

The totality of the dynamic interplays among direct and indirect jobs throughout the economy in the public, private, and nonprofit sectors—making and maintaining peace; securing America's borders; making, delivering and repairing vehicles; growing and supplying food, providing care for victims of domestic violence; ensuring the containment of epidemics, and ensuring that bridges are built and safe, for example—accounts for the well over 160 million jobs at any given time in America in the last decade. Although some jobs are being eliminated, others are being created to replace them in one fashion or another. A principal characteristic of the American economy remains its ability to continually renew itself from within. Both the direct and the multiplier jobs rely on other variables within the larger economy for sustainability, reinforcement, and renewal. From an anthropological perspective, these variables serve as rituals of transformation, reinforcement, and intensification for the employees and their jobs. We turn now to these variables.

Productivity by Other Means

Jobs provide employment, which assures that at the end of a work pay period (generally every 2 weeks), the employer will pay the employee a salary or wage. With that income, the employee is able to provide basic needs (food, shelter, clothing, etc.) for himself or herself and the family. Admittedly, with earnings falling behind the cost of goods and services in the past decade, an employee needs to be creative in maximizing his or her earnings in order to optimize the purchasing power of his earning. Put differently, an employee needs to explore and exploit the many opportunities available for enhancing productivity. It is no longer enough to work hard (20th century paradigm). One must also learn to work hard and work smart (the 21st century paradigm). This requires enhancing productivity by other means, including the use of other capital within the economy that is at the employee's disposal.

Human Capital – Training, Skills Development, and Education

An employee's most important asset is himself or herself. He/she converts his/her labor to income by being employed. An employee can boost his/her income through promotion, but promotion requires performance beyond the current level of performance. This may require additional training to develop new skills or enhance existing skills. Generally, upward mobility assumes a commensurate level of education, as discussed in above. Education provides the skills, knowledge, and ability needed to perform at a higher level. Additionally, upward mobility can use a boost from networking, which higher formal education provides.

Investing in career development and professional growth is one way to maximize an employee's earnings. Career development leads to additional responsibility, promotion, and upward mobility, and, in effect, increased productivity. Furthermore, an employee with a family should consider investing in the development of the human capital at his or her disposal, namely, the spouse and/or children. An educated family with diversified revenue streams (two or more incomes), tends to increase its purchasing power and, thereby, overall family productivity. One income can go only so far, especially in an era of job insecurity.

Economic Capital – Savings, 401K, Certificates of Deposit (CD)

The American economy is aptly described as a capitalist economy. That is, the economy embodies the principles and philosophy of a free market where people are free to work, trade, and acquire property to the best of their abilities. The government's role is to set the rules of the markets and monitor them to ensure that everyone is playing by the rules. People are free to pursue their interests to improve their conditions, provided those interests are legitimate as prescribed by society and mediated through the apparatus of the government. In principle, the limits of economic pursuits are the limits imposed by the knowledge, skills and abilities of the individual. In reality, though, humans are, by nature, fragile and severely limited by the constraints of time and mortality. To survive, humans must do what they know best—acquire resources from the environment and seek ways to maximize the scarce resources for optimal utilization. American citizens and immigrants alike are not immune to these realities and must take advantage of the economic capital available to them in order to make the most of their earnings from employment.

Life is short and individuals can only work so many hours in a day and hold so many jobs. Even if an employee could possibly hold several jobs and work 24/7, he or she is likely to incur as many expenses in healthcare costs, automobile maintenance, and home repair, to list just a few. After all, a dollar can only go so far. One way to stretch earnings from employment to optimize short- and long-term productivity is to take advantage of what we might call, for lack of better term, economic capital. Economic capital comes in different packages, such as interest-bearing savings, individual retirement accounts, money market accounts, certificates of deposit, low risk bonds, and more. Many of these schemes are designed to give a break to hardworking Americans who have gotten their hands dirty, paid their dues, and worked their way up over the years. The schemes provide safety nets during their golden years of retirement. Smart employees take advantage of them to ensure a better future for themselves and their posterity. Financial institutions structure the schemes to motivate employees, and anyone for that matter, to save through earnings from both the formal and informal employment.

Employees in formal employment, especially in the public sector and in mid-size business and major corporations, have benefits packages that include savings for retirement. However, the traditional retirement benefits (Social Security, pensions, annuities, etc.) are no longer provide enough income to enjoy a comfortable retirement after years of hard work, raising a family, and, in many cases, putting children through college. Employees can maximize earnings by investing in tax-deferred investment schemes such as individual retirement accounts (IRAs) or a 401K, a Thrift Savings Plan (TSP, for federal employees), and other less popular but safe retirement accounts.

Other avenues for maximizing earnings from both formal and informal employment include traditional savings accounts, money markets accounts, and certificates of deposit (CDs), government issued bonds, to list a few. These accounts pay very low to moderate interest rates. The accounts are insured by the full faith and credit of the federal government, to the extent that the financial institution in which these accounts are held is insured and regulated by the Federal Deposits Insurance Corporation (FDIC)—an arm of the federal government.

More aggressive avenues for maximizing earnings include the stock market, where investors invest employees' money in companies in hope of receiving higher returns on investments (ROI) as the companies grow and make a profit. These schemes are not federally insured and so there are risks of losing money with these schemes as well as making money from them. Last but not least, there are the nontraditional avenues for investments opportunities, depending on your level of risk tolerance. These nontraditional schemes include precious metals, real estate flipping, peer lending, historic real estate, company-issued bonds, and annuities. It is advisable to use the services of a licensed professional in the investment industry before engaging in any of these avenues as a way of maximizing your hard earned money.

There is consensus in literature about economic capital maximization that what an employee should not do is stash his or her hard-earned money under their mattress in the form of cash. Such a practice can only lead to a lose-lose situation. Not only does a person risk losing the cash to thieves or fire, but he or she will actually lose out on the cash due to inflation and declining purchasing power. The purchasing power of a dollar put under a mattress today will be worth much less than that of a dollar a decade from now, even adjusted for inflation, whereas, that same dollar will be worth much more than a dollar if it is invested wisely. The kind of investment plan you choose depends largely on a number of variables beyond the scope of this study. Suffice it to say here that an employee's level of risk tolerance should play a role in the decision to invest and which plan(s) to invest in. After all, it's your money.

Social Capital – Network, Family, and Friends

Hardworking employees spend their free time with friends and family. Hardworking and smart employees network with family and friends as well as with strangers and foes alike. We observed in the previous chapter the important role of networking as a way to build social capital. We also noted that social capital—knowing people who know you—is a necessary habit of productive people. It is important to point out here that networking is not an end in and of itself, but a means to an end. Networking does not automatically lead to productivity. Networking as a social capital must be calculated and measured in order to ensure results; it must be planned, orchestrated, and targeted toward a specific goal or goals.

Quality networking is effective and desirable for productivity maximization. But quality networking also takes time, costs money, and can sap one's energy. If an employee must spend his hard-earned money on networking, the entire endeavor must be treated as an investment. Investment assumes returns on investment (ROI). From this perspective, an employee must always ask what is in a particular networking event or activity for him and for the other parties involved. The returns do not necessarily have to be immediate or have monetary value. However, at the end of the day, there have to be some social benefits from attending the networking event. The social benefits should, at some point, lead to economical or other benefits. Social benefits in this regard can be tangible things (e.g., references, job opportunities, business deals), intangible kinds (earning the trust and integrity of others, useful advice, useful knowledge and tips, general awareness of and exposure to the good life), or a combination thereof, such as a place to hang out where people actually care enough to know your name and are glad to see you. The people trust you enough to loan you money for a business investment, in a time of crisis, or when you are low on cash.

Political Capital – Get Involved at Some Level

In the words of President Abraham Lincoln, the government of the people, by the people, and for the people shall not perish from the face of the earth. America, as a collection of states, counties, and municipalities, is an enduring nation. It is an enduring nation because the governments are enduring. The governments are enduring because the people are enduring. America takes its body politics and governments seriously as evidenced by citizens' participation. For Americans, democracy and capitalism are inseparable elements of a just and civil society.

As a democratic society, any citizen can run for any public office, and anyone can support anyone else to run for political office. Although only citizens can run for and hold public office, anyone who is a legal resident can participate in the political process by helping to elect the most qualified citizens who share their views and values. People can donate money and/or volunteer time and talents to their candidates of choice. They can help a candidate canvas for votes, and join a political party to make difference. Immigrants ignore these political activities, especially at the local level, to their peril.

One way to build political capital is to get involved at some level of the political process in your community or state. It is not enough to participate in politics randomly without clear objectives. To build political capital, much like networking, a person must invest time in studying and learning about candidates or a party and where they stand on the issues. You want to make sure that the views, values, and agenda of the candidates or the platforms and objectives of the party align with yours and will further your interests. The candidate's views or the party's platforms should certainly not be inimical to your beliefs and way of life. For example, if you are planning to start a family in the near future, it is wise to support the candidate who will fight for and support maternity leave. If you have parents with a chronic illness who will soon be moving in to live with you, you want to support that party and candidate who will sponsor laws that enhance or protect benefits for seniors, such as Social Security and Medicare.

You also want to make sure that the candidates you are supporting are persons of character and integrity as well as electable. There is not much political capital to earn from campaigning for a political aspirant who will not or cannot win an election. It is a waste of time and effort to back a politician who will not and cannot keep his word, win or lose. Attend rallies and listen to debates. Research and read about the candidates and pay attention to their track record of accomplishments. All of this will help you have an informed opinion and then decide the extent to which you want to support a particular candidate. After the election, you want to stay in touch with the office holders that you help elect, helping them implement their agenda, where feasible, and holding them accountable to the promises they made on the campaign trail.

By participating in body politics with your time, money, and efforts, leaders and officials begin to know you better. They notice your skills and ability to get things done. They may tap you to serve in their administration based on their firsthand knowledge of your ability to perform under stress. They may recommend you to others for appointment into an office or hire you to fill a critical position in government. You can count on them for a reference letter, based on their personal knowledge of you. Although government officials are required to serve all people in their constituency, they tend to pay closer attention to the citizens who have made a difference in local body politics, especially in times of need or crisis. In addition, most politicians are good at reciprocating, even if only with a state dinner or a seat at the inaugural ball. A seat at an inaugural ball can only help, not hurt, your resume.

Spiritual Capital – Developing a Clear Moral Compass

Freedom of speech, association, and religion are constitutionally guaranteed rights of all Americans. This means that people are free to express themselves as they see fit, gather if and when they so desire for whatever purpose, and practice their beliefs and faith as they choose without inference by the government or other associations, provided the speeches do not endanger the safety of the general public or are not libelous in nature. The purpose of the gathering should be legitimate and not injurious to the individuals involved or to the general public. If the gathering is for religious purposes, the religious beliefs and practices must not involve proscribed behaviors and conducts not allowed under the laws of the land. For example, the Supreme Court has pointed out in a free speech ruling that you have right to shout "fire," but not in a theater full of moviegoers when there is no fire. As the saying goes, you have rights to your opinions, but not the facts. Barring the exceptions given above, people are free to pursue their career, vocations, interests, and dreams to the extent possible. This is one of the geniuses of American culture—the freedom to be yourself, to chart your own course, and to pursue your own dreams. With so many people taking advantage of this freedom to exercise their rights, society and the economy can only boom.

The flip side of this freedom is that people do all sorts of things that you may not like and they have right to do them just as much as you have right to do things that others may not like. The entertainment industry can make and market movies that promote values that are different from yours. Department stores can use nude or semi-nude models to promote their products on TV and in the print media, for instance. Politicians and, in fact, the majority in a society can put a law in place that promotes a lifestyle that you find objectionable. The good news is that you are not under any obligation to watch objectionable materials on TV or at the movie theater. You can choose what products to spend your hard-earned money on and what products you do not. You can even choose to relocate to a city or a state that promotes the kind of lifestyle you believe in, and that is one where you would like to raise your family and/or spend your retirement years.

Making choices requires an investment in what we could call, for lack of a better term, spiritual capital. To develop spiritual capital, a person needs to focus on virtues. Virtues are those values, behaviors, and conduct that contribute to a person's overall growth and development, e.g., a decent education, exercise, healthful food, and fruits and vegetables. To further develop holistic spiritual capital, a person also needs to stay away from vices. Vices, as used here, refer to behaviors and conduct that chip away at a person's quality of life and overall well-being. Extreme types of vices include such behaviors as consuming alcohol to the point of becoming an alcoholic, gambling to the point of losing one's mortgage money and losing one's home, or testing positive for drugs at the workplace to the point of losing one's job.

The desirable and undesirable quantities mentioned above are best developed and treated through professional support groups and religious centers, respectively. Spiritually uplifting and ethically illuminating books written by well-known characters can be useful in this regard. Interestingly, centers for spirituality and literature on spiritual formation are in abundant supply across America. Having a lone ranger mentality is usually not a viable way to build spiritual capital.

Embracing virtues and eschewing vices are the easy part. These choices and their implications are as clear as day and night, making decisions about them a no brainer. The need for spiritual capital becomes more imperative when decisions involve gray areas of life, where there are no easy answers to life's perplexing questions. Such circumstances offer grim realities and the choices appear to be between two evils. Other situations call for a choice between two competing interests with equally valid moral claims. Then there are the inevitabilities of life— some humanly inspired, others by acts of nature, such as drunk driving accidents, road rage, hurricane disasters, or loss of lives to sinkhole. In these instances, there are many questions but few answers. There is enough blame to go around, but few solutions to share.

It is important to develop and sustain an inner moral compass that brings clarity to everyday life's decisions. Waiting for events to happen before trying to sort out right from wrong can be stressful. Making decisions under normal circumstances is difficult enough. Making life and death decisions or right and wrong choices in a stressful environment can be daunting. Decisions made under duress are almost always not the best. More often than not, those decisions are not the right ones. Wrong or hastily made decisions can be expensive, energy sapping, and a waste of hard-earned resources from employment and investments, as outlined above.

Bottom Line

Jobs are at the center of productivity. For a society to be productive, governments must create and maintain the conditions that make job creation possible. Private and nonprofit organizations must take advantage of the conditions to create jobs. And individuals must take advantage of available jobs to make a living. To maximize earnings and move up the food chain, a person must not only invest in himself for more rewarding opportunities and higher paying jobs, but must also invest in a wide array of economic, social, political, and spiritual capital. To maximize productivity from Little League to the major leagues, a person should consider controlling the very means of production, namely, a business. Just what this might entail is the subject of the next chapter.

CHAPTER 4

DOUBLING DOWN ON PRODUCTIVITY I – BUSINESS START-UP AND PHASES

So you want to be productive, rich, and wealthy? Very good! To be more productive on a scale larger than yourself, an assured route is to grow your own business. Yes, you heard that right: Business! Business! Business! It's the American way—the whole idea of rags to riches. Consider the following business facts in the United States based on the most current available data (for additional data and details, see Appendix 6):

Private nonfarm establishment, 2012	7,431,808
Private nonfarm employment, 2012	115,938,468
Total number of firms, 2007	27,092,908
Manufacturer's shipments, 2007 ($1,000)	5,319,456,312
Merchant wholesale sales, 2007 ($1,000)	4,174,286,516
Retail sales, 2007 ($1,000)	3,917,663,456
Accommodations and food services sales ($1,000)	613,795,732

Admittedly, the dream of starting or acquiring a business is the easy part. Owning and managing an operation that you can call your business is the hardest part. As the saying goes, the devil is in the details. The purpose of this chapter and the next chapter is to highlight those details and hopefully take some of the mysteries out of a complex and tedious, yet rewarding process. We begin this chapter by exploring the necessary link between career and business. Next, the triggers for the need for business are identified, followed by an examination of business focuses, life cycle, and types. In Chapter 5, we examine business structures, organizing instruments, processes, and operations. We conclude the discussion with a reflection about the bottom line—how business, if properly conceptualized, developed, and managed, can double down on productivity and wealth creation for the stakeholders, including employees, investors, and business owners.

Business as a Beginning of an End

As has already been stated, business is that sector of the economy that creates most jobs. Most Americans work in the business sector and make a living from business payrolls. In effect, business is a continuation of jobs and jobs are the reducible units of business. Where one ends, the other begins. One is a bridge to the other. This observation applies even in automated offices and robotic factories and assembly lines. Someone has to monitor and maintain the automated machines and the robots as well as supply the necessary accessories to ensure proper functioning of the robots. Furthermore, someone has to build, program, and install the machines and robots to begin with. Modern societies are born and built around jobs and business. Societies thrive and are sustained through the availability of jobs. This will very likely remain the same for the next millennium.

A common trend for a business start-up is for individuals to work as employees for others in a business firm for quite some time before they move on to start their own business. Most successful people usually move on to start business as a continuation of their career or along the type of job or occupation they have held for many years. This trend is very much like the school commencement concept, where the end of one endeavor is the beginning of a whole new undertaking. There are individuals who have never worked but started from scratch and grew a large successful business. These are usually anecdotal. They tend to be exceptions that reinforce the rule. After all, as a self-employed person, the individual was once an employer of one person—himself or herself.

From the point of an individual's economic cycle life, the goal is always to work hard as an employee and then move up the ladder—from entry level employee to mid-level employee, then to supervisory level, and so on. Ultimately, the options available to the individual include working and saving seed money to start or buy a business while in their prime; saving money to start or buy a business upon retirement; or working and saving through a variety of schemes to ensure sufficient income upon retirement to live out their golden years. Regardless of the options, the predominant determinant factor is the employee-entrepreneur nexus.

There are similarities and differences between being an employer and an employee. An employee works for somebody who pays him or her a salary and benefits (if any) at the end of each pay period. The employer also pays an employee severance benefits when the employee leaves or retires, whichever occurs first. The employer makes the rules and assigns the work. The employee follows the rules and does the work. The employer keeps the profits after all production and benefits expenses as well as tax obligations are deducted from the gross revenues. At the same time, the employer carries the burden of the success and failure of the business, making sure that there is enough work to ensure productivity and profits. The employer may hire employees or other professionals to perform operational or administrative functions, but the employer as the business owner is ultimately responsible for all of the fiduciary and paperwork responsibilities, especially tax obligations.

When an employee makes a move to own a business, he is now the employer, even if self-employed. He or she now performs all the functions and responsibilities of the business owner or employer. In fact, you now have to work longer hours, still have to work very hard, and, if you hire employees, still have to model a strong worth ethic for the employees. This is where most new business owners drop the ball and watch their business fail. Most people think only of the profits, benefits, and honor of being your own boss and becoming an employer. A failure to fully appreciate the responsibilities and risks associated with being a business owner is the first step on a slippery slope that usually leads to a business failure. Successful and productive entrepreneurs tap into their habits to network, do feasibility studies, and seek guidance from trusted friends in the industry before launching or acquiring a business.

Societal Needs and Finding Your Niche – Triggers

Career capital is a necessary ingredient in any business adventure. It is important to build career capital—experience, expertise, network resources—in your field of endeavor while you are still working as an employee. Put differently, networking and being employed in a business at some level are the starting point for owning your own business. With employment, you acquire experience, develop clarity about your goals and objectives, and, perhaps more importantly, save seed money. Money is the life blood of business much like air is to humans and water is to fish. Of course you need to know the business process of the business you have chosen to go into.

Even if you have the money and the expertise and know with clarity what industry you want to go into, the question still remains: How can a person be sure of business success in the industry? After all, there are few business areas that have not already been targeted or explored by some entrepreneur. As an America president once put it, the only thing that is new is the history you don't know. One way to approach this dilemma and the associated anxiety faced by all entrepreneurs is to ask: What are the needs in the society or community in which you intend to start your business? Based on an assessment of the societal needs, you should attempt to find your niche. That is, what do you do best that will help address the need or needs. As the saying goes, necessity is the mother of invention. Secondly, you must ask how you are going to make a quick buck from whatever you do to meet those needs. Successful entrepreneurs know and seize on what we might call, for lack of a better term, business triggers.

A number of events serve as triggers that create needs in a society. Natural disasters are the most common businesses triggers. Hurricanes, tornadoes, floods, and hailstorms, for instance, wreak havoc on societies and almost always cause damage needing to be repaired in the millions and sometimes in the billions of dollars. Such occurrences create enormous needs and, in effect, trigger business necessities for current and new firms in the affected areas. A wide range of industries are called upon to provide services and supply products to meet, say, housing repairs or rebuilding houses. The needs can be greater than existing firms can handle, thereby giving rise to business expansions and the emergence of new businesses in roofing, trash hauling, insurance adjustment, insurance claims, building materials, and moving and relocation, to name just a few areas.

Another trigger is volunteer work. America prides itself on neighbors helping neighbors and on communities helping the poor and those in crisis. The nonprofit sector is built upon the whole concept of volunteering and giving back to communities. Many youth programs are built around adults and parents volunteering to help run the programs. Volunteer opportunities can serve as an exploration platform for business adventure. Some companies started as volunteer organizations and eventually converted to business in order to be more effective serving the targeted population or be better positioned to manufacture better products in larger quantity to serve the larger society.

Human conditions have also served as the trigger for business adventure. Slavery, human trafficking, prostitution, infectious diseases, hunger, and pandemics are a few of the things that have stirred public consciousness while spurning a variety of service and product businesses in an effort to mitigate or eliminate these human conditions.

Social events can unlock a whole area of societal need for better service or products. Travel and vacations can also create a connection point to a need that is covert in nature or out there somewhere in a remote but exotic part of the world. Indeed, there are equally important but less noticeable business triggers, such as new government laws, regulations, and ordinances at the federal, state, or local levels; a major decline in the economy, leading to gross recession or depression; a major surge in economic growth in times of peace; wars and threats of war;

and a series of major violent occurrences and active shootings at public gatherings.

All of these events tend to create needs at the individual and societal levels. Responding to these incidents in an effort to mitigate them is human nature. Discovering the underlying societal needs and responding to the needs in a calculated fashion requires entrepreneurial discernment and determination. A savvy entrepreneur will somehow figure out a way to make the whole endeavor productive so that something good will come out of it to benefit all parties involved.

Someone with a college or graduate degree in business will recognize these needs. It takes a person with an entrepreneurial mindset and the determination to connect the dots in favor of finding his or her niche. As said, it is important that you love what you see and get excited about it. Business ownership is a long haul and involves a lot of hard work. The secret to successfully converting a societal need into a business necessity is doing what you love and getting paid for it or making a buck or two out of it.

Business Orientation: Products and Services

There is consensus in literature about business specialization that a business is either primarily product oriented or predominantly service oriented. Although this may seem like an oversimplification of reality, because there are degrees of overlap or a combination thereof in some businesses, it remains that businesses tend to look alike as newer businesses tend to follow the examples of existing businesses, especially successful ones. Overall, this is in line with my observation over the years in Africa and in America that people tend to fall into two categories—the thinkers and the doers. The thinkers tend to have unlimited wonderful ideas of what can and should be done, but do not focus enough to do any of them. Doers tend to have only a couple of ideas because they are too focused on and busy putting the idea to work that they have little time to churn out unlimited, untested ideas. There is element of truth in the saying "Those who can do, and those who can't teach."

Businesses owners who reach out into too many areas of business adventures tend to spread themselves too thin and risk failure. They are a mile wide, but only an inch deep in their business undertakings. Successful employees turned business owners tend to be doers. They focus on an idea and bring it to fruition. Little wonder that businesses tend to fall into two broad categories—service and product. In principle, a business stands a better chance of successfully meeting societal needs by focusing on a service or a product. In reality, the two are not mutually exclusive. One feeds off from and reinforces the other.

Product-Oriented Business

Businesses that focus on products deal with goods that are consumed by the general public, including government, society, and other businesses. Many businesses only manufacture products, such as vehicles, appliances, and building materials, and sell them wholesale to retail companies. Some manufacture their products and sell them as goods directly to consumers or customers. Others do a combination thereof in making and marketing their products.

The manufacturers, wholesalers, and the end user retailers focus primarily on the products. They do provide a wide range of services, but only to the extent that the services support the products. The products drive their business. The lion's share of the business revenues come from the product lines. To increase the bottom line, these businesses make and market a wide range of accessories and supplies in support of the products. Some companies manufacture these supplies, and others contract them out. Additionally, manufacturers do a lot of subcontracting with smaller business called multipliers. In this regard, smaller companies make and supply the components the manufacturers use to make the final product. For example, auto makers make cars, but use parts like tires or wipers made by other companies. This means that multiple large and small companies contribute a piece of a final product, such as a car. In return, the companies get their fair share of the revenues from the sale of the car or cars. At the end of the day, a significant number of large and small business owners double down on their earnings and profits.

Service-Oriented Business

In the service business, the emphasis is on providing services to clients. Hospitals and hotels fall into this category. The goal is to provide a wide range of services to the client in return for payment for the services provided. Service industries hire a variety of skilled, unskilled, and professional employees to provide a wide of range of services to the clients (see Appendices 20 and 21). Hospitals hire doctors and nurses to treat patients, lab technicians to do bloodwork, and medical recorders to ensure proper filing of papers associated with a patient visit to the hospital.

Service businesses do sell merchandise and supplies, but only to the extent that the merchandise and supplies relate to the services being provided. Hospitals sell medicine to patients and hotels sell food and beverages to customers staying or attending conferences in the hotel facilities. Revenues from these merchandise and supplies supplement but do not supplant the overall revenue streams from services.

Service industries sometimes subcontract services out to other smaller or highly specialized service industries. These service subcontractors or multipliers help the service company to keep the price under control to the benefit of all parties involved. Using subcontractors also allows major service companies to focus on their primary mission of providing services. This creates many great opportunities for existing service businesses to grow and for new businesses to emerge. In the end, the overall business culture affords many business owners the opportunity to double down on earnings and profits.

As has already been said, product-focused businesses and service-focused businesses are not diametrically opposed to each other. Later in this chapter we'll see that the need to stay focused is driven by a company's business strategies. In today's business environment, businesses face stiff competition and must stay focused in order to be competitive. A business's assets and resources can go only so far in enhancing productivity and the bottom line. Thus, a business must also find a way to leverage all revenue streams associated with its business interests in order to survive. The key is to know which of the two—product or service—is your primary focus and which is secondary. Scarce resources should be allocated accordingly as the business grows through different phases in the business life cycle.

Business Structure

A business generally has four main domains, also called divisions of labor: decision making, planning and policy, administration and research, and operations. These domains overlap and are basically performed by one or a few people in a business start-up. As a business grows into a full performance organization and matures, these interrelated domains evolve into the following four elaborate structures:

> Senior Management
> Middle Management
> Administrative Support and Research and Development
> Technical Core/Operations

Appendix 12 contains a visual representation of how these domains fit into the overall structure of a business organization. The roles and functions of these structures are discussed later in this chapter under Business Process and Operations Management. To fully appreciate these domains, it is important to understand the life cycle of business organization.

Business Life Cycle

Regardless of the area of focus (product or service), all businesses grow painfully through phases. Life sciences have observed that almost all living organisms, including humans, go through phases: we are born, we live, and we die. Anthropologists have observed similar trends in societies and cultures: we rise, we thrive, and we decline. Organizational researchers have noticed the same organic metaphors in business organizations: start-up, growth, maturation, and decline. As has been said, each phase has its unique structures, characteristics, and challenges that a business owner must take into considerations when planning, if he or she is to double down on productivity throughout the business life cycle.

Entrepreneur Phase

All businesses started from somewhere through an action or inaction of a person or group of persons. That is, almost all businesses start at the level of entrepreneurship. An entrepreneurship is a result of a combination of startup and creativity. Which one comes first—the idea or the action taken—is like the chicken and the egg debate. We'll pass on the debate, as it serves no useful purpose here. What is important is that an entrepreneur is someone who put an idea and an action together in response to a real or perceived need and then finds a way to make quick buck out of the exercise. The resulting business is very much a one person show. There may be a couple or even several people involved from the very onset, but one person drives the whole business experiment.

This individual is the lead person and sort of takes charge in delegating assignments and ensuring that things are done. He or she always scrapes by to get the initial human and financial resources to get the business up and running, including drafting needed documents, filing necessary business tax and registration forms with the appropriate government authorities, setting up computers, turning lights on and off, handling the mail, and picking up the trash. That is, the individual serves as the employer, employee, manager, and janitor. The person's name and the business are synonymous and everything very much revolves around this individual.

It is well known among business researchers that entrepreneurs are very creative and possess the ability to see things differently and then connect the dots. As mentioned previously, ordinary individuals sometimes stumble into opportunities and grow a business over time. These anecdotal stories only reinforce the assertion that a business start-up involves a level of creativity. Even individuals who stumble are smart enough to put two and two together to end up with business out of nowhere. In other words they are creative. One important area where creativity is evident is in determining the location of a business. Like real estate properties, businesses thrive on a common denominator: location, location, location. An ordinary person may see a societal need. Another person may see a prime location. It takes entrepreneurial foresight to put the two together to strategically position a business in time and space to respond to a societal need. Meeting people's needs at the right time and place is, in my opinion, the necessary ingredient for the emergence of a business that will thrive.

As the business takes off, additional functions and tasks emerge. This requires helping hands. At this stage, the entrepreneur has a decision to make that will make or break the new business. That is, the decision will impact the future growth or decline of the business. This is when new business owners make a number of mistakes in choosing from a wide range of approaches. One mistake is the owner trying to do it all without hiring helping hands. This approach keeps the owner in full control of the business, limits risks, and of course he or she keeps all the profits. The common mistake here is that the owner limits the opportunity for the business to grow. After all, the owner can only do so much in a day and there are only so many hours in a day, not to mention business-induced stress and long hours, which sooner or later take a toll on the owner's health.

Another mistake, at the other end of the spectrum, is the tendency for the owner to hire too many helping hands. This temptation stems from the fact that the owner has very likely been toiling alone for months and perhaps years, to the point of being burned out, and now finally can begin to see the business taking off. The desire to hire people intensifies when there are friends and family members who are readily available to "help." The word "help" is in quotes because new business owners tend to get more help than they bargain for—new ideas, fantastic suggestions, and never-ending criticisms, to name a few. As the saying goes, "too many hands do, in fact, spoil the stew," (the business stew, in this case). And then there is a possibility that too many employees can bloat the payroll more than the new business revenue streams can sustain.

A more productive approach usually is to assess the business performance within the context of the continued growing demands for the business products and/or services. The demand will inform the current and expected cash flow, which, in turn, should inform how many permanent and/or temporary helping hands will be needed. The business owner should put his entrepreneurial hat on and come up with creative ways to fund and staff the business. Whatever scheme is put in place, it should be flexible enough to allow for steady growth, additional staff when needed, and staff reduction when the demand slows.

One thing that the entrepreneur must not do is abdicate his role as the business creative mind to someone else, certainly not at this phase of the business. There may be a need to hire a manager or two at this phase, since many entrepreneurs tend not to be very good at managing. Such a move will put two very important variables—management and creativity—in full force, in time for the next phase—growth.

Growth Phase – Concentration, Verticals, Horizontals, Diversifications

Do you ever hope to make more than a buck or two from your business? If, as expected, your answer is yes, then you must grow it. After all, what was the point of getting into business if you are not going to make money. You might as well have remained an employee, making money for yourself and someone else, or you could have joined a nonprofit business where you can achieve a lot of social good. Not that anything is wrong with being an employee or working in helping services and ministry-related organizations. To paraphrase an American thinker, the mind, especially the mind of business, is terrible thing to waste. As Thomas Paine put it: "Lead, follow, or get out of the way!" After all, the business of business is to create jobs; the other is profits.

The point is that businesses, by their very nature, tend to grow. Time and again I have observed business owners make terrible decisions and implement bad ideas that made me wonder: "What in the world was he or she thinking?" One could almost hear the business saying, "I have met the enemy, and the enemy is my owner." The secret to unleashing new business to grow is to develop a set of business tools that will serve as a guide or guides to direct the future growth of the business. These tools, which include a business plan, a business model, and a strategic plan, are discussed at greater length later in this chapter. It is sufficient here to say that these tools help chart a course for business horizontal or vertical growth, or a combination thereof.

Business growth literature recognizes the following discernible paths that businesses tend to take to ensure steady growth: concentration, vertical integration, horizontal integration, and diversification.

Concentration Growth – This is where a business increases what it does (products and/or services) and establishes dominance in that line of business. Over time, the business organization becomes robust and controls a lion's share of the market. In concentration growth, the business adds more product lines to its line of products (for example, adding a line of fresh produce to a grocery store or opening additional supermarket stores).

Vertical Integration Growth – This is where a business expands its base of operations. If the vertical integration is *backward*, the business seeks to develop its own supply of raw materials and integrates its input operations into the overall operations management. If the vertical integration is *forward*, the business seeks to develop its own outlets and integrate its output operations into the overall operations management.

Horizontal Integration Growth – This type of growth entails expanding the business to other areas that are closely related to or associated with your business. In a *related* horizontal integration growth, a business seeks to expand by adding a related product or service line. For example, adding a car wash to a gas station. In *unrelated* horizontal integration growth, a business seeks to expand by adding a line of products and/or services from an unrelated business industry, such as adding a café to a bookstore.

Diversification Growth – In diversification growth, a business simply diversifies its products or services within the industry. Related diversification involves increasing a variety of the same or similar product lines, including generics and brand names, (for example, selling assorted ties and hats, both brand name and generic). Unrelated diversification involves different product and/or service lines within a broadly defined industry or industries, e.g., operating a library, a movie theater, and a gym in a co-location, or buying, selling, and repairing sewing machines, vacuum cleaners, and shoes in one store.

The secret is informed planning. As the saying goes, "If you fail to plan, you plan to fail!" The implication is that you do need to plan to grow your business. From my observation, though, wishful thinking or a laundry list of do's and don'ts is not enough. You need an informed plan based on sound data and data analysis, or a well thought out plan with input from seasoned advisors if sound data is not available. No plan at all is better than a poorly conceived and badly implemented plan.

Each growth structure means additional workload and hence the need for additional employees. A common mistake is to overwork current employees in overtime to the point of burnout. Maintaining a healthy and happy workforce is critical to sustainable business growth. However, any additional employees should be added incrementally to allow for flexibility and adjustments along the way as the business continues to grow. Also important in this regard is the need to avoid the temptation to have more chiefs than Indians, or more managers than employees to do the work of the business. If you must err, let it be on the side of having more staff in the operations department than in the management department. Sometimes there may be more seasonal staff than is needed, especially during down time. All you need to do to correct the problem is to drum up more work for the staff by creating the demand for your product and/or service through advertisements and social events. Think of ways to drum up business through any of the growth strategies identified above and discussed in more detail later in this chapter.

Full Performance Phase – Quantity vs. Quality Strategies

At the full performance level, a business has come of age. At this phase, the business has succeeded in finding its niche in the community and the industry. It has succeeded in "convincing" society that there is a need or that its products and services are needed and will continue to be needed to meet that need. In this regard, all public and private sectors are "guilty" of actually sustaining a need and in so doing justifying its continued existence under the sun. Over time, governments become bloated in bureaucratic red tape. Nonprofits develop complex organizations with intractable overheads. Businesses become arrogant and behave as if, in the words of a business mogul, greed is good.

Admittedly, societies have a tendency to want more, not less, of a culture once it has been created. After all, habits are easy to form but hard to break. Are businesses and society doomed in a seemingly intractable tangle of demand and supply pathology? The way that a business industry and society respond to this human drama will determine the survival of the business industry involved. Societies have many options, including finding other ways to meet persistent needs, moving on to other interests, or ignoring or accommodating the need. These options are beyond the scope of this book.

The literature on business strategy recognizes many long-term approaches that businesses adopt to respond to societal needs. In general, businesses that make it through the start-up and growing pains phases generally are better positioned to work with the limited options available to them, such as making a calculated determination about whether to go with quantity or quality in its strategies.

Quantity-Focused Strategy – With a quantity-focused strategy, a business targets the larger society or the pop culture and makes an effort to reach as many people as possible. To reach this goal, a business focuses on making a large quantity of products or services to reach a large number of people. It can be expensive and time consuming to produce a large quantity of products and services. Overall production and services costs stay astronomically high if not controlled. Yet most people in a pop culture cannot afford to pay the high price to buy a product or pay for a service. So the business has to cut costs, most notable in the area of product or service quality, to make a large quantity while keeping costs/prices down. The low cost strategy, as it is also called by business researchers, controls the price but at the expense of quality. There are several variations of this scheme, but the overall goal is to meet the needs of customers who just want their needs met without being overly concerned about durability or the quality of service. For example, a fast food restaurant around the corner will do just fine to quench the desire for a soda and a burger rather than needing to eat in the comfort of a high end restaurant located in an area with a high end zip code.

Quality-Focused Strategy – With a quality-focused strategy, a business focuses on providing quality products and services to a targeted customer base that can afford the price of quality products and services. Needless to say, quality products and/or services involve significant production outlay in input, transformation, and output—durable raw materials, skilled workers, refined processing, several quality control mechanisms, human touch, aggressive marketing schemes, high tech ads, and image-is-everything promotions, to name a few. There are many reasons that people shed a ton of money to buy a product that otherwise would cost less, such as durability, choice, social status, brand name, taste, trend, ignorance, stupidity, and ego. Whatever the reason, a capitalist economy assumes that all customers are created equal but some are economically more equal than others. To the extent that the need is there, real or perceived, businesses will seek to meet that need. Businesses sustain the need into perpetuity through the use of image making ads, public relations schemes, irresistible promotional items, and memorabilia. There is nothing wrong with targeting a high end customer base as long the quality is there and the customers are satisfied with what they pay for. Problems arise, however, when companies fail to deliver quality in line with the high price associated with the product or service. Generally, the high cost strategy controls quality at the expense of quantity.

Price-Focused Strategy – A third approach is what we might call, for lack of a better term, a price-focused strategy. This strategy is often overlooked in research or not well represented in the literature on competitive strategy. A price-focused strategy combines elements of the high price quality strategy and low price quantity strategy by seeking ways to produce and market quality products and services at a reasonable price. If quantity strategy targets primarily the lower class and the quality strategy targets primarily the upper class, the price-focused strategy targets primarily middle class Americans. This strategy controls production costs while ensuring the quality of goods and services by using quality control programs such as Total Quality Management (TQM), Six Sigma, and socio-technical work teams (STWT), to name just a few.

As a full performance organization, a business can afford the luxury of deciding whether to pursue one of these strategies or a combination thereof, although still within the confines of the environment in which it operates and its customer base. What is not acceptable, as a matter of business ethics and good business practice, is to produce poor or defective products and services and market them as quality products and services to unsuspecting consumers. It is strategically suicidal for a business to charge a higher price for poor quality products or service than justified by substandard goods and services. Such practices are very tempting and can be lucrative in the short term. However, these practices are not only unethical, but can also be criminally liable. Besides, such a bad business move almost always catches up with the business and can take down a full performance business. Widespread unethical and criminal business practices tend to affect and take down a whole industry or a segment thereof. In some cases, a need is created and new businesses emerge to fill the void created by a major business collapse. In other cases, an industry is able to work with the appropriate government authorities, nonprofit organizations, and other businesses to clean house and rebound.

This is the one of the geniuses of American culture, unmatched in most other cultures: the capacity and capability to self-monitor, self-police, self-correct, and self-revitalize, without the need for some external intervention from a foreign country or culture. Metaphorically speaking, American economy is a healer that heals itself.

As a business reaches the full performance level, it develops elaborate structures to accommodate growing functions, tasks, and responsibilities. At this stage, a business creates a number of divisions, departments, and units to handle internal and external demands and pressures. These structures are needed to manage the growth discussed previously, mitigate the risks and issues discussed above, and respond to external environmental pressures and obligations. The business owner is still the man, this time with many helping hands at the leadership, management, administrative, and operations levels. A business that is properly structured grows even bigger and begins to leave a business footprint in the industry. Such a business has crossed the point of no return while doubling down on the earnings, salaries, benefits, and wealth of whole hosts of internal and external stakeholders, including the employees, creditors, subcontractors, multipliers, or other smaller business, the nonprofit organizations, and the owner or owners.

Maturity Phase – Domination, Competitive Edge, Collaboration

Many businesses become a corporation at this phase and go public in order to raise more capital for yet more growth nationally. Some mature businesses even venture into international markets. They are capable of competing globally should they elect to do so. The literature on the evolution of business observed that, at this stage, businesses become increasingly complex, hierarchical, and bureaucratic. Expert opinions are divided as to whether this is a healthy development, especially with incessant red tape and production cost overruns. Bureaucracy is not necessarily a bad word in this regard, if properly managed. It is needed to ensure accountability and minimize friction at all levels and locations. The key is to avoid fractional or divided leadership. After all, when two or more proverbial elephants fight, the grass (i.e., low level employees) always bears the brunt of the fight.

For example, organizational development is needed to strengthen the overall performance of the business or aspects thereof. Organizational culture becomes just about as important as corporate rules, policies, standard operating procedures and technical cores in order to foster organizational cohesiveness, weed out bad blood and behaviors, and boost sustainable productivity. Public relations apparatus become imperative in crafting and maintaining corporate image. Concerted efforts are made to control business activities relating to social responsibility. At this phase, a business has matured and flexes muscle in terms of dominance, competition and collaboration in the industry and in the overall economy.

Dominance – A mature business may not only dominate the industry locally but also possibly at the regional or national levels. The name becomes synonymous with the industry. The general public recognizes the business and its facility as a community landmark and the location as a place to do business and also to socialize. The business contributes significantly to the local economy through employment, payroll, taxes, multipliers, and corporate social responsibilities. In fact, the municipal or regional authorities have a vested interest in the decisions and policies of the business' corporate leadership.

Competitive Edge – Mature businesses not only compete well with other businesses but also set or are capable of setting the tone, depth, and scope of the competition, from product and service lines to wages and prices. They maintain or seek to maintain the competitive edge. Without business watch dogs and regulatory agencies, mature businesses almost always tend to give in to the temptation of antitrust practices, price fixing, monopoly, and labor manipulation.

Collaboration – Mature businesses recognize their limits with regard to environmental constraints and production resources. They depend on resources from the environment—skilled laborers, raw materials, and innovative technologies—to function as business. To produce and market goods or provide services, they need reliable infrastructures such as clean water, energy or electricity, roads, and elaborate transportation apparatus (highways, bridges, airports, ports etc.). Inventions and innovations of new products and services can be astronomically expensive. Research and development can take years to bring a product from the lab to the market. All of these external demands dictate resource dependencies. To maximize the input operations budget, resource dependency demands require that business organizations collaborate with other business organizations in order to remain competitive in today's business environment in which investment capital is scarce and investors demand more returns on investments.

Mature businesses possess the capacity to convene and control meetings for collaboration purposes and do not hesitate to flex their muscles to engineer such collaboration. One way that they do this is by imposing astronomical membership requirements, thereby weeding out smaller or weaker competitors. Another way is by defining the collaboration endeavor as an exclusive working group of who's who in the industry, thereby triggering competition for membership application. Many mature businesses are able to use these and other mechanisms (discussed later this chapter) to guide their business into new or steady growth as outlined above.

However, danger lies in the tendency for large businesses to become so large and self-absorbed that they lose sight of their original mission and goals of meeting defined societal needs.

If and when this condition persists, a business begins to lose its competitive edge, a step on a slippery slope that, if not reversed in time, leads to a shell of the business' past glory.

Decline Phase

A business will eventually decline, no matter how careful or careless the leaders and those led are. A well-managed business will last for a long time—perhaps decades and even centuries. Even a great business will meet its waterloo at some point in time, however, due to changes in the environment, shifts in customer taste and loyalty, a community's decline, new inventions, technological advancements, and other developments. When this happens, many businesses close their doors for good. Some sell their operations and interests, while others break up or morph into smaller businesses, a mere semblance of their past. Poorly run businesses generally don't stand a chance. They either file for bankruptcy or simply fold, leaving many people out in the cold.

It is important to understand these dynamics in the business organizational life cycle in order to ensure that you are going into an industry or acquiring a business that has a future and is not in decline. This understanding is even more critical if you plan to use your life savings or other people's hard-earned money to start a business or acquire an existing one.

Organizational Types

Businesses are formed by way of planning and organizing tasks and functions that need to be performed by people and machines. The results of this exercise, properly conceptualized and implemented, are organizations and organizational charts. Although all businesses are one form of organization or another, not all organizations are business. Thus, there are two types of organizations – those that include businesses and those that do not include businesses. The latter are public organizations while the former are private organizations. Although they have similarities, there are also differences between the two. It is important to understand these distinctions with respect to the successful management of private sector organizations. Before we examine these differences and their implications for business success, however, let's examine first the structures of public and private organizations.

Public Organizations – Primary Culture

Public organizations are generally planned, structured, and implemented with the public's interest in mind. They are the governments at work. Public employees work in these organizations and structures to build or strengthen the primary culture and infrastructures of society. Public employees, organizations, and structures exist to serve the interests of the public at the local, state, national, and international levels.

Some public organizations are small, depending on their portable but nevertheless important functions and responsibilities. Small independent offices, commissions, and programs fall into this category. We call these offices, commissions, and programs—for lack of a better term—micro public organizations. Many public organizations are large, given the enormous public workloads, functions, and responsibilities they are tasked with. Large departments with cabinet status as well as independent and semi-autonomous agencies fall under this category. We call these large departments and agencies—again, for lack of a better term—macro public organizations.

Private Organizations – Secondary Culture

Businesses are private organizations. It is individuals (entrepreneurs) bringing people, machines and materials together (organization) to meet a need in society (business). The individuals do this by tapping the human and material resources within the environment to produce goods and services (capitalism) for public consumption and profits (markets) as defined by the representative government (democracy). That is, the government creates the infrastructures or primary culture (law and order, regulations, roads, bridges, energy sources, etc.) and the business owners build the multi-structures or secondary cultures. The latter is always within the limits and dictation of the former. The sky is essentially the limit, to the extent that a business owner can find ways to maximize human and natural resources in the environment within defined and enforceable laws and regulations. Thus, the ability to maximize resources accounts for the variations in the size and type of organizations.

Most businesses start very small or relatively large, depending on the real or perceived societal needs that they attempt to respond to and the ability to mobilize resources to meet those needs. Over time, some businesses grow into large companies and ultimately become corporations. Others grow into mid-size companies. Many remain small businesses for the duration of their existence. Small businesses generally require small structures and, in effect, small organization, given their focus and geographical span. Most business entities in America are small businesses of 500 or less employees, including

S-corporations, sole proprietors, and self-employed individuals. We call these businesses, for lack of a better term, micro private organizations.

Large and corporate business operations require elaborate structures and, in effect, become large organizations, given their enormous workloads, production and service capacities, number of employees, geographical span, and complex hierarchical structures. We call these large and mega companies, for lack of a better term, macro private organizations. These businesses are macro in nature, in that they control enormous resources—the number of employees, huge budgets, the markets, geographical span, and the scope and depth of influence on the economy. Their gigantic scopes and depths of influence are commensurate to those of big cities and/or large departments in the public sector. Although large businesses have a lot in common with public organizations, significant differences remain.

Similarities and Differences

The most obvious similarities are in the forms and structures of the public and private organizations (see Appendix 7 for visual conceptualization of these similarities). The structures of small public organizations and small businesses are essentially the same—few managers and supervisors managing a small number of employees. The size and scope of their respective forms and structures reflect the size and scope of their respective functions and responsibilities. In the same vein, the elaborate structures of the large public organizations and large business organizations are basically the same—senior management, middle managers, and a large operations department of supervisors and staff who do the bulk of the work. Again, the large size and scope of their respective forms and structures reflect the enormous size and scope of their respective functions and responsibilities. With regard to forms and functions, the macro private organizations look more like macro public organizations than micro private organizations, and micro private organizations look more like micro public organizations.

The most noticeable differences are in the area of revenue sources and the overall goals of public organizations and private organizations (Appendix 7 also provides a visual conceptualization of these differences). Public organizations are funded through appropriations from taxes. A few public agencies are cash funded. That is, they collect fees for services and products to the consumers. But the revenues from the fees are meant to cover the costs associated with the production of the products and services, without the benefit of a profit margin. The goal of public organizations is public good—the security, safety, and overall functioning of the general public and the economy.

Nonprofit organizations tend to retain the semblance of public organizations in that they raise funds primarily through donations and grants from the general public, including from governments and businesses, to accomplish their goals—namely, social goals. Profit is not the primary motivation of most nonprofit organizations (e.g., 501(c) 3 organizations), so these organizations enjoy tax-exempt status. Donors to tax-exempt organizations are granted tax deduction privileges in return.

Private sector businesses or organizations are funded through revenue from product sales and charges for services provided as well as from capital and other investments. Businesses must perform and be profitable to remain in business. Hence, the primary goal of business is to make money and ensure profits (total revenues minus costs of production and services, including company and payroll taxes). In this regard, private micro and macro organizations are more alike, and public micro and macro organizations are more alike. There is consensus in the literature on public-private sectors that public organizations and private organizations are alike in unimportant ways (forms), but different in important ways (revenue streams, functions, and goals).

In the next chapter, we examine business structures, organizing instruments, processes, and operations, followed by a reflection about business as a mechanism for doubling down on productivity and wealth creation for the stakeholders.

CHAPTER 5

DOUBLING DOWN ON PRODUCTIVITY II— BUSINESS STRUCTURES AND OPERATIONS

We began the subject of doubling down on productivity in the preceding chapter by exploring the necessary link between career and business. We identified the triggers for the need for business, followed by an examination of business focuses, life cycle, and types. In this chapter, we continue our discussion on the subject matter. We examine business structures, organizing instruments, processes, and operations. The chapter concludes with a reflection on the bottom line: how business—if properly conceptualized, developed, and managed—can double down on productivity and wealth creation for the stakeholders, including employees, investors, and business owners.

Business Legal Structures

Individuals are required to register their business and/or obtain the necessary and proper licenses before setting up and operating a business in America. There are regulations and obligations to be followed and honored at the federal, state, and local levels in order to own and operate a business. The types of rules to follow, licenses to obtain, and obligations to honor depend, in large part, on both the nature and type of business that the individual or individuals have decided to engage in. The requirements vary from state to state and municipality to municipality, and change from time to time, so it is important to stay current on business operations requirements. Overall, the business type determines which legal instrument to use, which, in turn, determines the requirements to meet in starting and operating a business. Starting and owning a business in America can be rewarding, but it can also be quite demanding regarding operations requirements and tax obligations. Information from friends and family, including the information here or in this book, is just that—information—and does not replace information from legal and business professionals. In America, ignorance is never an excuse for failing to meet business requirements and obligations. If you have specific questions or are not sure about certain circumstances, be sure to talk to legal and business professional for guidance. This is important when considering the type of instrument to use in setting up your business, including the ones discussed below.

Sole Proprietorship – Self Employed

Sole proprietorship involves an ownership by one person, as the name suggests. The owner may be the only employee in a self-employed operation, although he or she may elect to hire a couple of helping hands seasonally or on an ongoing basis. The business may have an office or operate out of the owner's home. It is important to understand the requirements and obligations associated with sole proprietorship and all businesses in general. For example, regardless of size, all businesses are required to apply for and retain a federal identification number (FIN) from the Internal Revenue Service (IRS) and are required to pay federal taxes in some fashion. Some states and municipalities require registration and/or a license to operate as a sole proprietor; others do not, depending on size and revenue streams of the business.

All state and municipal governments have websites and offices that cater to the interests of individuals wanting to start any type of business. Many public and nonprofit organizations across the country and online provide information regarding business start-up requirements. Notable organizations are Small Business Administration (SBA), SCORE, and Chambers of Commerce, to name a few. My observation is that friends and neighbors can provide useful information, but they do not always have complete and current information, well intentioned though they may be. As mentioned above, in America, ignorance is not an excuse for failing to meet business requirements and obligations, so talk to legal or business professionals if you are unsure about any business requirements.

Limited Liability Company (LLC)

An LLC is an undertaking organized by an individual or group of individuals for purpose of doing business. Another variation of this type of business is Limited Liability Partners Company (LLPC). The number of owners can be unlimited and may include American citizens and noncitizens. As the name suggests, the business is registered with the appropriate government authority as a limited liability company. The legal instrument imposes limited liability on the owner or partners of the business should anything go wrong with the products and services provided to customers or clients that would cause a customer decides to sue or hold the business owners liable. The partners certainly pay higher fees for registration and higher business insurance premiums than, say, a self-employed person. It is a good business decision to talk to a legal professional for guidance when starting a limited liability company.

Franchise

A franchise is like a business association with individual owners as members. Individual business ownership requires agreeing to the terms and conditions of owning a business in the franchise. The corporate headquarters set the rules, policies, structure, merchandise, branding, supplies, marketing, and services, among other things. Each operation is independently owned by the businessperson. In return for these services and the use of the brand name, the businessperson pays a start-up fee in the form of investment and adheres to the policies and standard operating procedures (SOP) of the corporation in operating his business. The independent owner is required to participate in initial and ongoing employee development and growth programs. Based on the agreement or business model, some of the revenues go to the corporate headquarters and the rest stay with the independent owner to meet his share of the agreed-upon business operations. Registrations, licenses, and taxes are handled at the corporate or local level, depending on the business model and structure. It is important that the independent owner understand and properly execute his or her responsibilities to the corporation, his employees, the creditors, government, and other businesses. As stated earlier, ignorance is never an excuse for failing to meet business requirements and obligations. For this reason, it is highly advisable, from a business standpoint, to talk to a legal professional for guidance before signing off on a contract for a franchise business.

Corporation

A corporation is usually set up by completing an application with and receiving approval from the appropriate state office. A corporation must apply for and retain a federal identification number (FIN) and a state corporate ID number from the state in which it operates, regardless of whether or not the corporation has employees or actually engages in business activity. The ID numbers are used to track the corporation's existence and business activities for purposes of applicable fees and tax obligations. A corporation is a legal entity that grants a status to the corporate owners to engage in business activities. The status separates the business from the corporate entity and limits business liabilities to the corporation's equity. An S-corporation is a small corporation of one or more persons who engage or plan to engage in small business activities. The number of owners is limited to 100%, and the owners are generally American citizens. It is more formal with strict requirements than, LLCs, which are less formal and have a degree of flexibility. A small business can remain an S-corporation to the extent that it remains portable. Otherwise it morphs into a large corporation as it grows into a large company.

Large businesses are generally structured and registered as C-corporations, with a board made up of many directors who are not necessarily the day-to-day employees or managers of the business operations of the corporation. C-corporations are formal and follow complex rules and regulations. The Board of Directors (BOD) is responsible for the broad policies and overall direction of the corporation and the business activities of the corporation. This allows for a fair and equitable balance between the interests of the various stakeholders in the company, such as the employees, unions, management, shareholders, government, customers, multipliers, and creditors, subcontractors, to name a few. The BOD, as a part of the overall corporate structure, inspires the public to invest in the company by buying company shares and motivates top talents to want to work there.

As with anything big, large businesses have their share of the business woes as they organize and go public to attract capital and talent, and improve their visibility. They must deal with union and labor organization demands for wage increases, improved working conditions, and benefits for union members working in the company. The corporation must comply with environmental and consumer regulations as well as attend to the public's demand for corporate social responsibilities. If other corporations are giving grants and scholarship to local and regional causes, the expectation is that you should be socially responsible as well. Government scrutiny of your tax obligations tends to intensify as does your need to lobby politicians and engage in body politics. At the expense of repetition, ignorance is never an excuse for failing to meet corporate business requirements and obligations in America. If you are not sure, talk to or hire a legal professional for guidance regarding how to set up a corporation or when to go public.

Business Process: SMART

Businesses are operated based on information. A product-oriented business needs information on what to produce, as well as when, where, how, by how many, by whom, and, occasionally, why. Similarly, a service-oriented business needs information on what service to provide, as well as when, where, how, by how much, by whom, and, sometimes, why. For business to be efficient and effective in its mission and in reaching its productivity goals, it is important that information be processed and transmitted from one level to another, from top to bottom and from bottom to top. Business processes live or die depending on the accuracy, consistency, and currency of information being processed and transmitted to and from individuals or a group of individuals at the leadership, management, and operations levels.

We call this dynamic interplay of key players and information at various levels of the business process SMART, for lack of a better term. The acronym stands for Senior Management, Middle Management, Administrative Support Management, Research and Development Management, and Technical Core/Operations Management. Appendix 12 provides a visual conceptualization of these independent yet related levels of business modeling. In practice, the levels are interconnected parts of a complex whole. The levels or parts are segmented for the purpose of analysis that follows. In a small business, one or a few persons play all or most of these roles. In full performance or fully mature business, many different persons play these critical roles. The discussion below pertains primarily to large businesses, although the concepts also apply to all businesses.

Senior Leadership – Decision Making

The senior leadership of a business shapes the overall vision, mission, broad goals and strategic management, and general direction of the business. They make decisions that impact the overall health of the business organization. The senior management team does this based primarily upon the information available to them from the next level below them. In some businesses, the senior leadership is made up of executive managers (President, CEO, Senior VP, VPs, COO, and CFO, to name a few) with extensive managerial and leadership skills. Although they perform management functions, broadly speaking their primary role is to serve as the internal stabilizer of the business by making far-reaching, organization-wide decisions. They also serve as the ultimate public face of the business organization to the general public via public appearances and statements in the media, especially in times of crisis or following a major organizational accomplishment.

The decisions that they make are driven by information. There is consensus in the literature on leadership and decision making that quality decisions are driven by quality data. Put differently, the decisions, broad policies and adventuresome commitments that the senior leadership makes are only as good as the information on which those decisions and commitments are based. Successful leadership teams are aware of this, which is why such importance is placed on investing in information technology and personnel to ensure accurate, concurrent, and consistent information.

A fundamental function of senior management is strategic management—planning and supervising the overall growth and direction of the business. By putting a strategic plan in place, the senior leadership outlines long-term broad goals and policies to guide the business in the foreseeable future in the following three strategic areas:

Corporate Strategies (overall direction of the organization)
Competitive Strategies (designed to gain a competitive advantage/edge)

Functional Strategies (internal/departmental
strategies to support competitive advantage)

See Appendix 8 for an outline of the elements within each of
these three strategies. Growth strategy was discussed earlier in
this chapter under Business Life Cycle – *Full Performance Phase*.
See also Appendix 9 for an example of a Strategic Plan, relative
to ongoing management plans, slogans, goals, and objectives.

In summary, senior leadership defines the vision (where
the organization wants to be), mission (why the organization
is in business), broad policies (how the organization does what
it does), and strategies (how to get to where the organization
wants to be) of the business organization. Senior leadership
also models the values (principles that guide actions) and the
culture (the prescribed and proscribed beliefs, attitudes, and
behavior) of the business organization. The overall design,
development, and management of the business organization
are subject to their review and approval. These functions are
generally delegated to the next level of managers below the
senior leadership.

Middle Managers – Planning, Organizing, Leading, and Evaluating (POLE/GMAC)

The middle managers serve as directors, administrators,
and managers of the business organization. They take direct
orders from and report to the senior leadership. Middle
managers define the day-to-day policies of the business and
are responsible for the successful implementation of policies to
ensure efficient and effective business operations. They work
with data, figures, numbers, and charts to make informed
policy decisions and allocate human and fiscal resources.

They possess extensive managerial skills and a deeper understanding and knowledge of the business. With their managerial skills, knowledge, and abilities, they are responsible for the functions of management, namely, managing, organizing, leading, and evaluation (POLE).

Planning – Managers are responsible for the planning of business activities in consultation with the supervisors and the workforce. Planning involves breaking down the broad goals outlined by senior managers and developing them into manageable goals and measurable objectives. Thus, the broad goals of the business organization are the foundations of planning. As stated previously, useful and reliable data are the foundation of sound broad goals. And planning, including manageable goals and measurable objectives, is only as good as the broad goals, and the broad goals are only as good as the data on which they are based. The data is only as good as the integrity of the data collection and analysis processes, which the middle managers are responsible for managing and controlling. The point is, middle managers are the invisible "mighty" hands of business organizations. They are the shadow leaders of the organization. One way that they exercise authority is through planning; another way they exert influence is through information control. As the saying goes, information is power.

Organizing – Middle managers are also responsible for organizing a business organization to reflect the environment in which the business operates. They structure the organization to be able to respond to environmental constraints, demands, and supplies. They design the organizational outlay to ensure a steady supply of human and raw material resources for the long haul. For example, middle managers use their invisible or shadow power to set business agenda in connection with dealing with power brokers such as unions and organized labor or other deal breakers in favor of their business.

Based on internal performance and environmental scanning information, middle managers generally develop and implement organizational restructuring from time to time with senior leadership review and approval. These restructurings enable the business to respond to acute pressure from market forces, other competitors, government regulations, and natural disasters or manmade catastrophes, or a combination thereof.

Leading – As noted earlier, if the senior leadership is the visible face of the organization, the middle managers are the invisible but very real leaders of large businesses. Although not all leaders are managers, all managers are essentially leaders in one way or another. Not only do they control information, they also use the information to influence decisions almost at all levels. In the wake of the Great Recession, it is important to adequately supervise or manage middle managers, given the enormous leadership powers they have at their disposal. Failing to manage this important role is managing to fail. As the saying goes, the graveyard is full of failed managers with good intentions.

Evaluation or Control – The last function of managers being discussed here is evaluation. Another term for evaluation in the literature on program and organizational evaluation is control. Evaluation or control is by no means the least nor the last of the many functions of managers, but most of those functions and roles tend to fall within the purview of those discussed here.

Although supervisors and team leads are responsible for evaluating the employees under their immediate supervision, middle managers are responsible for taking the pulse of the business organization from time to time. The organizational vital signs help managers evaluate how the business is performing and predict how it will perform in future. There is no consensus in the literature on evaluation and control regarding what should constitute vital signs and exactly how those vital signs should be taken (unlike medicine, which looks at weight, blood pressure, temperature, pulse, etc.). There is, however, consensus that businesses not only should but must have an evaluation and control program in place. Further, organizational evaluation is a function of management and ought not to be delegated or contracted out.

Based on my observations and on business literature, there is a common trend that can be summarized regarding how to measure organizational health. In order for a sound evaluation to control quality and growth, it should include at least the following four elements: goals, metrics, analysis, and control, referred to collectively as GMAC.

Managers often set *goals* for the business at the beginning of the year. They determine the **metrics** for measuring the goals and also ensure that there is a mechanism for collecting performance data throughout the year for periodic *analysis*. Based on the data analysis, an evaluation is conducted at the end of the year to determine if the goals are being met for the purpose of *control*. They control for command to repeat the process if goals are met. They control for correction if goals are not met. Managers should make corrective recommendations for the following year to senior leadership for their review and approval.

It is important to note here that managers can carry out these and other administrative, research, and analytical functions through the services of a vast array of employees who perform the work of these functions. Although some business scholars and researchers see these cadres of second tier managers and supervisors as a part of the middle manager category, others classify them separately right under middle managers in the organizational structure. My take is that since they are in the org chart, they should be accounted for, even if only for the purpose of analysis.

Administrative Support and Research and Development

Program offices, administrative support staff divisions, sections, and units belong in this category. The category includes the Procurement/Contract office, Human Resources office, Talent Development branch, Training division, Payroll section, Time and Attendance unit, Records office, Privacy office, and FOIA office. Also included in this category are the financial services divisions and branches, which encompass accounts receivable and payable, travel, and purchase cards, to mention just a few. Additionally, there are the Research and Development (R&D) offices and programs responsible for business creativity as well as new products and services. R&D's daily workload include such tasks as data collection, analysis, quality control, product research, survey, field research, and opinion polls, to mention just a few. There is no one best way to structure these offices and programs. Different businesses organize them differently based on their needs while controlling for optimal use of available virtual and physical spaces.

These cadres of employees range from mostly skilled workers (with college or graduate degrees) to unskilled workers (with a high school diploma or its equivalent). HR specialists and supervisors, program managers, management and program analysts, budget specialists, statisticians, IT specialists, and managers, to name a few, work in the offices, divisions, and branches as listed above. R&D employees do not generally fit here, since many of them have degrees in science, technology, religion, engineering, arts, and mathematics (STREAM). Others hold certifications in other disciplines with highly specialized technical and professional skills. They nevertheless tend to "serve" at the will and pleasure of the middle and senior leadership. After all, data don't have imaginations, people do.

Administrative support and R&D are much like the software that runs the computers. If you think about the software that makes it possible for humans to use computers to run machines, airplanes, ships, electricity grids, and nuclear weapons and plants, you begin to have a greater appreciation for these vast arrays of employees and their much-needed functions. Unfortunately, they nevertheless tend to be the sacrificial lambs during periods of budget crunch, slow demands for products and services, or economic downturn.

Overall, they make technical and administrative decisions, but primarily follow rules, guidance, guidelines, instructions, eligibility requirements, standard operating procedures (SOP), instruction manuals (IM), job aids, and frequently asked questions (FAQ) in the performing their duties. Many of these documents are generally drafted and put in place by the administrative employees, work groups, and teams, subject to clearance through circulation and supervisory approval. The documents tend to reflect the broad goals and policies set by middle and senior leadership. The administrative support and R&D staff not only service the overall administrative and management functions of the business organization, but they also serve as a necessary bridge between middle managers and the technical core and operations departments, especially in the area of information processing, repository, and retrieval.

Technical Core – Operations

Researchers sometimes refer to this component of business operations as the beast of burden—where the work of the business is actually done. The very location of the technical core on any visual conceptualization of a business organization only serves to reinforce this observation. The weight of the other structural levels rest on the technical core level, also called operations management. A business must perform and make a profit to stay in business. That is, business must produce products to sell for money and/or provide services for which to charge fees. Thus, operations management does the heavy lifting of whatever the business is in business for, whether product or service, or a combination thereof.

The expertise and the skills for performing the tasks, functions, and work of production and service delivery reside with this department. The workers in this department possess the specialized knowledge, skills, and expertise need to do the core work of the business. All business operations have an abundance of these workers. These workers do the core work of production and/or service, hence the term "technical core." The general public associates these workers with the business and a business is occupationally defined and classified based on the sheer number of these workers in that business. For example, doctors, nurses and medical technicians are the technical core workers in hospitals. A person visiting a hospital would rightly expect to see an abundance of doctors, nurses, and medical technicians. Lawyers and judges are in abundant supply in courthouses as the technical core professionals. A sports team's players are at the core of, say, a basketball or football organization. Meat cutters dominate meat factories, teachers drive schools, and roofers are in charge in the roofing industry, to name a few occupations. The core workers do the core work for which the organization is in business.

The core work is performed based on the information provided by the managers. For example, how many vehicles in what category and brand to produce daily or weekly on the assembly line, or the number of patients to admit to the emergency room, intensive care, outpatient and inpatient care daily or weekly based on the hospital's capabilities. As the core work is being performed, data is fed back to management with respect to how many products are actually being produced or services are actually being provided. This information is used to make adjustments up or down at various levels of the business organization. To be efficient and effective in achieving its goal, business operations management is structured to include three major divisions: the input, the transformation, and the output.

Operations Management and Process

Large businesses generally have a Vice President or Chief Operating Officer (COO) who is responsible for the overall operations management. This ensures that the technical core work is represented at the executive table, where the broad policies and general direction of the business are decided. The COO usually appoints or hires managers to head the major divisions of operations. The managers hire supervisors who, in turn, hire employees to do the actual job. The layers and complexity of the hierarchical structure depends on the complexity and size of the business organization as well as the number of operations locations involved. The most important thing is that everyone knows their own responsibilities and what is required of them within the context of broadly defined divisions of labor: the input, transformation, and output.

Input

The input component is primarily responsible for the supply of raw materials for production or services. Raw materials include a wide range of things that must be managed to ensure a steady supply of raw materials: human resources, material resources, transportation, contracted raw materials, physical plants, machines, and warehouses, to list a few. Decisions have to be made as to whether it is cost effective to acquire the raw materials directly or contract this out to subcontractor to supply the raw materials. Sometimes it is necessary to do a combination—direct supply of the core raw materials while contracting out the supply of supporting raw materials.

Additionally, input managers and supervisors must decide whether any cost savings will be realized by teaming up with other companies in the same business to access hard-to-reach raw materials or to lobby the government to provide infrastructure access to the raw material. If there will be cost savings by teaming up with others, it is not necessary to go it alone. Sometimes a combination of solutions is the best way to go. For example, an ice company could team up to access clean mineral water located up the mountain or convince government to pave the road to the mountain where the clean mineral water is located. Alternatively, the manager can work with R&D to come up with another way to make mineral water from ordinary clean water from a local dam located down the highway.

Input managers, supervisors, and employees are faced with challenges to find ways to ensure a steady supply of quality raw materials at the lowest price possible. They work with high level managers for budget allocation, R&D for innovative information and discoveries, and competitors and "foes" for collaborations;

the list goes on. After all, no raw materials means no production, and no production means no business! It's that simple! But this observation also highlights the important role and functions of the input department in operations management and in the entire business organization.

Transformation

Business is about combining the forces of labor and machines to convert or transform materials into products, goods, and services. The transformation department encompasses this process, which is at the center of operations management. Transformation is the core of the technical core; the cream of the crop, or the icing on the cake. In manufacturing, it is the process of converting raw materials into products—beating, bonding, bending, and torturing steel and iron into a fashioned object, called a car, at the end of the process at the end of the day. In a service business, it is the process of converting skills, expertise, and labor in combination with tools to produce a service (e.g., taking vital signs, making a diagnosis or prognosis, writing prescriptions, cutting an incision, extracting semen) for a patient during a visit. The patient receives something of value—treatment, cure, health, prescription drug—at the end of the hospital visit.

Skilled Workers and Professionals - The higher the risks associated with a transformation process, especial in service industry, the higher the level of education, training, refresher courses, licensing, regulations, and professionalism required of the personnel performing the work of the core functions (see Appendix 20 for examples). In traditional manufacturing, skills were acquired over time through rote learning or on-the-job training. In today's high tech environment, assembly workers are required to have some level of education, particularly in computer technology and factory automation.

Quality Control - Additionally, the transformation department, (also called manufacturing or just production) tends to be the most expensive part of a business operation with respect to capital investment and personnel costs—salaries and benefits, recruitment, relocation and retention expenses, training, refresher courses and career development costs, to name just a few. The aspect of business operations can also be expensive regarding the overall upgrading and maintenance of physical plants and keeping up with applicable accreditations and regulatory standards. Within the transformation division and to some extent in the high level management echelon, the expectation generally is that what can go wrong will not or should not be allowed to go wrong. The adverse effect of errors in production or defective rolled out products can be enormous in terms of cost: damage control, recalls, fines, lost revenues, litigations, low morale, and brain drain. In principle, management at all levels is aware of these probabilities and the consequences. In reality, rather than correcting a quality control problem, managers sometimes make decisions to cut corners to the extent that they can get away with it, even though a stitch in time would save nine, as the saying goes. The operative term is "in time." Management sometimes delays actions until the corrective measures that are implemented are too little and too late. As quality control suffers, so do the products and services. Ultimately, the overall business organization suffers the consequences of inaction.

Communication and Information - A common underlying cause of production errors and poor quality control is the tendency for a business to adopt a quality-focused strategy, but fail to live up to the standards in production and service delivery. Rather than revisiting business strategies, making the necessary structural adjustments, refocusing business goals and objectives, and communicating these changes to operations management, senior management usually leaves operations management to their own devices to come up with ways to meet unrealistic quotas. And even if communicated, the information is poorly transmitted to the operations managers and supervisors who sometimes are the last ones in the loop about the recommended changes in goals and objectives. A clear line of accurate, current, and consistent decisions from the top to the operations more often than not solves all the problems discussed above. Bottom line: Communication, communication, communication! Information, information, information! Communication and information are two sides of the same proverbial coin. The transformation department needs accurate information to be communicated to them in a timely manner in order to stay on target to reach the quality and quantity goals.

Output

The output department's primary function is rolling out the products and services for marketing. Output managers handle all functions associated with the display, sales, and maintenance of products. They are also responsible for follow-up services. The goal is to position the product or service for public consumption. The objective is to bring the product and services to customers where they are and to bring the customers to the products and services where they can purchase them. The customer service associates, sales personnel, account managers, floor designers, visual and virtual designers, and inventory specialists, to name a few, work in the output division. What good are products and services if customers are not buying them? Thus, the sales pitch, what is trendy, and "flying off the shelf" are the buzz words in this department. Customers are always treated with respect and presumed to be right, to the extent that they can and will buy the products and services.

Multiple Distribution Channels - The key is to use multiple distribution channels (radio, mass communication, and social media) to get the word out to targeted consumers. For example, radio works better for customers in the rural areas. Social media (Internet, Twitter, email, smart phones, tablets) work better for reaching young people, while newspapers or print media and direct mailings are more effective when trying to reach older folks and baby boomers. Race car events would be a location or broadcast of choice for an ad targeting middle class males in the southeastern part of America. Hockey games are a more effective channel for an ad that targets middle class Canadians. Where cost is an issue in getting the word out, low-cost, old-fashioned outlets can be used to reach the target audience. Interestingly, radio continues to be the least expensive mass communication outlet among the various times and places to get the word out.

Repeat Customers Effect – Many output divisions rely heavily on marketing research and surveys to identify the right audience and to sample customers' tastes and preferences. Since research and surveys can be expensive, output managers and supervisors can use the services of in-house R&D to leverage marketing information. Prior year sales data can serve as a guide for charting the roll out and marketing strategy for future products and services. Perhaps the best approach is to make quality products and provide excellent services while controlling for cost and price. To the extent that the products and services meet the needs of customers, not only will the customers come back for the same or similar products and services from the company, they will also tell their friends, family, and neighbors how satisfied they are with the company's products and services. We call this phenomenon, for lack of a better term, repeat customer effect. There is consensus in the literature on output management that customer satisfaction with product and services and "word of mouth" are still the most efficient and effective ways to build a lasting customer base for new and current products and services.

Money in Bank – The output division must be properly managed and controlled to account for all sales and charges of all products and services. This is where most businesses fall far short and hemorrhage revenues due to products and services that are unaccounted for. Proper inventory and recordkeeping usually correct these problems. A transparent accounting system must be put in place to ensure accurate and complete receipts of all sales, charges, and refunds/returns. A business must be making money and profits in order to continue to stay in business. Put differently, as the saying goes, there has to be money in the bank. The output division has a responsibility to make this happen.

Bottom Line – Doubling Down on Productivity

The bottom line is that a business must find away make money and stay profitable. A business must continuously explore all available avenues to optimize the resources at its disposal and, in the process, create wealth in some fashion for the stakeholders, including the business owners.

Profit or Perish

A business must be profitable to thrive in the long run or it will perish. All businesses start from somewhere, notably as an entrepreneurship. Chances are that many people will start or attempt to start in business as entrepreneur at some point during their lifetime. My favorite definition of an entrepreneur is a person who meets a need or two and figures out a quick and honest way to make a buck or two out of it. Let's unpack the elements:

> Meet – doing something
> Need – a societal felt need
> Figure out – creativity, being creative
> Quick – fast-paced approach; you snooze, you lose mindset
> Honest – a value that separates an entrepreneur from scammers
> Way – a calculated plan that links reward to action
> Make – earn a living
> A buck or two – a reasonable profit by a reasonable person's standards

Diversified Investment Portfolios

Admittedly, a business will not double down your earnings and productivity any more than a job will until one thing happens—diversification. You need to diversify the investment portfolios of your business to ensure continuous growth, productivity, and profits. Diversified business investment portfolios ensure a degree of immunization against risks. You will never completely eliminate the risks associated with entrepreneurship and growth strategies, but you certainly can minimize them. By diversifying your business focus and orientation, you can also mitigate the impact of recessions or market failures.

Wealth – Real Property, Intellectual Property, and Proprietorship/Patents

Wealth associated with business ownership includes, but is not limited to, real estate property, intellectual property, and proprietorship/patents. As a business grows, it will need to acquire the space and property to operate and expand. That is, at some point the business will own property to save on rental and leasing costs. The same can be said about intellectual property, proprietorship, and patents (the list goes on) arising from the company's research and developments, and innovations and inventions. Put another way, if you take care of your business (investments), your business will take care of you (return on investments). It's the American way. As the saying goes, what goes around comes around. Cast your bread upon the waters, says the preacher, and you'll find it after many days! Your sense of accomplishment, personal wealth, and business legacy are additional benefits to your achieving financial success. Now, that's doubling down on productivity!

CHAPTER 6

IMAGINE A MORE PERFECT UNION

In the preceding four chapters, we discussed the elements that form the means of productivity in American culture. We examined the human and economic elements that make America productive: the habits of productive people (Chapter 2), jobs as a mechanism with which individuals pursue an honest living and productivity (Chapter 3), and businesses as mechanisms for doubling down on productivity (Chapters 4 and 5). It was acknowledged that the interplays between individuals, jobs, and businesses do not happen in a vacuum; these human and economic elements are an integral part of the American culture. To fully appreciate the dynamic nature of the means or capabilities of productivity, it is necessary to dissect the context, namely, the American culture.

Thus, in the next four chapters, we will seek to answer the question "What makes America tick?" The short answer: A lot! For purposes of analysis, we will formulate the many responses to this inquiry in the following order: the quest for a more perfect Union (Chapter 6), an appreciation for diversity under one big tent called America (Chapter 7), law and order as conditions for peace and justice for all (Chapter 8), and the acceptance that life is good but not always easy and fair (Chapter 9). Together, these genres form the hardware or pillars of American culture. Put differently, these genres represent the core ideas and values that make America tick and, in effect, allow productivity to be possible.

The Declaration of Independence – "Resolve to Conquer or Die"

It is important to understand that the early settlers, and later the colonies, were not interested in founding a country that was independent from Europe. There doesn't appear to be historical evidence that this was the case. The colonies named cities, towns, counties, and landmarks after the monarchies and stayed in close ties with Europe. As noted above, settlers' quests for a just and free society where they could worship freely, accumulate wealth, and pursue happiness were paramount in their primary preoccupations and objectives.

In the Declaration of Independence, the founding fathers made it abundantly clear that the government is established to preserve the fundamental rights of the people and to protect the people against any abuses of their inalienable rights. They made the case that if and when a government fails in these obligations, the people have the right to abolish or sever their relationship with that government. But the evidence must be abundantly clear that this was the case, which is exactly what the founders did in the Declaration of Independence. By my count, there were an estimated 75 counts of abuses of power by acts of omission and commission leveled against the monarchy. Of these, 27 were abuses relating to colonial authorities, 25 were abuses relating to the societies and the people, and 23 were abuses relating to unfair, arbitrary, and capricious laws.

The founders were willing to do whatever it would take to secure and guarantee these rights for themselves and posterity. The stakes were high and they understood this. In the words of the founding president, George Washington, in his letter to General Thomas, July 23, 1775, during the Revolutionary War:

A people contending for life and liberty are seldom disposed to look with a favorable eye upon either men or measures whose passions, interests or consequences will clash with those inestimable objects.

And in his address to the Continental Army before the Battle of Long Island, on August 27, 1776, he made the case for a free and just society for them and their posterity, no matter the cost:

> The time is now near at hand which must probably determine whether Americans are to be freemen or slaves; whether they are to have any property they can call their own; whether their houses and farms are to be pillaged and destroyed, and themselves consigned to a state of wretchedness from which no human efforts will deliver them. The fate of unborn millions will now depend, under God, on the courage and conduct of this army. Our cruel and unrelenting enemy leaves us only the choice of brave resistance, or the most abject submission. We have, therefore, to resolve to conquer or die.

It is important to underscore here that the founders and, in fact, the armies of the Revolutionary War were considered rebels at the time and, I might add, rebels with a cause—a cause for inalienable rights. These rights would later be enshrined and guaranteed in the Constitution. The Bill of Rights and subsequent Amendments and Statutes would guarantee these and other rights to all. Thus, if the Declaration of Independence was a repudiation of the State, Society, and Statutes that the Colonial system represented, the Constitution was a representation of the new system that the founders craved.

The wisdom of the founders was forward looking in nature. Hence they ensured that these ideas were encapsulated in what we now view as sacred documents—the Declaration of Independence, the Constitution, and the Statutes. As the saying goes, a short pencil is better than a long memory. In the Declaration of Independence, the founders ensured that Americans then and thereafter were committed to ensuring inalienable rights for all—life, liberty, and the pursuit of happiness. In some of the Colonial American constitutions and charters, which served as precursors to both the Declaration of Independence and the Constitution, the right to property, along with the other three inalienable rights, was always considered and understood to be at the core of the inalienable rights of individuals.

The Quest for "a More Perfect Union"

I taught a course on Critical Thinking and American Culture for many years at Metropolitan State University of Denver. I would begin the first day of class with the question, "What is the secret of a great nation or country?" Of the many responses that the question would elicit, my favorite answer would always be along this line: the quest for a more perfect nation or country. This response captures the essence of what has made America tick since the dawn of colonial America in the 1600's and the founding of independent America since the 1770's.

The founders of independent America said it very well in the Preambles to the United States Constitution: "We the people ... in order to form a more perfect Union ..." The founders committed themselves and the people of the United States, then and thereafter, to forming a more perfect Union than the one they lived in and the one they intended to pass on for posterity. The Constitution was drafted as a framework, the supreme law or blueprint, for perfecting the Union. Since then, each generation has worked very hard to improve on the Union that is handed them and then pass an improved Union on to the next generation. My observation is that this quest for a more perfect America sets and drives Americans to be the best that they can be in all of their undertakings, both privately and publically. Hence the quotes "You can do better than that," or "We can do better than that."

The quest for a more perfect Union also inspires in Americans the ability to self-renew, self-critique, and self-govern. As an American Christian thinker puts it, the quest to do better or to be all that we can be tends to create a sense of restlessness in Americans. That sense of restlessness prevents them from settling for less or for the status quo. Laws are enacted to bring the Union up to speed with modern technology and human innovations. New policies and programs are created and implemented to ensure the perfection of decaying and outdated programs and policies. New goals are set to inspire competition and collaborations in new generations. These constant efforts toward renewal contribute to both the perfection and the greatness associated with a more perfect Union from one generation to the next.

As mentioned previously, America has been criticized because it constitutes only 4% of the world's population but consumes 20-24% of the world's energy. What these critics often omit or ignore is the cost of maintaining peace, humanitarian services, and philanthropy around the world (see Appendix 1). America produces more (if not most of the) Nobel Prize winners, Olympic medalists, patents and inventions, scientists, and millionaires and billionaires, and welcomes more immigrants, tourists, and conferences than any other nation in the world. It has the highest GDP, military expenditure, and per capita income of any nation. America is a beacon of hope and the destination of choice—more than any other country—for migrants, refugees, asylum seekers, tourists, and businesspeople alike.

For the founders, a perpetual perfecting of the state, society, and the statutes was not a luxury or even a necessary evil. It was a duty. The nation as a Union would have to be free from evil, injustice, and the imperial power of the oppressors (evidence of which was well documented in the Declaration of Independence) and perpetually seek a perfect balance between the leaders and those who are led or the state and society as well as between the absolute and the relative laws of the land from generation to generation. These elements—State, Society, and Statutes—of the American Experiment have evolved over the centuries as a process of perfecting the Union. We will dissect these elements briefly.

State – Vertical Reach

From the point of State-Society framework of the Union, the State is the representative government of the people. That is, the government represents, serves, and works for the interests of the general public. In order to fully represent and work for the people, the State is designed to have what we might call, for lack of a better term, vertical reach. That is, the State works for the people at the federal, state, and local levels. To ensure fairness and equitable performance of the responsibilities of all three tiers, each level of government is further divided into three branches, a form of division of labor.

Federal Government (FG)

The federal government (FG) serves the entire nation and represents the nation in the conduct of foreign policies. The FG has the primary responsibility of national security and safety. The founders, in crafting the Constitution as the supreme law of the land, divided the federal government into three equal branches and assigned each one specific roles and responsibilities. Thus, there are three branches of the FG: the executive branch, the legislative branch, and the judiciary branch. Broadly speaking, the legislative branch makes the laws, the judiciary branch interprets the laws, and the executive branch enforces the laws. Several major observations emerge from this experiment.

First, the president as head of the executive branch is the nation's chief executive officer. He is the president of the country and the commander-in-chief of the armed forces. In this regard, the American system of government is set up like a business with clear responsibilities and authority, with the "buck" stopping at the president. The president appoints senior leadership, made up of White House senior staff and cabinet heads (called department secretaries); middle managers (directors, administrators and commissioners), and multiple support staff, and R&D and operations employees, most of whom are located in the departments and agencies.

Second, as the legislative body, Congress is made up of two houses: the House of Representatives (elected from the people by the people in each of the districts in a state) and the Senate (two elected persons from the people by the people for each of the 50 states). In this regard, the FG is actually a representative government of the people by the people for the people. There are other territories and the District of Columbia (DC). These territories and DC are considered full members of the Union, but are not full-fledged states. Thus, they have no voting rights in Congress.

Third, the division of responsibilities ensures a balance. For example, the legislative branch makes laws which are actually bills until the president signs them into law. The president nominates judges, but the Senate confirms the nomination. The president submits an annual budget, but the Congress approves it before the president can sign it into law in order for the taxpayers' money to be disbursed accordingly. This ensures that even if individuals or a group of individuals did not vote for a president, a representative, or a senator not from the same party as the administration, they can be sure they'll be treated fairly and equitably, given the checks and balances as envisioned by the founders.

Fourth, if and when the executive and the legislative branches disagree with each other regarding how a Constitutional provision should be interpreted and implemented, they defer to the Supreme Court for resolution. If the executive branch or the legislative branch disagrees with the public regarding a policy, law, or interpretation thereof, the lower courts rule on the case. If disagreement persists, the Supreme Court makes a final ruling on the case. So the people can challenge their leaders if they feel that the leaders have strayed.

Fifth, the people elect the president, the vice president, and the representatives, and so hold the ultimate power over their leaders. The people reward the leaders by re-electing them for doing a good job or punish them for doing a bad or poor job by not re-electing them. However, Americans are very generous people and so sometimes give a president another chance by re-electing him even though he did a mediocre job.

Sixth, to carry out its ever increasing and complex responsibilities, the FG creates jobs and employs people by the millions. The FG also hires the services of contractors and grantees to do the work of governing and serving public interests. Contractors provide the government with products and services in return for payment, as agreed upon through the bid process. The FG gives money in the form of grants to individuals and nonprofits to provide products and services to the general public. Grants are also awarded to universities and think tanks to conduct research for the FG. The FG, through direct hire, contracts, and grants, creates job and business opportunities for Americans in all walks of life.

State Governments (SGs)

SGs are structured very much the same way as the FG. Each state has its own constitution, an elected governor and lieutenant governor, two houses of elected representatives, and a judiciary to ensure a balance of power as well as an equitable share of responsibilities and service delivery to the people of the state. The elected representatives are called different names in different states. There is consensus in the literature on governments that the powers and responsibilities that the United States Constitution did not assign to the federal government should go to the states. What is not clear is just what constitute these powers and responsibilities. Where differences in interpretation emerge or persist, the courts are usually called upon to sort out these differences. In general, FG laws tend to preempt state laws, especially where and when it is determined that FG has jurisdiction. Federal laws also take precedence over state laws in matters of national security and safety, especially when there are national/international implications.

Much like the FG, SGs create jobs and employ people by the tens and hundreds of thousands to carry out state responsibilities. SGs also hire the services of contractors and grantees to perform a wide range of duties, tasks, and functions. Contractors provide products and services in return for payment agreed upon through requests for proposal or sole bids. SGs give grants to individuals and nonprofits to provide products and services to the general public. They also award limited grants to universities and think tanks to conduct research for them. SGs, through direct hiring, contracts, and grants, create job and business opportunities for Americans, but mostly from among residents of the state.

Local Governments (LGs)

LGs include county governments, city governments, and town administrations, to name just a few. Cities are governed by elected mayors and council members who are either full time or part time, depending on the size of the city. Counties are governed by elected county executives, chairs, and/or commissioners. These governments do not have constitutions. They are technically functions of the state in which they reside. Their authority is derivative in nature. That is, they derive their authority from the state's constitution and laws. Much the same way that SG laws align with rather than contradict federal laws, LG laws, ordinances, codes, and charters do not contradict but, rather, align with state laws. LG laws tend to expand on state laws and apply to local situations and circumstances.

The functions of LGs are critical and very important in that this is where the proverbial rubber meets the road. The elected or appointed leaders and their employees of LGs interact with citizens and noncitizen residents in their jurisdiction on a daily basis. They are the direct respondents to residents' calls regarding all sorts of emergencies, disasters, and community concerns, security and safety breaches, and complaints. The bulk of LG budgets go toward law enforcement, and safety and security services: police, firefighters, medical emergency dispatchers. They deal with issues of employment and wages on a daily basis with local employers and employees, unions, and labor markets, to name a few. They ensure that trash is picked up regularly, that zonings are correct and in compliance, and that schools are open and children are being educated.

Like the FG and SGs, LG authorities, in order to carry out local responsibilities, create jobs and employ people by the hundreds, thousands, or tens of thousands, depending on the population of the municipality. LGs also hire the services of contractors and grantees to perform professional, regulatory, and enforcement duties, functions, and demands. Contractors provide services and products in return for payment agreed upon through requests for proposal and sometimes sole bids. LGs give grants to individuals and nonprofits to provide products and services to local residents. They award grants on a very limited basis to universities and think tanks to conduct feasibility studies regarding installations or similar services.

LGs, through direct hire, contracts, and grants, create jobs and business opportunities mostly for local residents.

Strict laws and guidelines are followed at all levels and in all branches of government when hiring employees and awarding contracts and grants, to ensure equal opportunity for all. These public laws and most of the guidelines carry over into the private and nonprofits sectors. Discrimination, corruptions and bribery are illegal. Undue influence on public officials and employees is discouraged. For example, businesses and nonprofits are prohibited from hiring based on favoritism and cannot deny hiring individuals on the basis of race, ethnicity, country of origin, sexual orientation, or disability, to name a few. Violations carry stiff penalties, in addition to creating a bad public relations image that can linger for years. Compliance inspires integrity in the hiring, contracts, and grants processes. Compliance also inspires public confidence in the organization as a great place to work.

The immediate implications of an integrated and welcoming workplace in the public and private sectors are many, including fair and equitable opportunities for all Americans and legal residents, in addition to the perception that the organization promotes an inclusive work environment. These practices enhance productivity and boost the overall economy in the long term for the benefits of all parties involved—governments, businesses, nonprofits, individuals, employers, employees, investors, unions, and new arrivals, to list a few. As a notable American Nobel Laureate observed recently, the American socio-political experiment was and continues to be tilted towards a productive society: What makes America great is the great public-private partnership in education, infrastructure, open immigration, rules of capitalism, and government-funded research and development.

Society – Horizontal Reach

The pillars or ideas and values of American culture are best represented in the personification of the inalienable rights for all people. These rights are:

> Life
> Liberty
> Pursuit of happiness, and
> Property

These four fundamental rights of individuals, great and small, represent essentially the seminal ideas underlying the American culture. At the practical level, they personify the genius that drives American productivity and, in effect, the American economy. Resources, great and small, primary and secondary, infrastructural and multi-structural, public and private are mobilized from generation to generation both to guarantee and secure these rights for all Americans. Ideally the government guarantees the rights through the creation and sustaining of the conditions that guarantee them. The people appropriate these rights to themselves and posterity through a variety of apparatuses such as jobs, businesses, markets, and properties, to name a few. People, not governments, must create and sustain these apparatuses for and by themselves.

If and when the government guarantees these rights as well secures the benefits of these rights for the people, the government needs large resources by way of taxes, personnel, and other mechanisms. In so doing, the government takes a lot away from the overall economy. The immediate effect is an expanded government, and the long-term effect is the status quo, at best, and, at worst, spoiled citizens, a nanny society, and a shrinking economy. In this regard, the ratio of the public-private sectors' share of natural and economic resources tends to disproportionately favor the public sector. Not a good problem to have as a nation!

If and when the government guarantees these rights for the people, but the people secure the blessings of these rights for themselves, the government takes less in human, natural, and economic resources and leaves a lot of these resources for the citizenry. That is, society secures the rights for themselves by creating jobs, businesses, investments, and intellectual and real property. The immediate effect is robust job opportunities, entrepreneurships, and booming markets. The long-term effect is a thriving and booming economy and a shrunken government. In this regard, the ratio of the public-private sectors' shares of economic resources tends to be disproportionately in favor of the private sector. A good problem to have as a nation!

The point of the foregoing is that the government must not do for the people what the people can do for themselves. Put differently, in the words of an American president, "... ask not what your country can do for you, ask what you can do for your country." The government should only intervene, albeit short term, when there are anomalies and distortions in the economy for whatever reasons, whether induced by humans or naturally. In this regard, the government is there for the same reasons all sporting events need referees and umpires. This is the kind of society the founders envisioned for themselves and their posterity. Subsequent generations since then have sought to perfect society and pass it on to the next generation.

This envisioned society was a far cry from the kind of society the founders left behind in Europe. Society in Europe at the time was ripe with bloated monarchy, oligarchy, and theocracy that exploited the people and distorted the markets. It was a society the European philosophers abhorred and condemned for denying individuals their inalienable rights of life, liberty, and property. The founders of independent America made enormous sacrifices to eradicate the oppressive society in favor of a just and free society and markets. We already noted above the sentiment of those days, in the words of George Washington, that the founders would settle for nothing less than a free and just society and would do whatever it would take to eradicate injustices in favor of justice, even if this meant death at the hands of the Colonial oppressors.

The envisioned society is a society that would celebrate the dignity and rights of individuals and families, the beauty of neighborhoods and communities, and the honor and glory of a nation. A nation where American citizens would later sing that they are "proud to be an American, where at least I know I'm free." It was an evolving society designed for what we might call, for lack of a better term, horizontal reach. The horizontal reach engenders society to reach out to and includes all individuals and families, neighbors and communities, and all cultures from "sea to shining sea." The immediate outcome of the horizontal reach is unlimited opportunities for economic productivity at the family, neighborhood, and national levels.

Individuals/Families

The rights and freedoms of an individual are paramount in American thoughts, beliefs, and everyday living. Americans admire individualism almost to the point of worshipping it. Such concepts as being "free to be me," "following your dreams," and "the sky is the limit" are taught very early on in kindergarten and grade schools. Children are raised and socialized to be independent, while respecting and valuing the rights and independence of other individuals. Team sports are highly encouraged, but recognition and rewards tend to be on the basis of individuals. A basketball team was once told to work together as a team, since there is no "I" in team. The team leader, a legendary basketball superstar and a hall of famer, chimed in later on, saying, "There is no 'I' in team, but there is 'I' in win!"

The nuclear family—two parents (usually mother and father) and their children—is considered the reducible unit of society. For the parents, their home is their castle. For the children, their home is a safe haven they can count on for love, warmth, safety, security, food, shelter, and clothing. Having a place to call home and raise a family is the essence of the American Dream. The picket fence, a car, and a dog and/or a cat are complementary in rounding out the dream. The extended family members—uncles, aunts, cousins, in-laws—are good to have and for the most part welcome. But the primary roles and responsibilities are defined around the husband-wife-children triad.

Then as now, parents are expected to not only be king/queen of their own castle, but also to take responsibility for raising their family. In the words of America's founding president, George Washington, in his letter to Dr. Boucher, dated May 13, 1770:

> A natural parent has only two things principally
> to consider, the improvement of his son (and
> daughter [*added*]), and the finances to do it with.

To provide for the family, the expectation was and is that parents will work and be productive. Again, President George Washington, in a July 20, 1794 letter:

> I know of no pursuit in which more real and
> important services can be rendered to any
> country than by improving its agriculture, its

breed of useful animals, and other branches of
a husbandman's cares.

Neighborhoods/Communities

Americans take pride in their neighborhoods and
communities. This is evident from the many businesses, schools,
athletic teams, associations, and estate communities that take
their names from the neighborhood name. If individuals are
raised in the safe haven of the family, the families are raised in
the nurturing environment of the neighborhood. Neighbors
are traditionally considered as the first line of defense against
intruders. They also serve as natural fit for social networking,
given the mere fact of sharing same physical space. Neighbors
form neighborhood watches to have each other's back and to
keep crime at bay. There are neighborhood churches, yard
sales, sports facilities, schools, events, recreational centers, and
parks. Cities usually consist of neighborhoods. Unincorporated
areas of a county usually form a town or a community around
conglomerates of neighborhoods.

Over the years, Americans have tended to live in social
space. Social space networking, made easier by the advent of
vehicles and social media, expands the cycle of neighborhoods
to include individuals, families, and friends who are not in
the immediate physical environment. Some businesses exist
to serve just the neighborhoods, such as a child care center,
dry cleaning, swimming pool, or tennis court. Social space
dynamics make it possible for these businesses to expand their
customer base. For example, with social space networking,
friends and families who move to other areas due to jobs or
other reasons are able to retain services in the neighborhood

that they left behind, especially if there are no similar or quality services in their new neighborhood.

The Genius of American Culture

America is productive because its people are productive. The people are productive because their ideas, culture, and values are inherently inclined or bent towards productivity. The notion of life, liberty, and the pursuit of happiness and property envisioned by the founders as a basis for a civil society laid a solid foundation for future generations to build on. It would have been counterproductive if America were not productive.

There lie the core genius of American culture: ideas that are capable of self-replication, self-correction and self-governing. The ideas, by their very nature, possess the DNA to self-replicate, self-refine, and self-regulate the various expressions of those ideas in the larger culture. The ideas are routed in a worldview that recognizes human imperfection yet is willing to strive for that perfect state, to the extent possible.

The process of striving to be the best lends itself to constantly and consistently rewarding and reinforcing productive ideas, conduct, and behavior, while weeding out views and values that are nonproductive, counterproductive, and intolerant. The American people hold on dearly to ideas that have served them very well. They seek new ways to explore, discover, and experiment with new ideas, always within the context of the rich traditions (or canons) handed down from the previous generation.

People are never afraid to change course when they find new and effective ways to lead a more productive life, run a business, or provide services. Such, for example, was the case of capitalism and the concept of the president being the nation's CEO. But the people will not fall in love with ideas simply because they are new, particularly if they are untested. Such was the case with communism, which was repudiated and contained. In the case of containing and eliminating anti-democratic and anti-freedom ideas and values, there is no price too high to pay or burden too heavy to bear. Further, the idea of a free and self-governed society recognizes human frailty and so built in its DNA the notion of a second chance and tolerance. Such is the case of the concept of presidential pardon for persons guilty as the devil, deserving no second chance but nevertheless granted a second chance by a sitting president.

People try to strike a balance between reality and ideas, recognizing that a perfect Union can be and often is elusive. But the beauty of this tension is that the process of striving for a balance between ideas and realities is, by its very nature, productive. I'm impressed with how Americans can always manage to make sense out of nonsense or pull victory out of the jaws of defeat. They never give up, even if that means not giving up on giving up. There are always meetings about "lessons learned" in the workplace, that "all things work together for good" sermon from the pulpit, that "what good could possibly come out of this" at the dinner table or in a family conversation, or that "I do not want this to happen to anyone else" speech in a press conference following a mass shootout in a school, mall, or theater.

Every victory, defeat, crisis, or tragedy is perceived of as an opportunity to learn a lesson, reinforce virtues, denounce vices, make behavioral adjustments, refine good ideas, root out bad ideas, volunteer to help the helpless, and start a business or a nonprofit to meet a need. Further, society polices itself by accepting bad news for what it is and cleaning up after a mess. Such, for example, is the case of crime-ridden Camden,

New Jersey; the Great Depression of 1929–1934; and the Great Recession of 2007–2009.

Statutes – The Umbilical Cords

America is a nation of laws. Americans exclaim all the time, "We are a nation of laws" or "No one is above the law." These assertions are frequently made in the broadcast and print media when a public official, a business executive, or a celebrity presumably breaks a law and appears to be getting away with it. The implication is that all Americas are expected to abide by the laws of the land, regardless of their status. The expectation assumes that a civil society is only civil to the extent that everyone understands and is guided by the same sets of codified rights, principles, regulations, and guidelines.

As mentioned previously, Americans cherish individuality and adore freedom. Put the two together and you have venerated individual freedom. Laws, while regulating civil behavior, if not guided, can infringe upon individual rights and freedoms. America's founding president, George Washington, in his address to the New York legislature on June 26, 1775 put it this way: "When we assumed the Soldier, we did not lay aside the Citizen."

Americans are aware of this other side of the effects of law, and therefore seek to balance the need for law and the rights and freedom of individuals. Hence, Americans would exclaim in protest, "A person is innocent until proven guilty." This assertion is frequently made when there appears to be a foregone conclusion, especially in the court of public opinion or in the media—that a person accused of certain crime or violations is guilty before the evidence is presented in the court of law. Thus, the need for laws and the need for freedom are held in tandem for the good of all. The laws serve both as glue—an umbilical cord—that holds society together and has rules by which all members of society must play. The guardians of the laws (justice department/offices), the judiciary (courts) and the associated legal systems (law enforcement, prisons, etc.), serve to hold members or individuals associated with society accountable to the rules of the laws.

Admittedly, there are myriad laws at the federal, state, and local levels, dating back to the 1770's. We call these myriad laws, for lack of a better term, the laws of the land. The laws of the land are far too numerous and too complex for us to discuss here in detail. Suffice it to say that the laws of the land fall into three broad categories: the Constitution, the Laws, and the Ordinances. We will consider these broad categories of law briefly and discuss their implications for productivity in America. It is important to keep in mind that the descriptive analysis below is based on participant observations, and not necessarily an exercise in legal theory or judicial philosophy.

The Constitution

The founders drafted, debated, and adopted the Constitution of the United States in September 1787 as the law of the land. Since then, the Constitution has been recognized as the supreme law of the land. Each state has its own constitution. State constitutions align with the provisions of the U.S. Constitution. Where there are disagreements, the U.S. Constitution prevails. Similarly, where there are differences of interpretation or rulings between a state Supreme Court and the United States Supreme Court, the ruling by the latter prevails.

As discussed above, the founders were mindful of the concerns regarding individual freedom and the reach of laws with regard to that freedom when they took it upon themselves to draft, debate, and finalize the Constitution. There are a total of eight Articles in the Constitution. Article I, divided into 10 Sections, defines the structures of the legislative branch or the Congress of the United States, including the duties, responsibilities and election processes of the members of the House and the Senate. Article II, divided into four Sections, defines the structures of the executive branch of the federal government, including the duties, responsibilities, election, and succession processes of the President and Vice President of the United States. Article III, divided into three Sections, defines the structure of the judicial branch, including the process of filling positions of the Supreme Court justices. The remaining articles cover issues of treason, debt, amendments, and ratification, to name just a few.

When it was all done, the founders realized that there was unfinished business about striking a balance between strong national governance and individual rights and freedom. So they went back to the drawing board, so to speak, to add Amendments, called the Bill of Rights, to the Constitution. The Bill of Rights ensures such individual rights as the freedom of the press, speech, association, and religion; the right to bear arms and own property; and the right to remain silent against self-incrimination and cruel and unusual punishments, to list a few. Since then, additional Amendments have been made to the Constitution, for a total of 27 Amendments.

In keeping with the Preamble to the Constitution, to strive for "a more perfect Union," the founders made provisions in the Constitution for amending the Constitution in order to allow for the possibility of perfecting the Union. The standards of the Amendments were set very high to ensure that the Amendments were not trivial or abused by a few powerful individuals or states. The same or similar standards apply in amending state constitutions to ensure that amendments are not abused by powerful individuals within the state.

Laws: Statutes, Regulations, Policies, EO's, Directives

Since 1787, the U.S. Constitution has served as a social contract document between governments, and between governments and the society who elected the governments. At the heart is the balancing act between the State and the society, between individuals and their governments, and between individuals. In addition to the U.S. Constitution, many laws have been passed at the federal, state, and local levels in various forms, such as statutes, regulations, executive orders, policies, and directives. Generally, they all tend to align with the Constitution in affirming a balance between the inalienable/ basic rights of individuals and their governments. Laws, in any form or fashion at the federal, state, or local level, that violate these fundamental principles tend to be struck down by the courts as unconstitutional, in violation of the spirit, intent, and provisions of the Constitution—the supreme law of the land.

Statutes are bills passed by the legislative branch or Congress and signed into law by the president. Statutes are codified into Public Law and/or U.S. Code. The Code or the Laws can be accessed by the general public in academic and public libraries, the National Archives, or through a search using Internet Explorer. If the president vetoes the bill, a two-thirds majority of Congress is required to override the president's veto in order for the bill to become law. The idea is for the executive and the legislative branches to work together to forge laws based on intense negotiations and compromises. The goal is to ensure that laws reflect the interest of the people via their elected representatives. After all, the governments and the enacted laws are meant to serve the public interest. With the powers to make laws shared between the executive and legislative branches, laws tend to rise above individual interests to serve the good of the people. Sometimes, interest groups hire lobbyists to help influence a bill in their favor. This practice, although useful in some instances, is regulated to minimize unfavorable or undue influence on elected lawmakers.

It should be noted that similar regulatory procedures apply at the state level to minimize undue influence on elected state officials and lawmakers. Efforts are made to ensure that state laws are consistent with state constitutions and that they serve the interests of the people in that state. They are so made to have undue influence on elected state officials and keep them in check.

Issuances such as Executive Orders, Policy Statements, Directives, Guidance, Guidelines, and Memorandums by the president or his designees are not laws in the sense of Statutes. These issuances are directed at federal political appointees and career employees in connection with the performance of their duties on behalf of the president. Ideally, the president, as the publically elected official, is ultimately responsible for the work of federal political and career employees in serving the general public. So these issuances serve as mechanisms for the CEO to outline standard operating procedures in connection with how the work should be performed and how instructions should be implemented. The issuances are binding and have the full force and effect of the law on federal employees and, to some extent, businesses, contractors, and grantees that do business with the federal government and receive taxpayers' money.

These issuances have serial numbers for tracking and reference purposes and are made available to federal employees primarily online. A few issuances are transmitted through secure lines, depending on the level of sensitivity or while still being developed. The general public via the media and Internet can and should access these issuances so that they know what they can expect from public employees regarding product and service delivery. After all, governments are more productive when informed citizens hold them accountable to standards. The same or similar standards and procedures apply at the state level with the governors and their designees regarding executive issuances to guide state public employees in performing their assigned duties.

Regulations are designed to unpack statutes. Lawmakers generally make laws in broad outlines and often using more legal language and terms than the ordinary citizen can fully appreciate. The general assumption is that Congress says what it means and means what it says in a statute. But this is not always the case. In reality, the laws are written for the most part to allow for interpretations in anticipation of new developments, outliers, and exceptions. Regulations are issued by the Executive branch to reflect the administration's view of an enacted law and how the administration plans to implement or enforce the law. The regulatory process gives the Executive branch one more avenue to spin a law in their favor, especially a law that the administration disagrees with or is not excited about but must honor and implement as a matter of constitutionally prescribed duties. The administration writes regulations and publishes them in the Federal Register for public comments before finalizing the regulation, or rule. The rulemaking process is spelled out in the Administrative Procedure Act (APA) of 1946 as amended.

The expectation is that the regulatory process must be meticulously followed because it is, in effect, a form of making laws. Regulations, like statutes, are binding on the general public, especially the industry or the segment of society that bears the brunt or blessing of the promulgated rule. If the procedure is not followed to the letter to ensure balance in the process by allowing for public input, the Executive branch or some zealous public employees will end up making laws, thereby usurping the functions of Congress. In extreme cases, enthusiastic public employees, by sidetracking public comments, can upend the will of the people through elected representatives. Such regulatory misconduct is generally in violation of the U.S. Constitution and the APA.

Final rules that meet all procedural requirements become "laws" of the land. The rules are codified into the Code of Federal Regulations (CFR) and are available to the general public through the Government Printing Office (GPO), the National Archives, and any internet explorer. CFR is the third "bible" of all public employees, the U.S. Constitution being the first and the U.S. Code being the second.

Ordinances, Charters, Codes, Guidelines

It would appear that most of what has been discussed thus far in this section applies mostly at the federal and/or state levels. But this observation is correct only to certain extent. As mentioned earlier, municipalities do not have constitutions or statutes, certainly not in the sense of state laws and federal laws, which apply statewide and nationwide, respectively. Ideally, local governments derive their authority from state constitutions and laws, since local authorities are, in effect, a part of the state or derivatives thereof. However, these municipalities—towns, cities, counties—are made up of Americans who live in America. Therefore, they rightly share in the assertion that America is a nation of laws. Not only do the federal and state laws apply to them, the local authorities actually serve as conduits by which the laws of the land are mediated to the people at the local levels. Local municipalities have a wide range of instruments which they use in carrying out these awesome responsibilities. The instruments of choice include, but are not limited to ordinances, charters, codes, injunctions, edicts, decrees, and guidelines. Local laws apply only to the town, city, or county over which the local authority enacting the laws has jurisdiction.

Small towns and cities usually have a part time or volunteer mayor and a few council members to discuss, debate, and, if necessary, vote on ordinances, codes, injunctions, edicts, decrees, and guidelines for the operations of the city. These "laws" tend to be in the form of codes and edicts regulating businesses, products and services, property, real estate, streets, street parking, domestic issues, peace, orderly conduct, smoking, prostitution, etc. The process is nevertheless democratic, or at least perceived as such, by the residents of the small communities/cities, where everyone knows everyone's name and one another's business.

Larger cities and certainly counties tend to be more formal and actually have council members or commissioners who function as legislators, with the mayor or county executive or chair serving the executive functions, much like the governor or president at the state and federal levels, respectively. Larger cities and counties make laws that legislate many of the issues listed above and a whole host of bigger issues, such as public policies, health care delivery systems, major road arteries, taxation, public and charter schools, libraries, and more.

It is important to note that the city and county halls actually represent the people's house more than does, say, the state or federal house. The people do actually attend town hall meetings and city deliberations and watch their elected official's debate and vote on bread and butter issues that directly impact them on a daily basis. My observations have been that citizens, especially naturalized immigrants or legal residents, tend to be in awe during their first visit to a city hall. They always describe the visit as intellectually stimulating and emotionally draining but a worthwhile experience. For some, these visits are usually the first time that they've witnessed democracy in action and can see the effects of the rule of law.

It should also be mentioned here that there are ethics, etiquette, and "reasonable, personal" rules and responsibilities that guide daily behavior at home, in schools, at the workplace, at social events, etc. But these are subject to the rules of law. Lawyers are trained in law and are licensed to help individuals or governments understand and navigate the laws of the land. Legal professionals help delineate laws that are binding and carry a penalty. Penalties can be severe, such as the loss of freedom and/ or a fine, depending on the laws a person has violated. Ethical and personal responsibilities are matters of noncompliance disciplinary actions, civil liability, integrity, and shame. The elaborate apparatus of the legal systems and the associated business opportunities are discussed in Chapter 8 of this book.

Bottom Line

It should suffice to summarize here that the founders, by enacting the U.S. Constitution, set in motion profound social engineering of not only the primary culture but also of the secondary culture. The Constitution and a host of other laws (statutes, regulations, executive orders, and issuances) served as templates for creating and perfecting new and improved infrastructures of government at the federal, state, and local levels. These documents, in turn, served as models for structuring society, business, and nonprofit organizations.

That is, over time, the private and nonprofit sectors take their cues from the public sector regarding laws, organizational structures and cultures, vertical and horizontal divisions of labor, bureaucracy, and personnel. Businesses, nonprofits, and many associations have Articles of Incorporation, constitutions, and bylaws that guide management functions. Managers have a duty to ensure that organizations are functioning as planned. They do this by creating a host of policies, guidance, guidelines, manuals, instructional memos, job aids, and standard operating procedures (SOP) for business processes, operations management, and performance of duties by employees. These documents tend to be in sync with the organization's articles of incorporation, constitutions, and bylaws, much like in the public sector.

Small businesses at the entrepreneurial level generally tend to operate in neighborhoods, communities, cities, and counties. As a business takes root and grows exponentially, it reaches out to other states and regions and develops more rules, policies, and organizational hierarchy. At the full performance and maturity levels, businesses develop highly evolved structures and organizations as well as complex "laws," executive issuances, and policies. At these levels, businesses establish regional, national, and even international offices, with regional managers, vice presidents, and directors heading these offices. Large corporations maintain corporate headquarters at one location, with subsidiary headquarters in other locations. The overall structure of large organizations bears a resemblance to the vertical and horizontal reach of the public sector at the federal, state, local levels.

Businesses place great emphasis on the importance of everyone following the organization's "laws," which are a reflection of the bylaws and the general public laws. With the strokes of a pen or pens, the founders unleashed what we might call, for lack of a better term, a "forest-trees" model of society. The State and the individuals/societies together form the Union. It is a unique architectural model that is truly an American Experiment. The public and the private sectors not only mirror each other but also reinforce each other. The two sectors are independent of each other in structures, yet interdependent of each other in operations and productivity. What is more, the forest-trees model requires that a great deal of work and tasks be completed in order for the model to work. Translation: jobs, businesses, and opportunities in the private, nonprofit, and public sectors for all at the local, state, and federal levels. What a great Union indeed!

But wait, there is more. As an experiment, the Union was and is a Union with the capacity and capabilities to self-renew. There is no room for complacency and settling for the status quo with respect to the dynamic interplays between the State, Society, and Statutes. If all that is necessary for evil to prevail is for good people to do nothing ... it follows that for good to prevail, good people must do something. And the founders did something. They gave us the Constitution, among other things. Thus, America started out as a nation of laws from its humble beginnings. The laws of the land have evolved over the years, as has the perfecting of the Union. Can you imagine even a more perfect Union as the laws are continually refined to be more inclusive of all people while celebrating diversity? In the words of a famous American president, You ain't seen nothin' yet!

The concept of diversity as yet another aspect of the American Experiment is the subject of the next chapter.

CHAPTER 7

AMERICA, THE BIG TENT: DIVERSITY AND INCLUSION

Why did the chicken, the peacock, and the parrot leave the kitchen? Answer: Because they were not getting along. The peacock was too pompous; the parrot was too preachy; and the chicken was, well, too chicken. If only the kitchen could speak, one wonders what it would say. Perhaps the kitchen would ask, in the words of Rodney King, "Can't we all get along?"

The year was 1992 when deadly riots broke out in Los Angeles (LA) due to what the residents perceived of as a miscarriage of justice when a jury acquitted the police who reportedly used excessive force in the arrest of Rodney King, a suspect. Another jury eventually convicted two of the four police, but not until after violent protest humbled LA, economically, racially, and socially with a loss of over 50 lives. A great deal of property and businesses were burned to ashes by the protesters. When Rodney King finally appeared, he plead for peace and asked the now famous question: "People ... Can't we all get along?" Neither King nor the general public quite answered that question. My observation in the past decades is that the question captures the essence of the issues surrounding diversity and inclusiveness in America. As the saying goes, as LA and California for that matter goes, so goes the rest of the nation with respect to the diverse demographic, race, social economic status, and civil rights fitting into one big tent, called America. Attempts to make all the fixtures and the various moving parts fit can be daunting. The purpose of this chapter is to dissect the opportunities and challenges inherent in the quest for diversity and inclusiveness in America.

We begin the chapter with an examination of the demographic characteristics of the American population, followed by an outline of various legal mechanisms that have been used to move the nation towards a more racially and socially perfect Union over the years. Next, we take a closer look at social realities on the ground. We conclude with some reflection on how more progress can be made by building on successes achieved thus far, thereby creating even more opportunities by all for all.

Demography

Based on the 2010 Census, as adjusted, the population of the United States of America is pegged at 309,000,000. Since then, different demographers have used different formulas and criteria to provide estimates for the population and to break down the population by race. There is no firm consensus on the exact numbers, some being more generous or conservative than others. Broadly speaking, the following is a breakdown of the population by race:

White	63.7%
Hispanic	16.4%

African American	12.6%
Asian	4.8%
Native American	1.5%
Others	1%

Although a significant number of Americans live in big cities – Atlanta, Baltimore, Boston, Buffalo, Charlotte, Chicago, Cincinnati, Cleveland, Dallas, Denver, Detroit, Green Bay, Houston, Indianapolis, Jacksonville, Kansas City, Los Angeles, Madison, Miami, Minneapolis, Nashville, New Orleans, New York, Philadelphia, Phoenix, Pittsburgh, San Diego, San Francisco, Seattle, St. Louis, Tampa Bay, and Washington DC, to list a few, many Americans live in suburbia and rural America. The urban areas tend to be more socially integrated than the suburbs, which, in turn, are more socially integrated than rural areas. With respect to income distribution, income per capita is more concentrated in the suburbs where real estate is pricier. But businesses are more concentrated in the urban areas and cities where there are more economic activities (jobs, businesses) as measured by productivity (output, products, services). Rural areas have always been the hallmark of agriculture and are dominated by agricultural produce, ranches, grazing, hunting, and similar occupational activities.

However, the population shifts are dynamic and not necessary stagnant relative to space. Once there was a great shift in population from rural to urban setting, manufacturing became the predominant determinant of economic activities. Then there was a shift to the suburbs due, in part, to urban decay and crime as well as the availability of smart vehicles. Mass upward mobility, due to the rise in income following the post-World War II boom, gave rise to a robust middle class. This is not to suggest that all was always well with everyone and all segments of society all the time. That would assume a utopia. America would be the first to disassociate itself from such a proposition, which would deny the hard work and sacrifice countless people have put forth over the years to get the nation to where it is today. These efforts resulted in civil rights laws and regulations that have succeeded, to a great extent, in ensuring that the tenets of equality become a reality for all Americans.

Key Diversity and Inclusion Statutes and Executive Orders

America as we know it has evolved and perfected itself over a long period of time. The concepts that all men are created equal and are endowed with inalienable rights were and still are fundamental tenets ingrained in the nation's psyche. But some 230 years ago, these rights were just that for many—concepts and tenets. Men, women, races, social status, and even religions were not equal in any conceivable way when the tenets were acknowledged and made the central thesis of such canon documents as the Declaration of Independence, the U.S. Constitution, and the Federalists, to list a few. The concepts were like a small leavening or yeast that, over time, leavened the whole bread. We already noted how the structures of the Union have improved over time in the previous chapter. In the words of Abraham Lincoln, the U.S. President during the Civil War for the soul of the Union and the principles of equality for which it stands:

The assertion that "all men are created equal" was of no practical use in effecting our separation from Great Britain and it was placed in the Declaration not for that, but for future use.

Events of recent decades are a testament to that forward-looking perfecting process of the Union, of which Lincoln spoke and to which we are eyewitnesses.

The 1980s and 1990s were decades of economic boom, with the baby boomers coming of age. Jobs and businesses were in abundant supply, and the Internet and computers changed the ways people worked and did business locally, nationally, and globally. Minivans, and then SUVs and compact cars, were everywhere. Dot.com businesses were springing up from coast to coast. The stock markets broke records and real estate skyrocketed, and then came a series of pauses in the economy.

The terrorist attack on U.S. soil on September 11, 2001, was followed by wars in Afghanistan and Iraq, which slowed years of unprecedented growth in the first half of the millennial decade. The Great Recession in the second half of the millennial decade almost brought the economy to a standstill—the stock market crashed, the housing market bubble burst, unemployment skyrocketed, dot.com businesses collapsed, and real estate equity and retirement savings vanished, to list the most obvious.

The stock markets have since recovered and are breaking records again. Businesses are slowly recovering and jobs are gradually coming back, though mostly in services, energy, and information technology industries rather than in manufacturing. America has witnessed booms and busts throughout its history. That is the nature of the economic beast, also called Capitalism. There are winners and losers, and a whole lot in between.

Of course an essential genius of American culture is its resiliency and ability to bounce back, with all hands on deck. On the part of the government, many mechanisms have been put into place over the years to help weather the storm by providing for the affected segments of society and by bringing into mainstream America those who, for some reason, have been left out or behind. The most significant of these mechanisms were or are the laws and executive orders that enhance and expand the big tent for the benefit of everyone.

Equality as a Matter of Laws

As a nation of laws, America prides itself in making laws to address acute and chronic issues, such as the lack of diversity and inclusion in the public and private sectors and society at large. The following are key enactments and executive orders put in place to ensure diversity and inclusion in the Union as a matter of law (see Appendix 13 for a more detailed list).

In 1865, The U.S. Constitution was amended to include the 13th Amendment, which abolished slavery, following a bloody civil war. The Amendment was passed by Congress on January 31, 1865 and ratified on December 6, 1865. With this milestone Amendment, slavery became illegal. African Americans who were slaves were free and were legally equal to any and all Americans as a matter of rights. In principle, at least, the big tent was expanded to have new full members. President Abraham Lincoln put the importance of the abolition of slavery in perspective when he pointed out that, "Whenever I hear anyone arguing for slavery, I feel a strong impulse to see it tried on him personally." For Lincoln, freedom for all was the essence of democracy: "As I would not be a slave, so I would not be a master. This expresses my idea of democracy."

A similar milestone event happened in 1919, when the U.S. Constitution was amended to include the 19th Amendment. The 19th Amended granted women the right to vote. The Amendment was passed by Congress on June 4, 1919 and ratified on August 18, 1920. With the Amendment, women were no longer prohibited from voting or being voted for as a candidate. Again, this was a landmark step in perfecting the Union, as women are now fully integrated members of society with voting rights to determine their future and the future of their fellow Americans.

In 1935, the Wagner Act became the law of the land. With this law, private sector labor unions and organizations were recognized and granted unprecedented rights to organize in the workplace, including the right to strike to put pressure on management for legitimate demands. There were unions and the labor movement as far back the Reconstruction, following the Civil War. But the labor movements and their leaders were always in a cat-and-mouse relationship with business owners, manufacturers, and the authorities. The labor movement used all manner of tactics to maneuver its way into companies to organize and enter into negotiations with management. The relationships were frosty, with violence and intimidation on both sides. The Wagner Act was a breakthrough in bringing unions and labor movement into the fold, including the private sector and society at large. They were granted the right to represent workers and to negotiate Collective Bargaining Agreements for employees they represented in companies and industries. In 1962, President John F. Kennedy signed Executive Order (EO) 10988, extending the same or similar rights to public sector employees. One exception was the right to strike. Since public employees are allegedly well compensated already and, for all practical purposes, serve the interest of the general public, it would probably be counterproductive if public employees were allowed to strike. A strike by public employees would, in effect, hold hostage the very public they have taken an oath to serve without mental reservation or pressure.

In 1961, President John F. Kennedy issued EO 10925 on Affirmative Action, which was designed to promote the inclusion of minorities and women in hiring, admissions, and contracts. In 1965, President Lyndon B. Johnson issued EO 11246, followed shortly by EO 11375, reaffirming Affirmative Action. The Order acknowledged the reality that minorities and women are grossly under-represented in the federal workforce and public schools. The provision was and is designed to compensate for these segments of society who have been shut out of employment opportunities or admissions opportunities for far too long. By these presidential executive actions, the underrepresented and underserved populations were brought into the fold and were given equal opportunity to have a shot at the American Dream.

The Equal Pay Act was passed and went into effect in 1963. The Act entrenched the principle of equal pay for equal work, regardless of gender and race. Thus, the workplace was rid of pay discrimination based on gender or race for equal work performed. This Act and the Kennedy Affirmative Action EO served as precursors to the Civil Rights Act, which was enacted in 1964. The Civil Rights Act, as amended in 1972, extended civil rights to all Americans beyond the pay disparity in the workplace. Title VII prohibited discrimination based on race, color, religion, national origin, or gender in the workplace and in society at large, including schools. In 1965, EOs 11246 and 11375 extended these rights in the workplace by going on the "offensive." The Orders ordered active recruitment and retention of minorities, women, persons with disabilities, and covered veterans in the workplace and employment.

The Age Discrimination in Employment Act of 1967 extended these rights to include age. The Act as Amended 1978 prohibited employment discrimination based on age for those

40 years and older. With this Act, in combination with the provisions of the Mandatory Retirement Act of 1978, employees cannot be discharged of their duties (in effect, of their livelihood) or forced to retire because they are old. No forced retirement of employees anymore, except in select occupations due to physical demands. The Pregnancy Discrimination Act of 1978 extended the rights to expectant mothers or employees. The Act stipulates that there should be no employment/workplace discrimination against pregnant women, child-rearing, and associated medical needs. The Family and Medical Leave Act of 1993 extended these rights to include medical leave to take care of family members for up to 12 weeks of unpaid leave.

With the Americans with Disabilities Act of 1990, persons with disabilities were brought out of the shadows to become active members of the workplace and the larger society. Before that, individuals with disabilities were often treated as handicapped and/or retarded. A handicapped person was at the mercy of the employer, even if the person had the needed skills and abilities to do the job. Persons with a disability tend to be laid off quite easily, even though they can do and have done the job more effectively and efficiently than other nondisabled employees. What is more, many employers would rather not deal with the added burden of reasonable accommodation, even though they could afford to prove accommodation based on their profit margins.

The Act prohibits discrimination against individuals with physical disabilities and chronic illness in hiring, the workplace, schools, and sports to the extent that these individuals have the skills and abilities to perform the job. Employers are required to provide reason accommodation for employees with disabilities. The Genetic Information Nondiscrimination Act of 2008 extended these rights to people with genetic challenges. The Act

Sunday A. Aigbe

stipulates prohibition against discrimination based on genetic information regarding disease, disorder, heredity, size, height, and shape, provided the person has the ability and skills to perform the job.

It is important to mention here that these laws have the effect and full force of the laws of the land. Violators of these laws, if convicted, can be penalized and punished, including fines and, in extreme cases, imprisonment or both. In the federal government, punishment can include dismissal. As said, these provisions are matters of law and so are not to be taken lightly. Neither is the need for diversity and inclusion.

Elements of Diversity and Inclusion

The above enactments and similar laws have been portrayed as protective rights. The term "rights," in this respect, is defined pejoratively by critics. There is this notion that there are too many more protected classes in America than the founders contemplated. This, the critics argue, is not good for the Union. My observation is that where people stand on issues of diversity and inclusion depends in large part on where they sit at the table, and where that table is located in the big tent.

From the point of human equality (the created equal principle) and equal protection under the law (the due process principle), these enactments can and should be seen as adding rich diversity and inclusiveness to the big tent. Some 250 years ago, a meeting in the public square would probably have included mostly white males. Not that anything would be wrong with the composition of such a gathering at the time. After all, a nation has to start somewhere. Besides, that composition was likely all that was needed at the time as opposed to what would be needed in a complex world with complex issues today. Thus, the same public square meeting today would attract a more complex demographic. This would only be possible primarily because of the enacted laws and EOs outlined above.

The nation can now celebrate diversity and inclusion that truly embraces people from all walks of life and backgrounds, age, language, and culture, to list a few. This is healthy and welcoming news, especially for a nation that is founded by immigrants for immigrants. Because all sorts of discrimination are outlawed, any gathering at, say, the National Mall in Washington, D.C., Times Square in New York City, or a Super Bowl anywhere in the nation, would look much more colorful in terms of faces, age, shape, language, and gender. The same thing can be said in many workplaces, churches, communities, towns, and neighborhoods across America, especially in the urban metropolis. However, advancements in diversity and inclusion are more noticeable and celebrated in the public workforce and workplaces than in the private sector, where progress is coming along slowly but steadily.

By progress, we mean a concerted effort in diversity and inclusion that embodies most if not all of the rights listed below. For example, a business organization can be said to be diverse and inclusive when the following elements of enacted laws and EOs are fully integrated into its workforce and workplace (and less diverse and inclusive when the elements are not represented):

Gender (sex and sexuality)
Race
Color
Ethnicity
Persons with disabilities
Religion/no religion

Sexual orientation
National origin
Language
Persons with different cultures, values, and beliefs
Social Economic Status (SES)
Physical attractiveness
Obesity/thinness
Job seniority
Intellectual abilities/lack thereof (intellectually
challenged individuals)
Parental status
Protected genetic information (genetically
challenged individually)
Whistleblower (reprisal)

Imagine for a moment the contributions of all of the following people represented by these elements to the economy: women, folks 40 years and older, colored people, persons with disabilities, genetically challenged individuals, immigrants from other countries other than Europe, to list just a few. Then think of the following alternative outcomes, if all these people were excluded from the public square, workforce, and workplace: loss of elected women in public service, including Congress, loss of disabled persons' contributions to the workforce, loss of purchasing power of these individuals, increased welfare and public liability, etc. The wisdom of the founders and subsequent generations regarding diversity and inclusion make sense. The economic and productivity benefits add up very quickly.

Compelling as the above analysis seems, it remains that the reality on the ground does not paint a desirable picture. This is, in part, because the founders also assumed individual responsibilities. Acceptance of these responsibilities makes a big difference where individuals will eventually sit at the table and where the table will ultimately be located in the big tent.

Social Reality

We have noted above that America is made up of at least five distinctive racial/ethnic groups: White, African Americans, Hispanics, Asians, and Native Americans. Social commentators have observed that these groups, except Native Americans, might have come in different ships, but they are all in one big boat or one big tent now. The reality of inalienable basic rights (life, liberty, pursuit of happiness, property, free press, speech, religion, and association) is that there are two sides to the proverbial coin. This observation has several implications for a society in search of a balance.

Dilemma of a Free Society in Search of Integration

Take, for example, the evolution of a society. Society integrates as people freely move into a neighborhood or community. By the same token, people are free to move out of the same neighborhood to a neighborhood where they choose to live or raise their family. This open-ended freedom to associate or pursue happiness creates a dilemma for a society in search of integration. The more a city or county integrates, the more its neighborhoods and communities are segregated. This conceptual reality explains in part why social integration continues to be elusive in America, many decades after the Civil Rights laws and subsequent efforts in integration.

Dilemma of Self Segregation

Another social reality is the tendency toward self-segregation. By nature, birds of the same feather flock together. Interestingly, this observation holds true in human and social evolutionary trajectories. Research on physical and cultural anthropology reveals that humans possess three essential elements: natural/biological equipment or genotype; environmental conditioning or phenotype; and socialization/nurture/enculturation or socio-type. The three elements account for why certain individuals from certain regions of the world have similar physical characteristics, act in about the same way, and pursue identical interests. We see how this plays out on a daily basis in, say, sports and entertainment where one ethnic group appears to hold occupational rights to a particular sport or entertainment industry. Ideally, people are free to pursuit their interests with people of the same interest. Consciously or unconsciously, the selection is based on or influenced by genotype, phenotype, and socio-type factors.

The immediate implication of this observation is the tendency for self-segregation. So far so good! Problems arise when self-segregation carries over into other spheres of society, such as religion. Someone has observed that the most segregated hour in America is 11:00 AM on Sunday, when churches are packed with congregants of the same feather across America. Similarly, the public housing projects rank high on the list of most segregated residential neighborhoods in America. These practices make societal integration elusive. Self-segregation, combined with elusive societal integration, is a recipe for a host of social issues.

Economic Disparity

A primary manifest of a less integrated, self-segregated society is economic disparity. Minorities and immigrants tend to live in cities and large urban settings where poverty is concentrated, with fewer economic opportunities, fewer jobs, few businesses, and, in effect, fewer or inadequate community resources. Unemployment tends to hit these communities the hardest. They are the first in line to experience the brunt of an economic downturn and the last to recover from a recession. Lower incomes lead to lower standards and property values, which, in turn, lead to less revenue for schools. Lower revenue streams lead to poorly funded schools and poor student outcomes. The poorly educated graduates recycle back into the local economy with fewer economic opportunities. Poorly educated graduates are also unable to perform in the larger society where they have to compete with graduates from well-funded schools with better student outcomes.

The end game is a huge economic disparity, with minority and immigrants overrepresented in the lower class and, by default, underrepresented in the middle class. White Americans who are poorly educated or possess little to no education experience a similar economic fate. In absolute numbers, poor whites suffer the same plight as minorities on the economic food chain. Together, poor whites living in suburbia and rural settings in addition to whites, minorities, and immigrants living in poor urban areas account for the well over 42 million people who reported economic insecurity in America in 2013, according to a recent survey (*Washington Post Express*, July 29, 2013).

Tangle of Social Pathology/Culture of Poverty

Although liberty can open the door to creativity, innovation, and entrepreneurship, it can also breed what we might call, for lack of a better term, a tangle of social pathology. By tangle of pathology, we mean intertwined social problems with intertwined social causes. As noted, America has come a long way in perfecting the Union. We've also noted above how good intentions or natural phenomena can lead to unintended consequences. When these consequences are left unchecked, they become a breeding ground for social problems, such as unemployment, teen pregnancy, drug dealing and addiction, alcoholic, homelessness, prostitution, vandalism, burglary, and violent crimes. When these pathologies are concentrated in a segregated locale, the outcome is a culture of poverty that reinforces the tangle of social pathologies.

Individuals or groups of individuals caught in the tangle of social pathologies or in the culture of poverty develop a sense of hopelessness, helplessness, and disenfranchisement. They have difficulty trusting authority, especially the politicians who promise so much change during elections but do so little after elections. They also have difficulty relating to law enforcement personnel, who are doing the best they can under the circumstances but do not quite understand realities on the ground. Under this condition, an "innocent" encounter with or honest mistake by law enforcement personnel is usually the last straw in a string of causes leading to a social volcanic eruption that has been building for quite some time. In such an encounter, the larger society seems to focus on the immediate cause-and-effect facts at the scene, while the affected community appears to have a different narrative of the eruption, based on the longstanding contextual cause-and-effect factors. Both sides are in a way only half correct. The two sides speak over each other's heads, making a meeting of the minds virtually impossible.

It is in this context that we must seek to understand and dissect trends for the purpose of finding lasting solutions to recurrent social upheavals, such as the Hilo Massacre, also known as Bloody Monday in August 1938 in Hilo, HI; Rodney King in 1992 in Los Angeles, CA; Caesar Cruz in 2009 in Anaheim, CA; Kelly Thomas in 2011 in Fullerton, CA; Manuel Diaz in July 2012 in Anaheim, CA; Trayvon Martin in 2012 in Sanford, FL; Andy Lopez in October 2013 in Santa Rosa, CA; Eric Garner in 2014 in New York City, NY; and Michael Brown in 2014 in Ferguson, MO; to list a few.

Any lasting solutions to the tangle of social pathologies identified above should involve three elements: diagnosis, prognosis, and prescription. Problems should be thoroughly diagnosed by experts in the field in consultation with the people affected by the social pathologies. The diagnosis should indicate the level of problem: infrastructural level, multi-structural level, or a combination thereof. The prognosis should determine the chances whether the problem is solvable or not solvable. That is, whether there is hope or no hope. The prognosis should indicate whether the chance of solving the problem resides within the immediate community (multi-structure), at the larger society (infrastructural), or both. Prescription involves identifying realistic solutions. Efforts must be made to avoid political correctness, which only postpones obvious problems by kicking the proverbial can down the road. Prescription should specify where the solution lies—with the people, the government, or a combination thereof?

Take, for example, a large city with urban social decay. Diagnosis: culture of poverty due to middle class flight; Prognosis: there is hope, given that the community is teeming with children and young people/families; Prescription: individual responsibility and societal responsiveness from the point of primary-secondary culture paradigm. For the individuals, there is a need for an understanding of life's reality—that there is no there, there. A hand-out can only take an individual so far. The proverbial fish can only feed him or her for a day. At the end of the day, what he really needs is a hand up, and not just a handout. The individuals must be willing to pull themselves up by their bootstraps. In this regard, they need to learn to fish.

But the larger community has a role to play in reversing the diagnosed social decay. The city should be willing to invest in and create jobs and business opportunities for the citizens trapped in the culture of poverty. It is not enough to train citizens how to fish. The city in collaboration with state and federal authorities and primarily with the private sector must ensure that there are fishing accessories, boats, and rivers teeming with fish to make productive fishing happen. Otherwise, learning to fish would be unproductive for individuals who are trapped in urban decay with few opportunities. A well-thought-out comprehensive approach can and will reverse urban social decay and culture of poverty to the extent that the approach is based on sound diagnosis, prognosis, and prescription.

Affirmative Action (AA) – The Case of AT&T

At the national level, many programs have been instituted to address the impact of economic disparity on the many Americans who are trapped in a cycle of poverty without any escape route to job and business opportunities in the larger society. One such program is Affirmative Action (AA), which aims to open doors in institutions and businesses in which women and minorities are underrepresented. As noted, President John F. Kennedy issued EO 10925 instituting AA in 1961 and it was reiterated in 1965 by President Lyndon Johnson in EO 11246. AA was designed to promote inclusion of minorities and women in hiring, admissions, and contracts. Johnson institutionalized AA in the spirit of civil rights and the "Great Society" philosophy. Since then, conservatives tend to attack and limit the program as a quota system.

The purpose of this case analysis is to dissect the ethical issues involving the hiring practices of AT&T in the 1970s, a case of Affirmative Action aptly documented by Robert K. Fullinwider in *Ethics and Politics* (Gutmann et al, 1990: 211-219). It all began when AT&T was charged with allegations of discrimination in its hiring practices. In its effort to respond to the allegations, AT&T undertook a process that aimed at righting past deeds while setting its future hiring record straight. The question remains, however, whether, in its attempts to respond to the pressure of discriminatory hiring charges, AT&T's action was an example of equal opportunity or an exercise in preferential hiring? Central to the debate is the notion of distributive justice (DJ) and the unintended consequence of reverse discrimination (RD).

Critics of AA (Thomas Sowell, William Bennett, Shelby Steele, Rush Limbaugh, Alan Keyes, Heritage Center) pointed out that it is not morally justifiable to rob Peter to pay Paul, so to speak. The critics will admit that, in the case of AT&T, women and minorities were underrepresented and, in effect, wronged. But they will argue that AT&T's action was unacceptable, as it was an exercise in the quota system. For the critics, AT&T's back pay and subsequent comprehensive plan did increase the number of women and minorities in the underrepresented areas of the workforce, but this was at the expense of a policy dubbed reverse discrimination (RD). Even some women and minorities, argued the critics, were not spared the adverse effect of robbing Peter to pay Paul.

Supporters of AA (Jesse Jackson, Paul Rockwell, Equal Employment Opportunity Commission) posed the question rather differently: "Are there occasions when it is morally justifiable to rob Peter in order to pay Paul?" The emphasis here is on *occasions*. Thus, EEOC argued that an 800,000 employee strong company in which women make up 50% of the workforce but are represented by only 1% in management positions is one of the many occasions. The racial and gender composition of AT&T workforce in the early 1970's was quite dismal, and even the most vocal critic of affirmative action admitted that some kind of action was needed to reverse the trend. AT&T's decision to take a corrective measure was an informed business and ethical decision.

AT&T, by vigorously pursuing an AA policy, did narrow the racial and gender gap in its management workforce by 1979. To some extent, DJ was realized and AA has done wonders. But the question remains: "Did AT&T act properly when it instituted override as a feature of the consent decree?" Admittedly, AT&T would have had difficulty realizing its goals, if the override provision had not been implemented. The consent decree, however, was based on the faulty assumption that the percentage of qualified minorities and women who were denied equal employment opportunity was representative of the percentage of minorities and women in the local population in general and in the workforce in particular. AT&T needed these statistics in order to, first, establish the depth and scope of the discrimination and, second, to develop an effective remedial plan based on sound data. Evidently, it had none of these.

When a company does not have statistics on minorities and women as represented in the local population but nonetheless designs a remedial plan based on the company's employment figures, an unhealthy scenario is likely to develop. In the case of AT&T, the percentage of the allotted slot for minorities and women was unusually higher than their representative percentage in the local population, given that the company was forced to pass over more qualified white males to hire less qualified minorities and women in an effort to reach the unusually inflated allotted percentage for minorities and women. This flies in the face of DJ. AT&T recognized this mistake, hence the decision to override the override provision in the consent decree in January 1979—a decision that was morally justifiable.

Based on my observations, the long-term effect of an override provision, as evident from the AT&T case, is the unintended consequence of RD. Indeed, the AT&T case brings into focus the dilemma of AA: you're criticized if you do practice it, and you're criticized if you don't practice it. Thus, President Clinton's advice to "mend it, but don't end it" appeared to follow in the tradition of AT&T who mended the program but did not end it.

But in the face of diminishing employment opportunities, salvaging AA or the consent decree does not address the fundamental questions of DJ. How should a society distribute its wealth or job opportunities to its members so that wrongs are righted without creating new wrongs? AA appears to suppose that a fair distribution of the employment pie is possible, hence the term equal opportunity. The AT&T case revealed the flaw of this supposition: that there is not enough pie to go around forever.

An AA policy is ethically defensible insofar as it is a penultimate means to an ultimate end. If the ultimate goal is socio-economic justice, and the equitable availability of jobs for all is the means to reaching this goal, it would follow that any

AA policy is and should be seen as a temporary arrangement. AA should be seen as a short-term plan calculated to adjust a maladjusted employment practice. If and when the goal has been attained in a company, then the corrective elements in the AA policy must be dismantled. To continue the arrangement as is, is to abuse the corrective and short-term nature of the program and, in effect, assure RD. Hence, my slogan: "Use it, but don't abuse it!"

AT&T acted properly by junking the override provision. However, a more permanent solution was for AT&T, and any company for that matter, to seek ways to increase the size of the pie. Rather than rationing the existing jobs, a company ought to explore and invest in new markets. Exploration, investment, and new markets carry with them the need for experienced managers and, in effect, expanded management position opportunities. The expanded-pie approach means sound business decisions, which preempt or mitigate tough ethical choices.

Implications for Productivity

As discussed in the previous chapters, new legislation can serve as a trigger for new business and jobs opportunities. Some statutes are actually put in place for purpose of stimulating growth in a sluggish economy or to expedite recovery from a recession. Others are enacted for purpose of correcting or perfecting imperfections in the Union—to make amends for those who have been wronged for so long. In this case, Congress provides the funding mechanism and appropriates funds for the enacted statute for purposes of implementation. Members of the targeted population are granted the right to participate fully in the economy. Unhindered, they are empowered to become productive members of society.

Corrective measures create jobs opportunities in the business organization or in the public agency tasked with implementation. Structures need to be put in place and tasks need to be accomplished. This means work to be performed, jobs to be created, and positions to be filled. Businesses opportunities become available when major statutes are enacted involving a large segment of the population at the national or regional levels. Infrastructures need to be built. Rules and regulations need to be written and published. In some cases, structures need to be developed, standing up and running at various levels of governments and in society. This means that offices and programs will to be created internally, and grants and contracts will be solicited, processed, and awarded to the general public—businesses and nonprofit organizations. Translation: jobs, jobs, jobs; businesses, businesses, businesses!

Bottom Line

America has done a great job of perfecting the Union through the power of ideas, laws, policies, and programs. Many people have been brought out of the shadows to become active productive members of society. We also note that far too many are still not able to realize the American Dream. A significant segment of society needs to be brought out of the shadows. The well over 40 million poor Americans yearn for economic freedom and to sit at the table in the center of the big tent. A renewed effort on the War on Poverty is long overdue in order to afford them full participation in the tent.

The 11 million illegal immigrants yearn for freedom from the infamous shadow economy. They want to come out of the shadows of the permanent underclass and a culture of fear and hopelessness. They will not go away or be deported. It appears that they will continue to be a source of irritation and inconvenience until their conditions are addressed. The larger society will be enriched if and when it finds a way to extend opportunities to them so that they can become productive members of the American culture as the newest members in the tent.

As Dr. Martin Luther King, Jr. noted, America must learn to live together as citizens or fall as fools. The threat to the continued perfection of the Union is not so much from outside as from the inside. In the words of President Abraham Lincoln:

America will never be destroyed from the outside. If we falter and lose our freedoms, it will be because we destroyed ourselves.

As he pointed out:

A house divided against itself cannot stand.

For him, if America sticks together as a nation there is no reason why the nation cannot be the best that it can be:

My dream is of a place and a time where America will once again be seen as the last best hope of earth.

The bottom line is that diversity and inclusion is good business, because it gives a business organization a competitive edge on a productivity scale. Tokenism is not a strategy and so not an option. Comprehensive diversity and inclusion is a time-tested strategy and most probably the only realistic option if the Union is to continue in its path towards an enduring tent.

Perhaps I should mention here that the chicken, the peacock, and the parrot did come back and figure out a way to live together in the kitchen. So, you might ask, why did the chicken, the peacock and the parrot come back to the kitchen? Simple: Because they needed each other. Only the chicken really knows the kitchen very well, after all they share a common name albeit in reverse. Only the peacock has what it takes to beautifully dress the table, and only the parrot has what it takes to entertain.

Can't we all get along? Yes we can all get along in the one big tent called America! To get along with each other or to create and claim your share of the pie, there are rules to follow. These rules of engagement are also commonly referred to as law and order, the subject of the next chapter.

CHAPTER 8

LAW AND ORDER

As stated in the previous chapters, jobs and business are the backbone of the American economy. We also noted that ideas such as inalienable rights and the quest for a more perfect Union within the context of the State-Society paradigm or Forest-Trees models of social representation are the geniuses of American culture. Statutes were discussed and acknowledged as the spines or the umbilical cord that hold it all together. In this chapter, we take a closer look at law and order as the ties that bind. We begin with several observations regarding the concept of law and order. This is followed by an analysis of the institutional representations of law and order and the roles of these institutions in the construction and implementation of laws and order. Particular attention is paid to law enforcement—an integral part of the American legal system. We conclude the chapter with the implications of law and order as they relate to productivity.

Sunday A. Aigbe

Law and Freedom: An Oxymoron?

Laws suggest regulations of individual and societal behaviors in a collective manner. Freedom implies uninhibited or unrestricted pursuit of individual and societal choices and decisions without external interference. The two propositions beg the question of whether a nation of laws or the inhabitants thereof are indeed free. Put differently, is law and freedom an oxymoron? The answer to this question depends on one's definition and experience of law and freedom. If freedom is equal to lawlessness and law means punitive restriction or infringement on an individual's inalienable and civil rights, then the two are an oxymoron, from the point of the law of non-contradiction.

However, natural laws have also taught us through experience that a society is not possible without laws, albeit rudimentary ones. Individuals are, by nature, social beings as philosophers have pointed out, hence the quote "I belong therefore I am." We find meaning in life through social interaction. Social interaction, by its very nature, suggests some basic principles of interaction if civil interaction is to occur. Thus, we are both free and bound by nature. We can sit anywhere we want to, but we only sit on seats and not on ceiling. Pure freedom or liberty is an illusion in this regard.

All civil societies, individually and collectively, need law and order to function as a cohesive social entity. Further, law and order is needed to ensure freedom for members of society, both to live and to make a living. This need for law and order to ensure freedom is not new, though. The foragers, hunters and gatherers, and horticulturists as well as sedentary agricultural societies had law and order in order to survive and make the most of their environment. What is new is the level of complexity that each generation has added to the evolving law and order to ensure a more efficient and civil society. A case can be made that the more a group of people evolves into a civilized society, the more rules, law and orderliness they create in order to maintain or improve on the achieved civility. As we have noted throughout this book, America is a case in point of this observation.

Law and Order – A Conceptual Framework

Some societies are way ahead on the civilization scale, while others are far behind. The difference depends largely on a nation's ability to make laws and enforce them in order to effectuate the desired results, most notably, order. Many societies have laws on the books that are not enforced, either because they are unwilling or unable to do so, or both. The result is a lawless society with a high rate of crime and very low productivity. In these kinds of societies, not only are people doing what they are not supposed to be doing by violating the law, they are also not complying with the laws. The outcome is chaos and disorder, a recipe for social decay and lack of economic productivity.

As a nation of laws, Americans generally share the view that laws are good and necessary for society. Law and order is seen as an integral part of a complex whole. The expectation is that if laws are properly constructed, implemented, and managed, they will lead to order. The resulting effects are orderly society, businesses, commerce, employment, and human relations as well as fair and equitable criminal justice. American laws can be viewed at many levels or fall into two broad categories—prescriptive laws and proscriptive laws.

Sunday A. Aigbe

Prescriptive laws

Prescriptive laws are laws, statutes, ordinances, edits, regulations, and EO, to name a few, that are meant to encourage positive behavior, actions, and rewards. These laws pertain to such activities as business loans, mortgages, students loans, starting and operating a business, applying for and maintaining a job, and credit records, to name a few. These laws regulate activities of members of society. Prescriptive laws and regulations set the parameters and basic rules for all Americans as they exercise their inalienable and civil rights (life, liberty, and the pursuit of happiness and property), constitutional rights (freedom of religion, association, speech, press, etc.) and civil rights (equal opportunity, diversity and inclusion, freedom from discrimination based on age, gender, national origin, race, etc.). These laws level the playing field for all.

Proscriptive laws

Proscriptive laws are laws, statutes, ordinances, edits, regulations, and EO, to name a few, that are meant to discourage negative behavior and actions. These laws not only outlaw bad behavior, but also state clearly the punishment for violators or perpetrators. Paramount among these laws is the prohibition against the destruction of lives and property. These laws hold and value rights to life and property, hence the specificity and severity in the punishment for violations of this type. Societies thrive or fizzle based on how well these values are held in high regard, preserved, and protected.

Law and Order Principles

Americans place a high value on law and order and have spent time and money over the centuries to perfect the system and ensure that it functions properly. There are more laws than any American could possibly know, let alone master the details. These laws embody the principles by which Americans lead their everyday lives, governments govern, and laws are enforced. There are many principles, but the following stand out (in no particular order):

> Innocent until proven guilty
> Equal protection under the law
> Due process of law
> Right to trial – present evidence, challenge evidence
> Equal application of laws – no one is above the law
> Double jeopardy
> Cruel and unusual punishment, proportionality of punishment
> Fifth Amendment – right to not self-incriminate
> Right to remain silent – Miranda rights
> Evidence as the basis of litigation and the verdict
> Legal remedy – anyone can seek legal remedy for anything (winning is another story)
> Do not take the law into your own hands
> Government monopoly of law and order – use of force, taking life, liberty infringement
> Right to bear arms – self defense
> Property rights
> Others …

Admittedly, most Americans go about their daily business and do not necessary memorize elements of the laws. However, they are aware of these basic tenets that constitute the principles of law and order. These principles are ingrained in American culture and permeate the everyday life of Americans, to the point of being taken for granted. The principles come alive and are handy when individuals engage in conduct or actions that are not congruent with the expectations of a civil society or when one's conduct infringes on the rights of others. When this occurs, law enforcement personnel are involved; they, themselves, must follow yet another set of lawful principles in applying these and other applicable principles to remedy the situation and restore order. Hence, law and order.

Law and Order Agents

Laws are of no use if they do not have the desired results, namely, a societal order in which good guys are rewarded and bad guys are punished. Put differently, laws are only as good as the extent to which they are enforced fairly and equitably. Americans are aware of this dynamic, which explains the billions of dollars invested in elaborate law enforcement every year (see Appendices 15 and 16 for details). Generally, law and order is the business of all Americans, hence the Homeland Security slogan "If you see something, say something." The entire executive branches of federal, state, and local governments are committed to the overall enforcement, monitoring, and administration of the law of the land to effect a healthy and functioning society in an orderly fashion.

Compliance commissions, regulatory agencies, oversight boards, benefits and human services agencies, social workers and field specialists, to list a few, are in the business of administering programs as well as enforcing laws. The same can be said of multiplier organizations, such as nonprofit watch dogs, the media or press who police the police force, and business organizations that provide products and services in support of law enforcement.

Law Enforcement Personnel

There are institutions that are specifically charged with the responsibility of maintaining law and order through the making, administration, and enforcement of laws. Personnel in many of these institutions make and administer laws, while others enforce the laws by protecting the general public from the bad guys. We call these institutions and personnel law enforcement personnel (LEP). Within the LEP, there are various careers and professionals—law enforcement core personnel and law enforcement mission support and resource personnel.

The following are the key institutions and professionals that constitute the LEP (roughly in order of their involvement in the law enforcement process):

> Lawmakers
> Police
> Prosecutors
> Court – court paralegals, reporters, arbitrators and mediators, etc.
> Judges
> Lawyers
> Jury
> Probation officers/correctional treatment officers
> Prison/Correctional officers
> Others – Military, National Guard, etc.

These institutions and their associated personnel play interrelated roles to ensure law and order in communities and states across America.

Lawmakers

The lawmakers are that branch of government at the federal, state, and local levels charged with the responsibility of making laws in the form of statutes, ordinances, executive issuances, edicts, acts, and regulations, to list a few. At the federal level, there are 29,848 federal employees in the legislative branch involved with making laws, including senators, congressional representatives, and staff. See Appendix 15 for additional information. No numbers are available for lawmaker personnel at the state and local levels. With 50 states, 3,000 counties, and tens of thousands of cities from coast to coast, the number of lawmakers across the nation is astronomical. Lawmakers represent the people, so, therefore, the laws they make can be reasonably assumed to reflect the will and interest of the people.

Police

It is not an overstatement to say that the police are the bull's-eye of LEP, the core of the common core of law enforcement. They are charged with the responsibility of enforcing the laws on the streets and in the community, where the proverbial rubber meets the road on a daily basis. The police make sure that elements of the law or rules of engagement are adhered to by members of society on a daily basis in public spaces and, in some cases, in homes. The police are usually in the executive branch of government.

Social theory has observed that when a society is formed, members of that society usually give up some individual rights and delegate those rights to the representative government. Thus the government has an exclusive monopoly on the rights to both exercise and enforce certain rights (such as taking life or the death penalty and liberty infringement or imprisonment) for the benefit of all members of the society. One such right is the use of force to enforce the law of the land. In America, and in most societies for that matter, the police force is the most noticeable arm of government that performs these functions, hence the law enforcement motto: to serve and to protect. As part of the law enforcement institutions in America, the police come in various forms and shapes and have more different names and responsibilities than can be discussed here. The following are the most notable:

> Desk police who serve in the office
> Patrol or traffic police who serve in the communities
> Trainers at the police academy
> Detectives who investigate crimes
> Sheriffs who serve at the county level
> State police/troopers who patrol state highways and perform other state safety/security functions
> Marshals who patrol the airlines
> Police who patrol national parks, government buildings/properties and public installations
> Police who protect our leaders and public officials
> Others – office duty police, private security officers/guards, etc.

Based on Bureau of Labor Statistics 2012 data, there are an estimated 780,000 police and detectives in the country, performing a wide variety of functions. This number is expected to grow by 41,000 by 2022. (See Appendix 16 for additional information.) At the local level, the police ensure peace, safety, and orderliness in the community within their jurisdiction. They do this by protecting and serving law abiding citizens, and by issuing warnings to or arresting those in violation of the law. In this capacity, police are expected to function primarily to maintain the peace, safety, law, and order of the community. They patrol the streets to ensure that people follow driving laws and are safe. They promote law and order in the community through public education and campaigns. They arrest those in violation of such laws as disturbing the peace of neighbors, domestic violence, burglary, and active shooting, to name just a few. Sometimes they have to use force to enforce the law, especially when a person resists arrest and/or poses an imminent threat to himself/herself, others and/or the police. When police fail to adhere to basic tenets of the law in enforcing laws, citizens can file a complaint and ask for redress.

American police are generally trained in the law of the land. They are also trained in the rules of engaging members of society whom they are charged to protect and to serve. Most police are very professional and adhere to the rules of engagement. They use proportionate force in enforcing the laws. As in any profession, however, there are few bad eggs who do not adhere to the rules of engagement. These police have a habit of using disproportionate force to enforce the laws. Unfortunately, these few bad eggs tend to dominate the news when law enforcement goes awry, as discussed in previous chapter.

Prosecutors

If and when arrests are made, the police investigate, gather evidence and submit the case to the prosecutors in the appropriate office or offices at the local, state, or federal level, depending on the type and nature of crime or violation. The prosecutor, usually a trained and licensed attorney, examines the evidence or case and makes a determination as to whether to prosecute the alleged criminal or violator. The police make the arrest and conduct an investigation, the prosecutor prosecutes and takes to case to court. The prosecutor may or may not utilize the grand jury, depending on the jurisdiction and the types and natures of laws involved. As a law enforcement personnel, the prosecutor or his or her designee play a key role in holding the suspect accountable to the law. He or she makes the case for or against the suspect in the court of law and decides what punishment or lack thereof to recommend based on the severity of the alleged crime, the evidence, and applicable laws. Prosecutors are part of the executive branch.

Court

With the court's involvement, law enforcement comes full cycle: the legislative personnel make laws; the executive personnel enforce the law; and the courts interpret and apply the laws. There were an estimated 33,772 employees serving in the judicial branch at the federal level in 2012. (See Appendix 16 for details.) The number of personnel working in the judicial branch at the state and local levels is not available. Given that the bulk of court activities take place at the state and local levels, the number can be expected to be astronomically high. This speaks to the premium value that Americans place on law enforcement.

At stake are the freedom and the inalienable rights, of the person who is arrested and accused of a crime (or crimes). It is a given that the courts generally take great care to ensure that the rules of engagement are followed fairly and equitability from start to finish. This is important to ensure the integrity of the law enforcement process and to maintain the people's faith and confidence in the process. Further, the key players (police, lawyers, judges) are trained professionals who assist the citizens in navigating the law enforcement processes. Suspects or defendants are highly encouraged to retain a licensed lawyer/ attorney. If the defendant cannot afford a lawyer, a lawyer (also called a public defendant) is appointed to represent him or her. This is important because of the complexity of the laws and the court process, but also because an individual's liberty is at stake. The process has many moving parts and complexities beyond the scope of this book. Also beyond the scope of this book is an analysis of the elaborate court systems with many tiers and districts to handle all kinds of cases on issues ranging from murder to shoplifting and traffic violations. An experienced judge always finds a way to make the process as transparent and expeditious as possible.

Judges

All judges in the court of law are trained and licensed lawyers. Many of them have served in various capacities in law enforcement as prosecutors, trial lawyers, solicitors, administrative judges, and public defendants, to name a few. There are an estimated 42,300 judges and hearing officers in the country in 2012 and this number is expected to grow by 400 by 2022. Additionally, judges use the services of legal professionals to support the overall functioning of the court.

The legal professionals include paralegals, estimated at 277,000; arbitrators, mediators, and conciliators, 8,400; and court reporters, 21,200. (See Appendix 16 for additional information on these cadres of law enforcement personnel and the crucial roles they play.)

Judges rely on formal education, training, and experience to preside over the cases in their court. They or their back-up judges usually conduct the affairs of court proceedings. They advise all parties of their rights, the rules of engagement, and what the case is about. There are different courts for different cases and laws (family, real estate, civil, criminal) at different levels (administrative, local, district, superior, appeals, supreme, etc.), but the process is the same, broadly speaking. The key parts are the case, the plaintiff, and the defendant. The prosecutors and trial lawyers make their case and present and cross-examine evidence; witnesses, if any, testify; the jury, if any, listens to the presentations, evidence, and testimonies; and the judge and/or jury deliberate and render the verdict and judgment.

Lawyers

America is blessed with an abundance of lawyers in every facet of law enforcement. Lawyers are everywhere in society, so it is hard to think of any occupation, business, or individuals who do not need lawyers or feel the impact of lawyers' services. They are needed at every twist and turn of the law enforcement process. There are an estimated 759,000 lawyers in the country and this number is expected to grow by 74,800 by 2022. Additionally, lawyers use multiple paralegals to perform basic administrative legal functions – filing, research, scheduling, etc. (See Appendix 16 for more information.)

Lawyers serve in government as judges, prosecutors, attorneys, public defenders, counsel, solicitors, adjudicators, administrative judges and hearing officers, investigators, and regulatory specialists, to list a few. In society, they serve as family lawyers, trial lawyers, business and corporate lawyers, lawyers for nonprofit watchdogs, and in many other vocations. Lawyers pride themselves on being the defenders of the defenseless, the champions of the poor, and the advocates of those in need of legal representation. They also provide free legal aid for those who have been left behind or just forgotten in society. Nowhere are their services more obvious than in the courts of law across the nation where matters of law enforcement and freedom are paramount. A visit to a court, any court, would reveal the omnipresence of lawyers. Lawyers are almost always in black suits, carrying worn-out leather handbags and briefcases overflowing with files and folders.

In law enforcement, lawyers usually serve as the legal representative of their client as the defense attorney or the attorney for the plaintiff, depending on whether their client is the one who is suing (plaintiff) or being sued (defender). Either way, the attorney is there to represent the best interests of his or her client to ensure a fair hearing, due process, equal protection under the law, sound evidentiary process, and application of applicable legal principles. As the saying goes, a good lawyer knows the law, but a great lawyer knows the court, the judge, and the jury. The goal is for the lawyer to persuade all deliberative and decision making parties to see the case from the point of view of his client. This requires a keen knowledge of the law, but also the ability to develop a narrative (a legal theory) that aligns the evidence in such a way that it is convincing to the judge and jury. In the end, the decision is usually made by the judge and/ or jury, based on the evidence presented and a matter of law.

The police and the lawyers (including prosecutors and judges) form the law enforcement common core. Some police move on to become lawyers. From the abundance of lawyers, many move on to become prosecutors and judges. Police and lawyers make up the lion's share of LEPs nationally. Of the total 2,510,470 LEPs (not including uniformed military personnel), police and lawyers account for 1,539,000 of them.

Jury

Not all courts and cases use the services of a jury. A jury is made up of jurors who are usually citizens selected from among the members of the community. Jurors are instructed by judges with respect to the rules of engagement in performing jury duties. The primary duty of the jury is to listen to presentations and testimonies during the hearing and then deliberate and render a verdict on a case. Jurors are selected through a "randomized" process and vetted by the lawyers on both sides. There are different types of juries, most notably a grand jury and a traditional jury of peers. Prosecutors use the services of a grand jury to determine whether a suspect or an accuser of a crime should or should not be indicted. As noted above, a jury of peers hears, deliberates, and renders a verdict on a case.

Probation Officers and Correctional Treatment Specialists (POs/CTSs)

POs/CTSs come in at any phase of law enforcement once an arrest has been made or when a lawsuit has been filed, but the bulk of POs are involved in a case at the final phase of law enforcement. There are estimated 90,000 POs/CTSs in the country. This number is expected to slow by 2022 due to the introduction of automation technologies to perform some of the functions performed by these cadres of law enforcement personnel. (See Appendix 16 for more information.) The primary functions of POs/CTSs are in the area of monitoring and helping services. The goal is rehabilitation and positive behavioral modification.

Probation officers help those who have come in contact with law enforcement to rehabilitate back into society. If the clients have served time in prison, POs help them gradually re-enter society as they regain their freedom. The CTSs assist with the treatment needed to overcome their personal and/or skill deficiencies so that they can become fully functioning members of society. This requires a treatment plan and strict adherence to and compliance with the provisions of the plan.

Prison/Correctional Officers (PCO)

PCOs, much like POs/CTSs, come in at the tail end phase in law enforcement, once an arrest has been made or a guilty verdict has been rendered. There are an estimated 469,500 PCOs in the country and this number is expected to grow by 23,000 by 2022. (See Appendix 16 for details.) Upon arrest, suspects are placed in detention in police custody. Within days, the suspect is brought to court for an initial hearing. Depending on the nature and severity of allegations, the suspect may be released on bail or remanded back to jail without bail. If released, the suspect may not be back in prison. The suspect may be sent back to prison, depending on whether he or she is found guilty at the hearing and sentenced to do time in prison or serve probation. If the suspect is sentenced to probation, he or she has limited freedom and works with the PO/CTS. If the suspect is sentenced to do time in prison, he or she loses most of his/her freedoms and comes under the custody of a PCO, who follows strict guidelines and rules of engagement in housing and "caring" for prisoners in the correctional facilities for the duration of their imprisonment.

Others – Military, National Guards, etc.

On a broader scale, the military and the National Guard play an incalculably valuable role in maintaining law and order at the state, national, and international levels. The primary function of the military men and women is to secure the parameters of the nation so that the rest of the law enforcement personnel and all of us, for that matter, can go about our business. They do this by developing and maintaining superior military strength and strong military personnel, backed by a high level of public support. As shown in the Appendix 1 data, the national military budget, compared to that of other nations, speaks for itself. There are an estimated 1,551,000 uniformed military personnel serving in this capacity (see also Appendix 16). The numbers of National Guard and army reservists are not available.

These cadres of law enforcement personnel do the heavy lifting in the most unlikely places, whether fighting Ebola in West Africa, containing terrorists overseas or helping with Hurricane Katrina and Hurricane Sandy here at home. Like the police and detectives, they put themselves in harm's way and sometimes pay the ultimate price by taking the bullet so that we don't have to. By providing, building, and maintaining the infrastructures for national security, we can breathe more easily and enjoy the freedom and the benefits of a free nation. Who says freedom is free?

Ideological Divide

It follows from the foregoing that Americans agree on the principles of law and order and on robust law enforcement personnel. However, Americans differ on the approaches to take to reach a strong system of law and order. That is, although Americans subscribe to the principles of and the importance of law and order, they do not always agree on the way laws should be interpreted and applied. A significant number of Americans place emphasis on punishment as deterrent. Others emphasize rehabilitation and second chances. Generally, law enforcement falls into two broad schools of thought to deter crimes: punishment versus rehabilitation. The former focuses on tough enforcement, such as "three strikes and you're out." The latter focuses on rehabilitation, retraining, and reintegration of violators or perpetrators. These approaches reflect divergent philosophical views of a society and the role of government and individuals in that society.

As such, Americans fall into two broad ideological divides: conservatives and liberals. Liberals are also called progressives. For example, based on the general mid-term elections on November 4, 2014, roughly 87% of liberal voters indicated that they had voted Democrat, while roughly 85% of conservative voters stated that they had voted Republicans. (See Appendix 14 for details.) Republicans are generally conservative in their ideology, with emphasis on lower taxes and small government. Conservative budgets, as reflected in the budgets of Republican states (also called red states), tend to lower taxes, limit government programs, and place more responsibility on the individuals and families. Democrats are generally progressive in their ideology, with emphasis on wealth redistribution through taxes, government outreach to the poor and underserved segments of society, and in providing economic opportunities and jobs for all, especially the poor and the middle class. As the name suggests, liberals are, well, more liberal regarding government programs. Liberal budgets, as reflected in the budgets of Democratic states (also called blue states), tend to redistribute through higher taxes (especially on the rich). The liberal agenda places more responsibility on publically funded programs so that individuals and communities can flourish.

Admittedly, the above is an oversimplification of complex ideological realities, with conflicts and contradictions on both sides of the ideological divide. However, the impact of these two ideological camps are more nuanced and the outcomes more identifiable in the lives of millions of Americans who come in contact with law enforcement every day. There is a general perception that the conservatives tend to be strong on enforcing the laws, with emphasis on punishment and prisons. The common slogan is "three strikes and you're out," or build prisons and the prisoners will come. Red states or Republican-led federal administrations and Congress tend to build or spend more money on prisons than, say, schools. Conservative judges and courts tend to be tough on sentencing and send more criminals to prison. Conservative judges and prosecutors also tend to apply a restricted or narrow interpretation of the laws.

There is a general perception that progressives also tend to be strong on enforcing the law, but with the emphasis on giving violators and perpetrators a second chance by providing them with rehabilitation and reintegration services. Common mantras are "it takes a village to raise a child" or "teach them to fish and you feed them forever." Blue states or Democratic-led federal administrations and Congress tend to build or spend more money on schools and programs than, say, prisons. Liberal judges and courts tend to grant leniency requests and probation when sentencing. They send more criminals to rehab programs. Liberal judges and prosecutors have a tendency to interpret laws more broadly, allowing for wiggle room in law enforcement.

There is consensus in public opinion regarding the public trust in enforcing the law and maintaining order. The general public tends to trust the Republicans to do a more effective job in matters relating to law and order—national security, law enforcement, and crime reduction. On matters relating to the economy, jobs creation, and social justice, the public tends to trust the Democrats to do a better job.

What is behind the ideological divide is the level of commitment to patriotism, national pride, and the overall stability, growth, and development of the nation. This observation is self-evident in the elaborate institutions of law and order committed to making sure that there is law and order at the federal, state and local levels. The number speaks for itself: a total of 4,061,470 law enforcement personnel are committed to law and order across the land and in military bases and installations overseas. (See again Appendices 15 and 16.)

Thus, making laws is not enough if they are not enforced to regulate behaviors. According to this school of thought, law enforcement is very important and resources must be committed to this goal. The belief is that law enforcement not only protects lives and property and maintains order; it also deters bad behavior by regulating the behavior of lawbreakers or potential lawbreakers.

Law and Order and Productivity

Productivity associated with law and order can be viewed at two levels: at the level of law and order's contribution to society and at the level of the multiplier effect. President Abraham

Lincoln eloquently articulated the goal of law and order when he stated that:

> My dream is of a place and a time where America will once again be seen as the last best hope of earth.

American laws and the resulting societal order are by no means perfect and they have their share of criticism of what is wrong with modern nation states. Yet it remains, in my judgment and based on where most immigrants are coming from, it is heaven on earth that any nation would want to trade places with. This explains in part why more people seek to migrate and continue to migrate to America than to any other nation in the world. Not only are economic opportunities for a better life in great supply, its laws and social engineering remain the best that humankind has offered.

The American type of productivity is only possible in a society where law enforcement, as outlined above, works. Law enforcement is designed to protect law abiding citizens and to weed out criminals and trouble makers. Indeed bad arrests and perceived miscarriages of justice surface in the media periodically and dominate the news for days and weeks (not that anything is necessarily wrong with that, given the nature and function of free press as the watchdog of a civilized society). These unfortunate incidents are better understood when put in context.

It is important to note that there are millions of arrests made every year in an attempt to maintain law and order. Between 2009 and 2013, there were millions of arrests and adjudicated cases, as a matter of routine litigation business. In 2010, there were an estimated 13,211,110 arrests made in the U.S., and in 2013 there were 11,302,102 arrests (see Appendix 17 for details).

Two obvious conclusions can be deduced from these statistics. First, from the point of efficiency, law enforcement is doing its job enforcing the law—protecting citizens and removing the bad guys. Second, from the point of effectiveness, the numbers of arrests has gone down significantly—by nearly 1.9 million arrests between 2010 and 2013. This drop in arrests is also reflected in the drop in the overall crime rate in the United States in the past several years, based on data from the Federal Bureau of Investigation and the Departments of Justice's Bureau of Justice Statistics (see http://www.bjs.gov; http://www.fbi.gov/stats-services/).

Thus, American taxpayers in this regard can and should rest easier and go about their jobs, businesses, and the pursuit of happiness and property, knowing that their hard-earned tax dollars are at work for the safety and security of the nation and the communities. We've noted that it would have been counterproductive if the American economy were not productive, given its investment in ideas, people, and society with superb law enforcement to back it up.

At the level of the multiplier effect, refer to the occupations listed previously regarding the enormous numbers of jobs available to Americans in the public and private sectors as a result of law and order. Multiple legal and professional activities—formal education (law schools), continued education (training programs and centers and institutions), and licenses (professional associations)—are associated with law and order in general and law enforcement in particular. Paralegal programs are in steady supply to meet the demand for legal personnel. Many legal professionals are self-employed. Some are in LLC businesses, while others hold positions in large corporations at the national and international levels. These skilled white and blue collar professionals serve vital roles in performing law enforcement functions across the nation and internationally. They serve as defenders of the defenseless, protectors of freedom, consumer rights watchdogs, and advocates for noble causes, to list just a few. Their combined earnings and purchasing power contribute immensely to the economy.

Bottom Line

Business opportunities emerge when major laws are enacted affecting large segments of society or in response to natural disasters, human catastrophe, and economic negotiations. We discussed in previous chapters how these enactments and occurrences can serve as triggers for opportunities for jobs, business startups, and the expansion of existing business. As stated, law enforcement plays a significant role in these efforts, generating enormous economic output.

Further, law enforcement creates a level playing field for individuals and groups of individuals to pursue economic and social interests or simply to accumulate wealth. Provided a person abides with the laws of the land, the sky is very much the limit in pursuing legitimate dreams, whatever the dreams are. To the extent that the public continues to perfect, support, and collaborate with law enforcement, the future of the country is not only bright, but will continue on track to be the "last best hope on earth" for centuries to come.

CHAPTER 9

LIFE IS NOT EASY, NEITHER IS PRODUCTIVITY EASY

In this chapter, we pause to take the pulse of productivity in America. It would appear from the discussions thus far that productivity is a piece of cake as long as one does all the right stuff and pushes all the right buttons. If this were the case, productivity and economic opportunities would flourish in almost every country on earth and there would be no need for migration. Of course, there is no picture-perfect formula for productivity. In fact, another way to look at our discussion thus far is to say that productivity is predicated on a lot of conditions and terms, some within your sphere of control, others outside your orbital control. This is because productivity is, in the long run, part of life.

And life is not easy. If you think life is easy, you haven't lived long enough. Life as we know it is not always easy. Neither is productivity. If you think productivity is easy, you haven't been in the job market or in business long enough. My observation is that American success stories, the whole idea of rags to riches, are possible because America as a nation and as a collection of individuals has the resiliency to put good news and bad news in perspective and in parenthesis, respectively. The purpose of this chapter is to locate productivity within the context of life in America. We begin by observing briefly the elements that make life worth living, followed by an analysis of how these very same elements can make life rather complex and uncertain. Next, we examine how these complexities and uncertainties play out in our pursuit of economic opportunities in the larger society. We conclude with the implications of internal and environmental uncertainties for productivity.

Life's Social Elements: Family, Friends, and Faith

Life has many definitions and dimensions. Some dimensions are essentially inherent in us (genes, chromosomes, blood, heart, brain, kidneys). Others are essential but external to us (heat, air, water). Yet there are those dimensions that give meaning to our interiors and exteriors, but are often taken for granted. Among this last group of essential elements of life are family, friends, and faith. It is hard to imagine life without these three social elements, which, together give meaning to life and form the context in which we live out our lives privately, publically, and spiritually. They also form the stage where our interiors and exteriors interface with each other to give us a sense of direction.

Family

We are born into a family by a family. At any given time, we are a member of a family, even if that means a family of only one. Within this family we eat, sleep, talk, and move around freely. Yes, we may maintain some fears of and keep secrets from each other, and may even compete against each other as well as love and hate each other. It is nevertheless a family that we neither choose nor decide to be a part of. We are born into it and so are full members of the family, no matter how hard we try to excommunicate or ignore members of the family. We have a right to the family resources, at least until we reach the age of 12 or 18, depending on which resources we are talking about—food or a car. As the reducible unit of society, the family is the most basic habitat where we nurture and ultimately pursue and celebrate our humanness, hopes, dreams, socializing, language, values, and beliefs, to name a few.

Friends

As early as at the age of infants and toddlers, we recognize faces and voices that are friendly and not so friendly. As we grow older and have the love and hate of immediate family members locked in, we begin to realize that there are the "we and they" or the "us and them." As such, these categories give us choices in an infant and toddler world. Depending on how those in the "they and them" category behave and relate to us, we can move them away from or close to the "we and us" category. Since they don't share our blood line, we call them friends. Over time, we develop close or distant relationships not only with our family members but also with our friends. We have more latitude with our friends, so we make and keep many friends but like some better than others.

We eat, interact, and share our dreams and hopes with these friends at different levels in a web of intimate, casual, and distant circles. We fall in love with and eventually marry some in the inner circle; others remain friends forever. Many simply drop out of sight and out of mind but can be, nevertheless, long lost friends whom we encounter once a decade or quarter century. These coincidences can be fun or awkward, depending on where the casual friendship left off. All of these friends play a role in whom and what we are and have become as a person. Some friends are there for support and intimacy. Others are there to brag or lie to. A few serve as our reality-check mirror. We measure our mobility on the food chain against their ranking on the social economic status scale. We feel good if we are a step or two ahead of them; we feel terrible otherwise.

Faith

As humans, we all have fear. Fear of success and failure, and of life and death. Our faith or lack thereof helps us keep these inherent anxieties in perspective. The faith community comes in handy in this regard. Faith is something that we can't live with and can't live without. No wonder the ancient wisdom says that only a fool says in his/her heart that there is no God. Many people would rather claim to have no need for faith, a faith community, or God, for that matter. They see God talk as psychobabble and the faith community as something that seeks strength in numbers. That is, until a life threatening emergency strikes in an airplane, in the family, or in an active shooter situation. In these situations, almost everyone prays to an Almighty for protection and safety.

Mystery and Contradictions

Much as we love to admire and crave family, friends, and faith as the embodiment of life, these elements equally represent a stage where much of life's complexities are played out. For many a philosopher, life itself and the elements thereof—family, friends, faith—can be viewed as necessary evils. Another way to look at human narratives is that life is full of mysteries and contradictions, which makes the very elements of life all the more necessary.

Much as we need family, who doesn't know how annoying a family or family members can be. Social commentators have noted that Thanksgiving Day is the most anxiety-filled day in America, with family members fighting, screaming, and yelling at each other in between meals and football games. It doesn't make sense to work all year long, only to spend your hard-earned money to go to a fight. Yet, it is in those family fights that we learn about each other—and grow, develop, and mature to become functioning adults in society.

Life is a mystery that no one can explain. Stories abound of persons missing a flight and cursing their friend or kicking the flat tire that caused them to miss their flight. But then hours or minutes later the plane is involved in an unfortunate incident leading to unfortunate outcome. Or, imagine a person who kindly gives up a seat for a friend that is more in need of a seat on a tour bus. The kind person boards another tour bus that later is involved in a road hazard and no one survives.

When I was a social worker, I recall many couples who were street poor and homeless, with no health care insurance and who had never visited a doctor in years. They could not care for themselves let alone care for a child. Yet, a couple would give birth to a healthy baby, without pre- and post-natal care. Meanwhile, middle class couples (yuppies, as they were called in those days) would spend a fortune to have a baby, to no avail. Some would manage to have a baby, but the baby and mother would have severe post-natal health issues.

Implications for Productivity

I always wonder why appliances always break when insurance has just expired. Why do heating systems always break late on Sunday afternoon when the temperature is the sub-zero degree range. Why does an air conditioning system always fail to work on a weekend when it's over 100 degrees in the home of someone who is elderly or living on a fixed income? Why are countries with very low literacy rate and low technology awash with an abundance of oil and other natural resources, while countries with high literacy rate and high technology have limited natural resources with a terrible natural habitat?

Americans, and most civilized societies for that matter, are fully aware of life's dynamics, as outlined above. One response to these uncertainties in life is the invention of insurance, both in the public and private sectors. The importance of insurance of all kinds in this regard can hardly be overemphasized. This is important—especially for new arrivals to the United States from countries where insurance is an alien concept. Backup plans, savings, emergency funds, and retirement accounts can come handy, but that is the extent to which these contingencies are put in place in good times.

As the saying goes, opportunities tend to come only once. Even then, they don't always come without any strings attached. This is true whether in employment or when starting a business. In theory and in math, two apples and two apples make four apples. The reality is, however, is that two and two are not always four. That is, if you are fortunate enough to have two apples and again run into two apples twice in a row. When you need four good apples, chances are you'll get two good apples, one bad apple, and four good oranges. Put differently, there is always the proverbial monkey wrench that finds its way into the engine compartment to wreak havoc when least expected and at the moment when you can least afford a major repair or when the landlord has just reminded you that the rent is due.

Yes, opportunity comes but once. Most people in America get that. That is why America is also a nation of second chances, and the second chance of a second chance. At the same time, Americans are smart to strike a balance with the second chance principle to avoid abusing the principle. Such abuses can create fertile grounds for laziness and dependence on living on the dole. The principle or law of no double dipping is, in effect, primarily to prevent abuses and exploitations of second chance opportunities.

The concepts of living wage opportunities and having a second chance are very important to the concept of productivity in America. As stated, jobs and business are the backbone of the American economy. The expectation is that individuals, after education and training, should find a job and work to make a living and be productive. The problem is that most employers want applicants with experience—usually at least 2 years of experience—for high-paying jobs. The question is: "How does a recent graduate with hopes and determination get experience without someone giving him a job?" In this regard, living wage opportunities and second chance privileges come handy.

Without the availability of initial opportunities and second chances, individuals who move on to become national icons and status symbols would have had little chance. There are iconic players with great expectations from the public, but who end up not meeting the high expectations. A case in point is Robert Griffin III of the Redskins football team and Freddie Adu, formerly of the DC United soccer team. In this respect, a person's capabilities need to be recalibrated for realistic productive goals.

There are great players who were very productive with the right team, but whose performance was mediocre due largely to no-show teammates. Take, for example, the iconic basketball player, Michael Jordan, and the famous football quarterback, Peyton Manning. Michael Jordan met with great success with the Chicago Bulls basketball team, but had only mediocre success with the Washington DC Wizards. Peyton Manning had a great Super Bowl success story with the Indianapolis Colts football team, but met his waterloo with a mediocre performance in the Broncos 2013 Super Bowl. The opportunity and second chance concept came in the form of teammates. To the extent that the great players had great teammates, their greatness flourished. Absent those great teammates, their greatness was tempered with humility. But having the right combination to optimize productivity can sometimes be as much a game of chance as it is a game of planning.

Similarly, entrepreneurs are always required to have seed money in order to secure loans to invest in a start-up business. Banks, lenders, and investors all require an entrepreneur to contribute his or her share of the total capital needed for the business. This requirement is to ensure that the entrepreneur has a stake in the business. The rationale is that an entrepreneur is more prudent in managing a business and when making risky decisions when he or she has vested interest in the business. So far so good! But the question is: How and where does a young entrepreneur fresh out of business school or incubation training have enough money for a 20%–40% down payment or deposit without a job or business? Sure, the individual can borrow seed money from friends and family members. But this usual suggestion ignores several realities. Many entrepreneurs have creative minds but, as in life, the same individuals don't always come from a background with rich families and friends.

Secondly, even those who manage to scrape together seed money from families and friends are faced with the burden of paying back the loans to those families and friends and then some. A person can renegotiate payments with lenders, but not with friends and families. Additionally, the entrepreneur must also begin to pay back the loan to lenders, while striving to feed his or her family and at the same time grow the start-up business. Meanwhile, there are no guarantees that environmental circumstances will not throw a monkey wrench into the mix. Based on Murphy's Law, what can happen almost always will happen. In this regard, the living wage opportunity and second chance concepts comes handy. A low-interest Small Business Administration loan or a grant from a philanthropic organization can provide such an opportunity.

The Case of the Great Recession of 2007–2009

As noted in the previous chapters, America was founded on the notion of continuous improvement, long before the term entered the modern business lexicon. As in life, efforts at perfecting the Union don't always perfect the Union. Sometimes the efforts create more imperfection and unintended consequences. A case in point is the great recession that hit the nation with far-reaching consequences during the second half of the millennial decade. The recession officially began in December 2007, when unemployment climbed to 5.0% and economic growth came to a screeching halt, followed by a rapid decline in almost all economic indicators. The recession officially ended in June 2009, when signs of growth in the economy began to show again on Wall Street, but was barely noticed on the main street or among the general population.

The causes of the Great Recession have been documented and debated extensively. Economists, philosophers, business experts, and social scientists, to list a few, have weighed in on the causes and the theories behind those causes. (https://muddywatermacro.wustl.edu/node/92 ; http://en.wikipedia.org/wiki/Causes_of_the_Great_Recession ; http://stateofworkingamerica.org/great-recession/).

A comprehensive analysis of these causes and theories is beyond the scope of this chapter or this book for that matter. It is important to note that, however, that based on the most notable theories and causes listed below (in no particular order), there is consensus among experts that there was enough blame to go around regarding who caused the worst recession since the Great Depression of 1929—from mortgage lenders, subprime borrowers, bank managers and employees, Wall Street investors and agents, and global investors, to government officials and regulatory agencies (for more details, go to http://en.wikipedia.org/wiki/Causes_of_the_Great_Recession and/or http://stateofworkingamerica.org/great-recession/):

> Excessive private debt levels
> Across-the-board culture of greed
> Affordable housing policies
> Interest rates
> Home equity extraction
> Flawed housing speculation
> Corporate risk-taking and leveraging
> Subprime lending to unsuspecting consumers
> Aggressive mortgage underwriting
> Mortgage fraud

Down payments and negative equity
Predatory lending
Risk-taking behavior
Consumer and household borrowing
Financial market factors
Flawed financial product innovation
Inaccurate credit ratings
Governmental policies
Failure to regulate non-depository banking
Globalization
End of a long wave
Capital market pressures
Lack of transparency and independence in
financial modeling
Off-balance-sheet financing
Private capital and the search for yield
Conflicts of interest and lobbying
Role of business leaders
Boom and collapse of the shadow banking system
Run on the shadow banking system
Mortgage compensation model, executive pay
and bonuses

The annals of causes read like one big conspiracy involving many institutions, professionals, consumers, and schemes to dupe the overall economy. I recall many homeowners taking out a second and third mortgage against the equity on their home to buy a Hummer or a boat they neither needed nor drove other than to park it in their driveway or leave it at the marina, just to catch up with their neighbors. There were all kinds of lending schemes that no one could explain or understand. The untested theory of a never-ending evolution of home equity became very popular. The world of unlimited credit cards was presumed to be without end, or so it felt to the gullible but unsuspecting consumers, as was sold to them by credit card companies and banks. Every economic indicator seemed to be right on target—until the housing bubble burst.

The domino effect was like a long nightmare that would never end. First, there were pockets of subprime mortgage late payments, then a floodgate of defaults. The collapse of the Bear Sterns and Lehman Brothers financial institutions greeted a shocked nation. The domino effect of the bubble bursting reached the housing market, auto industry, mortgage industry, stock markets, and financial services firms. The multiplier firms and satellite companies that relied on the fallen giant corporations for business were not spared from the brunt of the recession.

Many of these small businesses operate from payroll to payroll, much like an individual or a family living from paycheck to paycheck. Small businesses hire the bulk of the American workforce. With the recession hitting home hard, many businesses let a significant number of employees go. The immediate effect was a skyrocketing number of bankruptcies filed by both individuals and businesses, as evident from the following bankruptcy figures (see Appendix 18 for details and links to additional data on bankruptcy trends):

Year	Total	Non-Business	Business
2012	1,221,091	1,181,016	40,075
2011	1,410,653	1,362,847	47,806
2010	1,593,081	1,536,799	56,282
2009	1,473,675	1,412,838	60,837
2008	1,117,641	1,074,108	43,533
2007	850,912	822,590	28,322
2006	617,660	597,965	19,695

The global impact was just about as catastrophic. As the saying goes, when America sneezes, the world catches a cold or a sore throat, depending on whether a nation is an ally or a foe. Almost all industrial nations suffered a high rate of unemployment and near-economic collapse. The PIGS nations (Portugal, Ireland, Greece, and Spain) were hardest hit and are still reeling from the worldwide impact. Third World nations were already struggling. These underdeveloped nations saw their permanent unemployment rates rise even higher than normal. Interestingly, the recession had little impact on nations that were already in perpetual state of poverty. Even so, the recession certainly did not help the already deplorable conditions in these nations.

Although the recession officially ended 18 months later, in the summer of 2009, the damage to the economy—the collapse of the housing market, stock markets, job market, businesses, and families—had already been done. When it was all over, the employment rate stood in the double digits—10% by some estimates. The effect of the worst recession of all time, except for the Great Depression, is still with us some 5 years after it was declared over. If there was a time that a significant portion of the perfecting of the Union, with all its checks and balances, failed to work, it was then. Many lost their jobs and businesses. Not for lack of trying, but from forces beyond their control. In effect, the recession was a reversed trickle-down economy. That is, a reversal of the economic dividends accrued from the trickle-down economy of the previous decade, assuming that the economy had, in fact, trickled down.

Employees and Seekers Overtaken by Events (OBE)

It is important to underscore here that productivity imitates life. As the economy tanked, many corporations and small businesses were forced to lay off workers. Many employees lost their jobs at Fannie Mae, Freddie Mac, Bank of America, JP Morgan, Ford, Chrysler, and in just about any industry in the economy. These employees in the millions ended up in the unemployment line, not for lack of trying, but because they were overtaken by events (OBE). So it is possible to develop all the habits of productivity (education, networking, knowing people who know you) and secure a decent job and yet be blown away from your job by a sagging economy through no fault of your own.

Millions of job seekers polished their resumes and honed their interview skills, yet found it difficult to land a job due to the high rate of employment. Understanding this dynamic nature of productivity, and indeed of life itself, does help to put things into perspective—that the downward spiral of a person and the economy is never the end. After all, where there is a beginning there will eventually be an end. Recessions come and go in a never-ending cycle of downward and upward swings. If you happen get on board the economic bandwagon during boom times, do all you can to save and build contingency plans to ride out the next recession(s). Should you get on board during periods of economic collapse, consider that the recessions are triggers for entrepreneurial opportunities. After all, if there was a time when necessity is the mother of invention, it is usually during these periods of uncertainty.

Impact on Entrepreneurs and Business Owners

Many entrepreneurs folded during the recession as did many long-established, existing businesses, partly because lines of credit and business loans dried up. As stated, others downsized their operations and streamlined their workforce just to survive the brunt of the recession. For small business owners, it was a sink or swim situation. Many never made it and so went under. It was not for lack of not playing by the rules of engagement; they were simply overtaken by severe economic events. It is important to point out that the businesses that operated efficiently and effectively, with pre-recession contingency plans, adapted relatively well to economic realities. These businesses survived to tell the story. A few businesses actually thrived and reported modest earnings and profits.

The key is designing a business model that is flexible enough to withstand internal and external environmental uncertainties. This requires the need to jettison or revise outdated business plans and models. It also requires the need to adopt business plans based on time-tested, evidence-based business management strategies, such as agile project management, horizontally structured management strategies, value-added supply chain management, and organizational development, to list just a few research-based strategies. To this end, business owners and managers do themselves a huge favor by heeding the advice of a great American army general who pointed out that a war plan goes out the window upon first contact with the enemy, but what general will go to war without a plan. The point being that rigid outdated plans don't work in military campaigns, but flexible plans do. And I might add that the same principle applies in some degree to business and productivity during tough times.

There is consensus among economists and businesspeople that the worst of the Great Recession is over, although the adverse effects still linger in some quarters more than others. The Dow Jones stock market, well under 10,000 points during the recession, was well over 17,000 points by December 2014. The unemployment rate hovered around 5.8 % around the same period, down from 10% at the height of the recession. In November and December 2014, the economy added well over 300,000 jobs and 250,000 jobs, respectively.

Almost all productivity indicators had pointed in the right direction by January 2015, indicating that the economy has slowly but steadily recovered from the recession. New regulations are in place to ensure that this serious a recession doesn't happen again. As in life, though, the only thing that is certain is change. The certainties and uncertainties of productivity are no exceptions to the rule. Meanwhile, the perfecting of the Union has essentially been brought back on track and life goes on!

Business Uncertainties and Providence

It is important to underscore here that, as in life, managers and business owners can still run into periods of turbulence even though they use and adhere to evidence-based organizational models and management principles, such as POLE (planning, organizing, leading, and evaluation), GMAC (Goal, Metric, Analysis, and Control), and SMART (senior management, middle management, administrative staff/research and development, technical core/operations), to list a few. (See Appendix 10 for a comprehensive list and details.) In this regard, the 4 Ps of Entrepreneurship— Products, Presence, Publicity, and Providence—in Appendix 10 are of particular interest.

There is consensus in the literature on business management that an entrepreneur and any business manager for that matter can meet all the product line requirements, establish a presence in the community and in virtual space, roll out an aggressive and well-planned marketing campaign, and still fail. But why would he or she fail? After all, all the T's are crossed and I's are dotted. Short answer: out of luck. Given, the fourth P (Providence) is of critical importance. The point is, after you've followed all the business rules of engagement to the best of your abilities, I recommend saying a little prayer; leave the rest to providence and go about your daily business.

Admittedly, American culture is, in my opinion, rooted in the spirit of human adventure, which, in turn, is rooted in the acceptance of divine providence in everyday life and in the moments of great crisis. This observation is not new. The practice of working like a dog and at the same time trusting divine guidance for success is an integral part of American history, dating back to the founders. The founders and subsequent generations have always invoked divine presence in their effort during periods of internal and external uncertainties: the Revolutionary War, the Civil War, the Great Depression, World War II, Segregation, civil rights unrest, and the Great Recession.

Bottom Line

In the final analysis, life is full of uncertainties and so is productivity. It is for this very reason that adequate preparation for life's uncertainties is very important. The more education and experience a person has the better he or she is in marshalling a wide range of options and tools to work with in response to uncertainties. Fewer tools mean fewer options to work with when adapting to new situations and challenges.

Further, the more diversified a person's repertoire of education and experience, the more effective he or she is in responding to uncertainties and in taking advantage of new challenges.

Education, experience, and abilities to respond to uncertainties must be planned and executed in a timely manner. Native-born Americans are aware of this. As the saying goes, time is money. But for many immigrants, time is often taken for granted in their pursuit of a better life and economic opportunities in America. Many immigrants usually do not have their family with them, have few friends, and are not attached to faith community. These deficits sometimes truncate the experiences they brought with them and limit their ability to deal with uncertainties in the new environment and culture.

Time is the enemy of life and, yes, of productivity. Productive people make wise use of their time for the purpose of productivity within the context of their family, friends, and faith community. After all, charity begins at home. These elements of life have a way of adding spice and meaning to the pursuit of jobs and business. Together they provide a rich context for learning important seminal qualities needed to make life a little easier in the workplace and in business, namely, the art of expressing gratitude and dealing with conflicts. Gratitude and apology are the subjects of the next two chapters.

CHAPTER 10

GRATITUDE AND PRODUCTIVITY: THE THANKFUL STATE OF THANKS

A long, long time ago, Grandpa Balewa had three grandchildren: Bello, Bitu, and Batuta. One day, Grandpa paid a visit to the grandchildren. Upon arriving, he announced that he had brought toys for them, hauling with him a big bag full of toys. Batuta, the first one to meet Grandpa, said, "Thanks!" Grandpa reached into the bag and gave him one toy. Bitu was next. She said, "Thank you, Grandpa!" Grandpa reached into the bag and gave her two toys. Last but not least was Bello, who stepped up and said, "Thank you, Grandpa Balewa!" Grandpa reached into the bag and gave him four toys. Batuta jumped to his feet and asked Grandpa why he gave Bitu two toys and Bello four toys, but gave him only one toy. Grandpa knelt down beside Batuta and wrapped his raggedy but loving arms around him and said, "Bitu said 'thank you, Grandpa' and so she received two toys; Bello said 'thank you, Grandpa Balewa' and he received four toys; you only said "thanks" and you received one toy." Batuta said "oh" and sat back in his seat quietly. Such is the power of gratitude when fully or not fully expressed.

Gratitude is a universal act of appreciation, which is expressed in many culturally conditioned ways in different societies. The various expressions of gratitude fall into two broad categories— namely, social gratitude and institutional gratitude. The former consists of everyday expressions of gratitude. These expressions are used more informally. The latter is more formal and consists of various ways of expressing appreciation in an institutional context. Institutional gratitude expressions serve as ways of motivating employees towards desired performance and conduct outcomes in the workplace. In this respect, institutional gratitude takes its cue from social gratitude. Expressions of social gratitude serve as ways of affirming and influencing desirable behaviors in social and cultural settings.

In this chapter, we discuss the good news and bad news of gratitude as a universal norm and as an abundant American cultural trait. This is followed by a brief examination of the roles of institutional gratitude in American workplace. We conclude with several observations in connection about the impact of gratitude on social life in general and on workplace productivity in particular.

Good News about Thanks – the Most Widely Used Universal Term

The most commonly used word in the gratitude lexicon is "thanks" or "thank you." Its various permutations are widely used in almost all cultures and languages of the world. According to cultural anthropology, almost all known and documented languages or cultures have a rich lexicon of gratitude, with "thanks" or "thank you" being the most obvious in the universal gratitude repertoire. Consider the following:

"Thanks" in English
"Gracias" in Spanish
"Merci" in French
"Obulu" in the Esan tribe of south central Nigeria
Others (add yours) …

Other culturally conditioned ways of expressing gratitude include thank you notes, tips, thank you cards, announcement banners, surprise parties, gift items, appreciative hugs, bowing, smiling, generous donations, and a pat on the back, to list just a few. These verbal and nonverbal expressions of gratitude serve important functions in building social relationships in local communities and in society. The following are the common benefits of social gratitude based on my observations and on literature about gratitude:

Daily expressions of gratitude boost relationships.
Regular expressions of gratitude reinforce good habits and, by default, discourage bad behaviors.
Spontaneous expressions of gratitude inspire and motivate generosity.

Bad News about Thanks - Casual Use, Brevity, and Loss of Its Luster

If the good news is that gratitude is a universal cultural trait, the bad news is the excessive use of its various expressions. As the saying goes, too much familiarity tends to breed disdain and loss of luster. Nowhere is this observation more applicable than, well, in the most used form of gratitude—thanks or thank you. Consider the following permutations of thanks:

Thank you, John
Thank you
Thanks
Thx

My observation is that on first contact people use "thanks" to express their appreciation along with the recipient's name ("Thank you, Joe"). Over time, the same people use thanks to express appreciation without the recipient's name but still with "you." Years later, the same people express appreciation with just the word "thanks" to the recipients. In email, "thanks" is reduced to Thx or just an Emoji smiling face. When used too frequently and casually, the various expressions of gratitude—saying thank you, giving a pat on the back or a certificate of appreciation, etc.—loses its luster and, in effect, its value.

Used appropriately and tactfully, gratitude can serve as a potent tool for building social relationships as noted above. A case in point is the vital role of gratitude in American culture.

The Importance of "Thank You" in American Social Relationships

The expression of gratitude by saying "thank you" is commonplace in American social relationships. That is, "thank you" tops the list of expressions commonly used in America to express gratitude.

As already mentioned, the most obvious forms of gratitude are the expressions "thanks" or "thank you." Although this observation is true of nearly all cultures, it is unusually true of the American people and culture. Immigrants, tourists, visitors, and businesspeople have made the observation that Americans are very grateful people who say "thanks" or "thank you" or a variation thereof all the time in almost all settings, even for the most common acts of kindness.

A group of international exchange students were asked to name the most obvious things about American culture they've observed that is different from their culture. On top of the list was the size of American trash cans, especially in restaurants and food courts. Second on the list was that Americans are very appreciative, always saying "thanks" or "thank you." Some students noted that some Americans would even go as far as thanking you for thanking them.

Americans say thank you with grace and admiration. That is, they say "thank you" with a polite smile. If you open or hold the door for them, they'll politely say "thank you" with a smile. If you pull a chair out so they can sit down or if you offer them a seat, they'll say "thank you" politely and with a broad smile. They usually do so with additional kind words, such as "that is so kind (or nice) of you," or "I very much appreciate that." If they inadvertently drop something and you bring it to their attention that they have dropped something, they say "thank you" politely with a smile almost to the point of adulation.

Acts of kindness are usually reciprocated with an abundance of thanks. If you perform your regular duties of providing services or supplying a product, they'll shower you with thank you's, and give you a polite smile. Even when people do not naturally like each other, these acts of kindness and responsibilities, followed by reciprocal acts of gratitude have mended frosty relationships and enhanced good relationships. The immediate result is the tendency for people to get along in social and business settings, even though they don't necessarily share common interests or know each other.

Expressions of gratitude to prescribed behaviors tend to reinforce those behaviors. Saying "thank you," giving a bonus to employees, or tipping waiters and waitresses serve as rituals of intensification that reinforce good conducts and manners. A corollary of this observation is that by withholding expressions of gratitude in response to a behavior, that behavior is by default being discouraged and proscribed. Withholding expressions of gratitude, such as saying "thank you" or a smile serve as a disincentive to desirable conduct and having good manners, which undermines mutually beneficial social relationships.

When gratitude is practiced in a routine or spontaneous way, it serves as leverage for shaping prescribed behaviors and perpetuating positive habits. An immediate outcome of targeted gratitude is in the area of generosity. Habits such as generosity, acts of kindness, and various expression of gratitude may be codified, but cannot necessarily be "legislated" for people to memorize and follow. These habits are more effective in influencing social behavior when leaders practice them.

The simple habit of a community leader saying, "Thank you, John" to a member of their constituency in likely and unlikely places goes a long way toward building a cohesive and generous culture in that local community. The common habit of a business manager saying, "Thank you, Jane" to an employee in both likely and unlikely places will go a long way toward fostering a high performance culture in that business organization.

Institutional Gratitude and Productivity

Institutional gratitude in business organizations includes various forms of expression, such as a simple thank you or pat on the back, and more tangible practices such as bonuses, awards, recognition, certificates of appreciation, a working lunch, birthday or anniversary celebrations, baby or wedding showers, etc. When gratitude is practiced in both routine and spontaneous ways, it serves as leverage for shaping prescribed behaviors and perpetrating positive habits in the workplace.

An immediate outcome of targeted gratitude is in the area of generosity. As pointed out above, habits such as generosity, acts of kindness, various expressions of gratitude may be codified, but cannot necessarily be issued as policies and directives for employees to follow. These habits are more effective in influencing organizational behavior when managers and supervisors practice them. A simple habit of saying, "Thank you, Jim" or "Thank you, Karen" to an employee in an all-staff meeting or at an annual holiday party goes a long way toward building a spirit of gratitude and generosity in an organization's culture. A grateful and generous organizational culture provides a solid platform for planning and implementing growth and productivity strategies. After all, as business researchers have noted, culture eats strategy for lunch. That is, even the best organizational strategies will falter if the culture is toxic.

Put differently, effectively planned and implemented institutional gratitude programs can serve as useful tools for enhancing productivity in organizations.

Forms of Gratitude as Productivity Tools for Employers, Managers, and Supervisors

Institutional gratitude can be an effective tool for boosting productivity in the workplace. In this regard, gratitude must be designed as a part of the organization's culture and performance management strategies. Employers, supervisors, and managers need to be trained in the art of using various expressions of gratitude as tools to motivate employees in the form of incentives, rewards, and salary increases. To be effective, gratitude in its various expressions and forms must be fair, consistent, and equitable across the board. It should be developed as an integral part of performance management.

A performance plan is a type of agreement between the supervisor and the employee regarding the work that the employee will perform under the supervision of the supervisor, usually over a period of one year.

A sound performance management program begins with a well-written and well-implemented performance plan at the beginning of the fiscal year. This should be followed by at least one performance review during implementation, a final appraisal at the end of the fiscal year, and a reward (once the appraisal has been completed).

There is consensus in the literature on performance management that a performance plan should clearly delineate the work to be done. A performance plan should also include measurable goals. That is, an effective performance plan consists of at least four elements, commonly known as performance SMART (specific, measurable, attainment, relevant, and time bound). Each identified work or task listed in the performance plan should be specific and measurable as well as relevant and time bound to the overall workload of the employee.

The plan should be written by the supervisor with input from the employee. The supervisor and the employee should discuss the plan in a meeting. At the end of the meeting, there should be a mutual understanding of what is expected of the employee, levels of rewards, if any, and under what condition the rewards will be awarded, such as based on availability of funds. Both the supervisor and the employee should have a signed copy for reference, with the original copy placed in the employee's file in the supervisor's office.

Periodic reviews and feedback are necessary in order to ensure that work is being done. There should be at least one mid-year review with feedback and one final review with feedback at the end of the year. A reward should be based on the final evaluation, which summarizes the year-long performance of the employee. Depending on the available resources, giving a reward as a way of saying thank you could be a promotion, salary increase, and/or a one-time bonus. A thank you reward can also be in kind, such as a gift certificate, time off, certificate of appreciation, lunch with the supervisor, a cubicle with a window, and recognition at an all-staff meeting, to list a few options.

Rewards as a form of thanks should be few and far between to retain their value and motivational effect. It cannot and should not replace the regular supervisor's and manager's expressions of appreciation and a pat on the back to say thank you for a job well done on a daily or weekly basis. This everyday thank you gesture should also not be done too frequently; otherwise, it loses its value and effectiveness. To be effective, it should be genuine, spontaneous, and proportionate to an actual challenging effort put forth by the recipient or employee.

Gratitude Dividends as Sources of Productivity for Employees

Gratitude dividends can be a source of an employee's productivity at two levels: the professional level and the personal level. As a recipient of gratitude, an employee can use workplace acts of gratitude to enhance his professional standing in his or her job in the organization. At the professional level, workplace cash and kind gratitude implies that the employee is in good standing with the employer. An employee will likely receive favorable responses to his or her requests for training, promotion, or reassignment, to name a few, when the employee is viewed in a favorable light with the supervisor and the overall business echelon. This is especially important when career development resources are scarce, amid fierce competition for limited resources. An impressive list of workplace acts of gratitude in the form of awards also enhances an employee's resume, a key to opening the door to the next major career move.

At the personal level, the employee has additional cash and in-kind resources at his or her disposal to meet basic necessities or to pursue happiness. A generous bonus comes in handy for, say, that long overdue repair on the house or new tires for a car. A boost in salary can mean additional steady resources for retirement account investment, investment in stocks, or savings towards a family dream vacation. A bonus can be used for a great weekend getaway with your spouse. An in-kind time off award can mean taking much-needed time for rest and relaxation from work-related stress.

There is consensus in the literature on work-induced stress that stressed employees are not only unproductive, but are actually more prone to making more costly mistakes than non-stressed employees. Burned out employees contribute to more than their fair share of workplace absenteeism. Further, stressed employees tend to lash out more often when faced with personal, family, and other social challenges than their peers. In-kind awards can come in handy for taking much-needed time to rest and decompress.

Bottom Line – the Generous Returns on Investment (ROI) of Gratitude

So, as was his custom, Grandpa Balewa paid his grandchildren a visit one year later. As usual, he hauled a bag of toys with him. Upon hearing Grandpa's deep, eloquent voice announcing his arrival, Batuta outran his brother and sister to greet Grandpa. This time he minced no words as he shouted, "Thank you, thank you, thank you, Grandpa Ibun Batuta Tafawa Balewa! Can I have four toys!?" Grandpa was so impressed that he gave Batuta 19 toys—one for each syllable. Such are the generous returns on investment (ROI) of the thankful state of thanks! Be generous with thanks as an expression of your gratitude and the ROI will be generous as well, socially and in the workplace!

CHAPTER 11

APOLOGY AND PRODUCTIVITY: THE SORRY STATE OF SORRY

John: Knock, knock.
Jane: Who's there?
John: Sorry.
Jane: Sorry who?
John: I'm sorry, Jane.
Jane: Oh, come on in, John.

Such is the positive power of a fully expressed sincere apology, while a not so fully expressed insincere apology leaves much to be desired. There are various forms of apology and many different ways to express an apology, from a simple "I am sorry" to signing a treaty of surrender. The term "I'm sorry" is, by far, the most commonly used expression of apology.

For the purposes of our discussion in this chapter, we focus on two broad categories of apology—namely, social apology and institutional apology. The former consists of everyday expressions of apology and is more informal, while the latter is more formal and consists of various forms of apology in a workplace setting. Institutional apology serves as a way of reducing and eliminating employee friction in organizations. In this respect, an institutional apology takes its cue from various expressions of apology in society, where apology serves as a way of reducing and de-escalating interpersonal conflicts in social and cultural settings.

In this chapter, we discuss social apology as a universal norm and as a much-needed tool for cooling culture war in America. This is followed by a brief examination of the roles of institutional apology in the workplace. We conclude with several observations in connection with the functions of apology in reducing conflicts in general and, specifically, in de-escalating frictions in the workplace.

Apology as a Universal Norm

Cultural anthropologists have observed that an apology is a culturally conditioned universal concept. Thus, an apology, like gratitude, is universally practiced. But, unlike gratitude, not all cultures embrace apologies with the same level of understanding and commitment. That is, while almost all societies have developed concepts of apology over time, it is important to recognize that apology as a normative behavior is expressed in very different ways from society to society and from one generation to another. In many cultures, people overtly and verbally express that they are very sorry to friends and foes when they are wrong or commit acts that warrant an apology. In many cases, that simple act of admitting wrong and saying we are sorry has reduced friction and de-escalated conflict between communities and, in some cases, averted wars between nations.

People in a different culture consider such an overt apology as a sign of weakness, especially when the apology is made to an enemy. In this culture, the aggressors may apologize to friends or those they consider in the in-group, but not to those they consider outside of the group or enemy. Yet, in other cultures, the aggressors would simply acquiesce to the dispute. Acquiescence in this regard is a way of admitting wrongdoing. In this case, a lack of aggression or withdrawal from conflict would be considered a form of apology.

Diversity as Source of Intolerance, Friction, and Conflict

As a nation of immigrants, American communities are made up of diverse people who hold divergent worldviews, temperaments, and styles. The implication is that people do not always agree in all matters. These disagreements tend to cause friction between individuals in a community or among members of an organization. At the individual level, disagreements can lead to intolerance of one another and interpersonal friction. At the societal level, intense disagreements about worldviews and tolerance of one another serve as the underlying causes of many social conflicts.

The symptomatic manifestations of intense disagreements surface in unlikely places, such as in the family, neighborhood, communities, organizations, and associations. That there will be these sorts of friction is not unusual. It is also not unusual that America, like most societies, develops elaborate mechanisms for reducing interpersonal friction and de-escalating social conflict. But, left unaddressed, these causes and the associated symptoms fester into a perfect storm as a basis for culture war, also called values war. Culture war rears its ugly head around us every day in the forms of broken homes, youth violence, scourge earth politics, to name a few.

Elements of Cultural War in America

An extensive analysis of the many faces of culture war and their long-term domino effects on society is beyond the scope of this book. Suffices it to point out here that the most noticeable and quantifiable representations include domestic violence, divorce, lawsuits, and workplace complaints, to name a few. The statistics on these samples and the costs to society are mind numbing, as noted below.

Domestic Violence

Domestic violence has taken its toll on American society over the years. An estimated 960,000 incidents of domestic violence involving spousal abuse are reported each year in America. Most of the abuse is perpetrated on women by their significant others or boyfriends due to disagreements and interpersonal conflicts. Other cases of domestic violence include child abuse, and disagreements between friends and neighbors resulting in violent situations. Then there are the cases of out-of control-parties, disturbing the peace, public humiliation, revenge and retaliation, to list a few. The number of incidents all types of domestic violence combined varies widely. According to the Bureau of Justice Statistics, an estimated 6 million incidents of domestic violence are reported annually, at a total cost of $5.8 billion to America.

For additional information and statistics on domestic violence in America, visit the U.S. Department of Justice website or click on the links below:

http://www.evefoundation.org/domestic-violence-statistics/
http://www.futureswithoutviolence.org/user files/file/Children_and_Families/Domestic Violence.pdf
http://dvrc-or.org/domestic/violence/resources/ C61/#hom

Divorce Rate

Divorces occur between two individuals or a husband and wife who once loved each other but over time grow apart. As the marriage evolves, irreconcilable differences or interests emerge. Many simply file for a no-fault divorce to avoid making an already tense situation more tense. In 2011, there were a total of 2.2 million marriages in America, or an average of 6.8 marriages per 1,000 Americans. During the same period, there were a total of 877,000 divorces in America, or an average of 3.6 divorces per 1,000 Americans.

For additional information and statistics on divorce in America, visit the U.S. Center for Disease Control and Prevention website or click on the links below:

http://www.cdc.gov/nchs/fastats/divorce.htm
http://www.cdc.gov/nchs/nvss/marriage_ divorce_tables.htm

Civil Lawsuits

Civil lawsuits have seen their share of exponential growth over the years in the culture war. On average, there are a staggering 512,000 lawsuits filed annually, at a cost of $233 billion to the economy.

For additional information and statistics on civil lawsuits in America, visit the U.S. Department of Justice website or click on the links below:

http://www.statisticbrain.com/civil-lawsuit-statistics/
http://www.bjs.gov/index.cfm?ty=tp&tid=45
http://www.uscourts.gov/Statistics/JudicialFacts AndFigures/judicial-facts-figures-2011.aspx

Equal Employment Opportunity Commission (EEOC) Workplace Charges

EEOC workplace charges include complaints and grievances filed by employees against management and sometimes against fellow employees and supervisors due to management's inaction or inappropriate actions. In fiscal year 2011, there were 99,947 complaints and grievances filed and about the same number—99,412—in fiscal year 2012.

Workplace grievances and resolutions can be costly and time consuming. Organizations hire people to perform tasks and functions. The expectation is that the employees will do the work and the employers will pay the employees the rate of pay or wages previously agreed upon. So far so good! But more often than expected, either the work is not performed as expected or the payment for work completed is not forthcoming as agreed upon, or a combination thereof. This can be due to performance issues or issues relating to conduct in the workplace.

Many performance and/or conduct issues are easily resolved by a meeting between an employee and a supervisor to identify the issues. This is followed by a plan and implementation of the plan. Some issues are more difficult to resolve, requiring verbal and written reprimands and, if there is no improvement, adverse action. In most cases involving adverse action, Labor Relations specialists from Human Resources offices are brought in to help sort out the issues and differences and come up with a fair and balanced resolution within the framework of human resources and labor laws and, if applicable, Collective Bargaining Agreements (CBA).

For additional information and statistics on employee charges regarding complaints and grievances at workplaces in America, visit the U.S. Equal Employment Opportunity Commission website or click on the links below:

http://eeoc.gov/eeoc/statistics/enforcement/charges.cfm
http://www.archives.gov/eeo/
http://www.fbi.gov/stats-services/fbi-resources

Labor, Management, and Collective Bargaining Agreements (CBA)

Workplace situations become more complex if and when the employees unionize to form a collective bargaining unit (CBU). In this case, the union representatives negotiate terms and conditions of employment with management on behalf of the employees they represent. Negotiations usually focus on the following economic items, which are usually most contentious between employees and management:

> Rate of pay
> Wages
> Hours of work
> Conditions of work

These items are commonly considered the hard issues or the bread and butter of union-management negotiations. Other negotiated items include seniority, leave and healthcare benefits, and space allocation, which are generally considered the soft issues of a bargained agreement between union reps and management. The outcomes of negotiations are documented and issued in a signed document by all parties involved. The document, called Collective Bargaining Agreement (CBA), is binding on the union, the CBU and the management. In principle, this process and the resulting CBA are meant to ensure a smooth and productive working environment for both the employees and management.

In practice, the process does not always work as it should, partly because the process is adversarial in nature. The CBA document is always interpreted in many different ways by the union, the CBU, and the management, usually to their respective advantages. The endgame is usually that of a lose-win situation, instead of a win-win situation. If the union gets what it asks for, management is portrayed as caving in to the union standoff or and giving in to union demands. This scenario emboldens the union to want to ask for more or dig in deeper the next time around. If management gets what it asked for, that spells one more death knell to the union or union leadership. The union is thus perceived as weak by management, who will likely flex more muscle the next time around. The CBU may want to vote out the union leaders or shop for another union organization.

The history of Labor-Management Relations (LMR), dating back to the Reconstruction era, is littered with disagreements, interpersonal conflicts, personal egos and workplace politics, deadlocks, hatred, anger, frustration, name calling, and occasional violent tactics. In some cases, employees have resorted to strike and walk out to force serious and honest negotiations. Not to be outdone, managements have attempted to burst the union or union leadership. In such situations, neutral parties such as arbitrators and mediators under the auspices of the Federal Labors Relations Authority (if private sector) and National Labor Relations Board (for if public sector) step in to break the impasse. These neutral parties help negotiate a settlement agreement within the framework of labor laws, regulations, and Executive Orders to the benefits of all parties involved and the general welfare of society at large.

My observation is that, by and large, a simple "I'm sorry" is the first major but difficult step for disputing parties to take. A sincere apology is an important but the least used tool in de-escalating disagreements and conflicts. We'll draw on some examples from a common source, the scriptures, to illustrate the point being made.

Examples from Scriptures

The following are examples drawn from scripture with respect to the difference an apology makes in de-escalating conflict and smoothing relationships. It should be noted here that we draw on these accounts as existential narratives of human and social relations, and not necessarily as an exercise in philosophical theology, which is beyond the scope of this chapter and the book.

The Garden of Eden Episode

The writer of the book of Genesis recorded an account of events that took place in the Garden of Eden, dating back to the earliest beginnings. According to the account, Serpent deceived Eve and Eve in turn led Adam to disobey specific instructions given to them by the landlord, the Almighty. When the landlord asked Adam and Eve why they disobeyed him, they went to great lengths into a blame game with finger pointing regarding what happened and who had done what. As could be expected, the landlord was not happy with the tenants (Adam and Eve) and the intruder (Serpent). He punished both tenants for their disobedience and the intruder for his deceptive role that began the whole saga.

One can only wonder what the landlord would have done if the tenants had simply admitted to wrongdoing and apologized by saying that they were sorry. Of course we will never know what the landlord would have done in response to such apology. But, if we can speculate for a moment, the outcome of the whole saga would most probably have been different, very likely for the better, than the tenants losing the Garden and the ensuing human and social conflicts.

The Primordial Cain and Abel Escalation

The writer of the book of Genesis also recorded an account of events documenting one of the earliest deadly conflicts. According to the account, the primordial incident involved two siblings, Cain and Abel, in interpersonal friction, which escalated into a fatal conflict. Both Cain and Abel were required by their landlord, the Almighty, to pay homage to him from the proceeds of their respective occupations. Abel followed the instructions the landlord gave them for paying homage. His homage impressed the landlord. Cain did not quite follow the instructions. His homage did not impress the landlord. Needless to say, Cain was not happy and eventually took his anger out on his brother, Abel, with him whom he obviously disagreed.

According to the account, events escalated into a conflict. When it was over, Cain had murdered his brother, Abel. Cain was indeed given many opportunities to get the homage right. When the landlord repeatedly brought it to Cain's attention to follow the instructions, Cain resorted to a series of blame games rather than admitted mistakes and apologies. The simple but much needed necessary first step would have and should have been an apology to the landlord: "I'm sorry." Then he could have taken advantage of the second chance afforded him to address the homage situation. Again, we will never know what would have happened if Cain had apologized. But the story would likely have unfolded in a different direction rather than the sorry end of promising careers and human relations. The power of apology to alter the outcomes of a conflict cannot be underestimated, as the following two accounts illustrate.

The Illicit King David Saga

According to the accounts in the scriptures, King David was one of the great kings who ruled Israel in the ancient Middle East, dating back thousands of years. One of the accounts of this great king pertained to his illicit affair with his army general's wife. The affair resulted in pregnancy. In order to cover up his misdeeds, King David had his army general killed in a war, that is after other attempted tricks failed. David married the widow. Problem solved! Right? Wrong! "Inquiring" minds shifted gears into overdrive. Soon enough, word got out regarding what had happened. A prophet confronted King David about his illicit affair and the ensuing murder—conduct unbecoming of a king.

Rather than complicating an already complicated matter, King David admitted his wrongdoing and sincerely apologized. This was evident from the chain of events that followed. King David did what he possibly could within his power to right the wrong. The incident had the potential to destroy King David, his kingship, and the kingdom. Indeed, the incident rowed King David's royal family and the kingdom in decades that followed. But King David lived to tell the story. He turned out to be one of the greatest kings, war strategists and statesmen of his time. His reign is remembered as the golden era in Israel's history. Of course, it would be overreaching to attribute all his successes to one incident of apology, given his many exploits.

Yet, history is replete with great leaders who met their untimely waterloo. It is not an understatement to say that the incident had all the indications of a waterloo for King David, given the powerful and influential roles of the prophets— the invisible rivals of his day. An apology de-escalated a scandal that was swelling around him and about to engulf his "presidency." King David himself recognized the rapidly rising tide of public opinion that was not in his favor by any stretch of the imagination. A fast, complete, and sincere apology tamed the rising tide of public opinion, beginning with the prophet or prophets to the royal court echelon, and the general public.

The Infamous Prodigal Son

A similar outcome was recorded in the scriptures regarding a young man who decided to go into a business venture. In this account, a young man asked for his share of his father's wealth so that he could launch his own business in a faraway city. It should be pointed out here that it was not unusual for individuals in ancient Middle East culture to launch out in search of a better life, taking their share of family inheritance with them. In this particular account, the young entrepreneur made poor business decisions. He invested excessive time and material resources into misguided networking and social adventures. As could be expected, he was soon out of resources and, subsequently, friends as his entrepreneurial dreams faltered. He mounted an effort to rebound by seeking low wage employment but to no avail. He came to the conclusion that he was now more of a hobo than an entrepreneur. Further, he reasoned that he actually would be better off returning home to be a servant. So far so good!

But the challenge was: how was he going to work his way back to his place at home, to which he brought no fame but shame? Ideally he had many options. He could engage in finger pointing, blame games, or making excuses, or a combination thereof. Instead, he decided in favor of apologizing for his bad decisions and misdeeds. He would ask for forgiveness and the opportunity to start all over as a servant in his father's estate. According to the account, he apologized to his father and asked for forgiveness. Because of his sincere and apologetic attitude and actions, his father received him back home with a warm reception and a huge party. One can only wonder what would have been the outcome of his return if he had started out by making excuses, a display of reverse psychology, or an aggressive attitude.

It should be pointed out that the young man is referred to as the prodigal son in contemporary literature. This is a label assigned to him by today's readers of the account. The label, prodigal son, does not appear in the original account of the story. His youthful indiscretions and entrepreneurial decisions and actions were indeed prodigal in nature. His analysis of the situation and the action he took to remedy the situation were premised on apology, hence a more appropriate label would be the apologetic son. He resembles an apologetic American president in the 1990s who was nicknamed the "Come-back kid." The president made serious illicit mistakes. After moments of unconvincing denials, he admitted to his human flaws. Further, his contrite spirits and humility propelled him time and again over his opponents, in spite of the ensuing career-ending, self-inflicted crisis he had to deal with personally and publically. Such is the power of apology to set the right tone for negotiation in a volatile situation.

Lessons Learned – Apology Boosts Relationships and Productivity

Many lessons flow from the foregoing discussions. The more obvious observations are listed below with brief analyses.

Disingenuous

We are disingenuous when we offer an insincere and incomplete apology. A disingenuous apology has a negative effect. An insincere apology is not any better than not apologizing at all. In fact, forced or convenient apologies sometimes actually make matters worse. Issues are swept under the rug rather than bringing them out into the open so that healing can actually begin. Insincere or incomplete apologies are identified by the way they are said or where and when they are said. For example, saying "sorry" underneath your breath over the phone to a person whose feelings you've hurt would qualify as an incomplete and insincere apology. This is disingenuous, especially when you have the opportunity to meet and tell him or her, "I'm sorry."

Denial

We are in denial of reality when we are wrong or hurt people's feelings but rationalize our behavior. Most people usually know when their actions are wrong and they hurt other people's feelings. This is what makes us human—a conscientious consciousness. A good test is to sincerely ask how you would feel if someone had done the same thing to you. In taking the test, be honest and do not rationalize; after all, only you know the correct answer. Denial only makes a bad situation worse. Sincere apology reverses the domino effect.

Defiance

We are in defiance when we refuse to offer an apology to people whom we wrong or hurt. You risk the potential to escalate an otherwise manageable situation. Further, a major problem with defiance is the unnecessary crisis of conscience that you create for yourself. You spend a considerable amount of time rationalizing your behavior, justifying your actions, and rehearsing the incident over and over in your head. The torment is like auto-rewind and auto-play in your head for days, weeks, and months, depending on the severity of the incidents and the issues. You would probably spend less energy and burn fewer calories if you stopped being defiant and just offered an apology. You'd feel a sense of relief when you did.

Defensiveness

Our defensiveness rather than apologizing undermines our credibility and damages social relationships. Being defensive when evidence dictates that an apology be given only makes you look as if you are a less honest and credible person. As the saying goes, honesty is the best policy. When co-workers and the management cannot count on your honesty and sincerity to do the right thing as well as do things right, your credibility suffers. And lack of credibility undermines trust—a necessary element in an enduring relationship with peers and superiors in social settings and in the workplace.

Duty

An apology is a duty. It is the right thing to do when we are wrong. Consider an apology a task that must be done when you are wrong or have wronged people. By apologizing, especially in situations involving deep wounds and strong feelings, you set healing in motion first and foremost for you and then for the other party. More often than not, you may not know the depth and scope of the pain you have inflicted on a person until you approach them. The need to mend relationships with people you wrong is very important in social interactions and in the workplace, where you spend a considerable amount of time five or more days a week. To do otherwise is to create a culture of stress that inhibits productivity.

De-escalation

When we apologize, we de-escalate and calm an otherwise volatile situation. As was said previously, my observation is that much friction and conflict can easily be reduced and managed if the parties involved can just say they are sorry. Recall many instances when you bump into someone and you immediately say that you're sorry. Usually the person will smile and say it's OK and move on. If you violate a person's social or physical space, his or her next move usually depends on your move: apologize (de-escalation) or ignore/refuse to apologize (escalation). The sorry state of sorry is our not using such a potent tool as often as we should in mending relations and amending situations.

Dialogue

When we apologize, we begin a dialogue that can lead to a lasting friendship. I have observed time and again people who became close friends for life, following a heated debate or a "fight." As the saying goes in our village back in Africa: "To live together is to ruffle feathers together!" Apologies open the opportunity for dialogue that would not have occurred otherwise.

The first four lessons (disingenuous, denial, defiance, defensiveness) are the negative effects of arrested apology and should be avoided. The last three lessons (duty, de-escalate, dialogue) are the positive effects of a genuine apology, such as saying, when we are wrong: "I am very sorry, Jane"; or, "I sincerely apologize to you, John."

Bottom Line – the Sorry State of Sorry

Sorry, as an obvious form of apology, shouldn't have to be in a state of sorry. We can make our family, workplace, and world a better place by bringing back the use of apology in its various forms and expressions. Together we can rediscover the glory days of apology by adding the practice of the admission of wrong and genuine repentance to our everyday relationship-building tool kits.

Admittedly, an apology would probably not eliminate all of the human friction and social conflict that unfolds in our societies every day, but this is not to say that apology does not have the potential to mitigate the impact of human friction and social conflict. This much is certain in the literature on apology: Cultures that appreciate and reward genuine apology have more social harmony and less social acrimony. The people in such societies live healthier and have more fun living the good life.

CHAPTER 12

STAYING HEALTHY AND HAVING FUN

Thus far, we've explored the culture of productivity in America and the ideas and values behind the culture. We noted that America is a nation of immigrants and a nation of laws. Americans are hardworking and law abiding people. After all is said and done, the question remains: "Where do the good, the bad and the ugly of productivity discussed throughout this book leave us?" A fair question! To respond fairly to this question, we must go back to where we started—the Declaration of Independence.

In the final analysis, ideas and values such as life, liberty, and the pursuit of happiness and property hold very little for people who are sick or who are not having fun. At the end of the day, the goal of the quests for life and freedom is predicated on the pursuit of happiness and property. This pursuit assumes two fundamental values—health and fun. A person has to be healthy enough to engage in the act of pursuit and the most obvious manifestation of happiness is having fun. It is not a coincidence that America spends more on quality healthcare than any other industry and most Americans look forward to vacations, holidays, and going places very much any time of the year. They work very hard, but also look forward to retirement and the golden years. In this regard, staying healthy and having fun are two sides of the same proverbial coin. One reinforces the other. Staying healthy requires staying active and having fun. And enjoying the good life requires a healthy lifestyle.

The purpose of this chapter is to briefly reflect on these twin seminal concepts as the defining cultural geniuses that both motivate and secure in place the geniuses of productivity we've discussed throughout this book. We conclude the chapter by examining the implications of the healthcare industry and the recreation and entertainment industries for productivity in America.

Staying Healthy

In America, you cannot afford to be sick. You need healthcare products and services to stay healthy or to keep from being sick. What is equally true is that healthcare in America is as good as it is expensive. So staying healthy is not an option—it is a "mandate." Treat your health as a task that must be done and you'll be off to a good start. Americans take their health and the need to stay healthy extremely seriously. This observation is supported by the sheer volume of human, economic, material, and institutional resources committed to this noble value. Consider the following healthcare resources statistics (see Appendix 20 for details or visit or click on these links: http://www.bls.gov/ooh/healthcare/, http://www.statista.com/, http://www.aha.org/):

Healthcare Facilities/Expenses:	2012
Hospitals (registered, community, public, private)	10,877
Beds	1,721,395

| Annual admissions | 70,578,316 |
| Medical expenses ($1.6 trillion) | $1,586,584,143,000 |

Healthcare Personnel:	**2012**	**2022 Projections**
Athletic Trainers and Exercise Physiologists	28,900	34,300
Audiologists	13,000	17,300
Chiropractors	44,400	50,900
Dental Assistants	303,200	377,600
Dental Hygienists	192,800	257,700
Dentists	146,800	170,100
Diagnostic Medical Sonographers, Cardiovascular Tech	110,400	153,100
Dietitians and Nutritionists	67,400	81,600
EMTs and Paramedics	239,100	294,400
Genetic Counselors	2,100	3,000
Home Health Aides	875,100	1,299,300
Licensed Practical and Licensed Vocational Nurses	738,400	921,300
Massage Therapists	132,800	162,800
Medical and Clinical Laboratory Technologists, Tech	325,800	396, 400
Medical Assistants	560,800	723,700
Medical Records and Health Information Technicians	186,300	227,400
Medical Transcriptionists	84,100	90,500
Nuclear Medicine Technologists	20,900	25,100
Nurse Anesthetists, Nurse Midwives, Nurse Practitioners	151,400	199,000
Nursing Assistants and Orderlies	1,534,400	1,855,600
Occupational Health and Safety Specialists	62,900	67,100
Occupational Health and Safety Technicians	12,600	14,000

Occupational Therapists	113,200	145,200
Occupational Therapy Assistants and Aides	38,600	54,500
Dispensing Opticians	67,600	83,400
Optometrists	33,100	41,200
Orthotists and Prosthetists	8,500	11,500
Personal Care Aides	1,190,600	1,771,400
Pharmacists	286,400	327,800
Pharmacy Technicians	355,300	426,000
Phlebotomists	101,300	128,400
Physical Therapist Assistants and Aides	121,400	170,800
Physical Therapists	204,200	277,500
Physician Assistants	86,700	120,000
Physicians and Surgeons	691,400	814,700
Podiatrists	10,700	13,100
Psychiatric Technicians and Aides	153,000	160,600
Radiation Therapists	19,100	23,600
Radiologic and MRI Technologists	229,300	277,900
Recreational Therapists	19,800	22,500
Registered Nurses	2,711,500	3,238,300
Respiratory Therapists	119,300	142,000
Speech-Language Pathologists	134,100	160,100
Surgical Technologists	98,500	127,800
Veterinarians	70,300	78,700
Veterinary Assistants and Laboratory Animal Caretakers	74,600	81,700
Veterinary Technologists and Technicians	84,800	109,800
Total	**12,856,900**	**16,230,700**

(Projected personnel growth of 3,373,800, or 26%, by 2022)

Hundreds of thousands of books have been written on how to stay healthy. Suggestions, recommendations, and medical opinions about how to stay well and happy are constantly being offered through a wide variety of media outlets. An analysis of these recommendations and opinions is beyond the scope of this book. Suffice it to note here that most of the recommendations and ideas fall into the following four broad categories, represented by 4 M's (not in any particular order):

Mind
Muscle
Mouth
Medical/Medicine

Let's consider each of these principles and how they can or have contributed to staying healthy in America and in any country for that matter. It is important to note that these principles are not prescriptions for any particular individual health conditions that require your consultation with your healthcare professional.

Mind

In order to stay healthy, it is important to develop and maintain a healthy mindset. After all, a healthy mind spells a healthy body. To develop a healthy mind, it helps to read evidence-based literature on staying healthy. It is also instructive to attend seminars and workshops on the subject matter presented by certified and/or licensed professionals about having a healthy lifestyle. Additionally, you can do your own research and interview trusted friends and family members who have started and maintained a healthy lifestyle. There is a lot of information in the print, broadcast, and social media that can be confusing as to what to believe and practice. Always check the sponsor of a study before buying into the recommendations of the study. Information from sources with no vested interests usually can be helpful in sorting out fact from fiction. Public agencies such as the National Institutes of Health, Food and Drug Administration, Centers for Disease Control and Prevention, and U.S. Department of Agriculture, to name a few, are usually reliable sources for research-based guidance and guidelines.

It certainly helps to set time aside for relaxation and meditation to rest the mind. Getting enough sleep definitely helps people get in the right mindset for the daily tasks ahead. Spending quality and quantity time with the people you love and care about—spouse, children, trusted friends, to name a few—can also help to relax the mind as well as maintain a healthy mindset. It is very difficult for a person to be productive at work or in business when they have a restless mind and are not staying healthy. Healthy people are well equipped to be productive at work and in business. Productive people tend to have a healthy and well-balanced mindset, which is needed to solve problems and to cope with work-induced stress.

More importantly, perhaps, it is difficult to engage in other activities that promote a healthy lifestyle without a sound and determined mindset. Drifting and dithering in the form of procrastination are enemies of physical exercise, which is a much-needed element in a healthy lifestyle menu.

Muscle

There is consensus in the literature of staying healthy that to be physically sound a person must maintain a healthy weight. To lose weight a person must move his or her muscles, that is, do exercise. The importance of maintaining a healthy weight can hardly be overemphasized. Being overweight and/or obese adversely affects a healthy lifestyle and life span. Numerous diseases are associated with this epidemic. The truth is that many of these diseases are treatable if the patient can find a way to lose weight. Losing weight requires doing exercise. As said, a healthy mind dwells in a healthy body. But it requires a determination of the mind to do exercise in order to stay healthy physically and mentally.

Usually it helps to start an exercise regimen on a limited scale and then increase the pace over time as you feel more comfortable. If a person has health issues and physical conditions, it certainly helps to consult your healthcare professional before starting to exercise. Guidance and guidelines from public and reliable private sources can be helpful in this regard. Admittedly, there are multiple nonprofit and for profit organizations these days with classes and programs on exercise. Many claim glowing results. It helps to shop around, check references, and compare programs before deciding on the one that will serve your interests and help you reach your goals.

Whether you join a program or set aside time for do-it-yourself routine exercise, it is important to keep in mind that starting to exercise is the easy part. The hardest part is staying the course when the going gets tough or when cramps set in. Also, other competing interests will rear their distracting heads just when you thought you'd turned the corner on your goals. As the saying goes, winners don't quit and quitters don't win. If you start, you might as well hang in there to reap the benefits of your efforts. Sometimes, quitting is inevitable. If you must quit, do so for good or higher reasons, but not for lack of determination or for a less competing interest. Doing nothing is not an option, especially for productive people.

Absenteeism due to obesity-induced poor health does no one any good in lost wages and productivity. Productivity, like charity, begins at home or with you. To be productive, you do need to be healthy. As pointed out later in this chapter, you also need to be healthy to have fun. A sound mind and good dose of exercise are healthy steps in the right direction. Watching what you eat is another step in the right direction.

Mouth

It is not an overstatement to say that there is nothing a person can do to lose weight and stay healthy until he or she does one thing: controls their mouth! No, not what you say or don't say, although that is also important to watch, too! By "control their mouth," the emphasis is on watching what one eats. As the saying goes, bulges in and bulges out!

Admittedly, it is very confusing these days to know what we can or cannot eat. What is purportedly healthy to eat one day is ruled out as being unhealthy the next day. One program approves a diet, another condemns it. We are constantly bombarded with diet ads that work miracles based on "evidence"—a magic pill, a fix-all caplet, prepared 10-day chores, to name a few. There are boxed meals shipped to you, with the claim of losing 10 pounds in 10 days or your money back ... no questions asked. Every New Year brings new claims, especially in January. By March, most of the ads have disappeared, along with the claims.

Again, public sources and reliable nonprofit and for-profit organizations offer sound guidance and guidelines on healthy food and beverages. Of course, your healthcare professional and dieticians can and should be useful sources in helping to craft a plan of healthy food and beverages that is right for you. Sometimes it takes several attempts and a few visits to your doctor and/or your dietician to get it right. A productive person is an active participant in the process. After all, it is your meal and your health that we are talking about here.

Man (or woman) does not live by bread alone. But man (or woman) does nevertheless live by bread. Starving is not an option. And a crash diet or a quick fix program serves no useful purpose in the long run. People who are serious about watching their weight incorporate a balance of healthy food and beverage choices into their daily routines. They watch their breakfast, pack a lunch, and enjoy a nutrient-filled dinner, with carefully chosen snacks in between.

My observation is that productive people tend to develop and cultivate sustainable healthy food and beverage choices over time. Hungry managers and workers with grouchy stomachs are not only grumpy but are also prone to making serious and excessive workplace mistakes, not to mention having a lousy attitude. The same goes for many obese and overweight workers and managers who are in poor health and constantly under perform in almost all respects, hence the importance of a healthy lifestyle that supports a productive lifestyle.

The point is that a person needs to stay healthy in order to stay productive in his or her pursuit, whatever the pursuit may be. And to stay healthy, a person needs healthy food and beverages, which begins with gaining control over your mouth or watching what you eat and drink. Staying healthy also requires healthy exercise and a sound mindset. In some cases, all these efforts may not be enough to effect a healthy lifestyle, due in part to biologically based condition(s). In this regard, the fourth piece of the puzzle—medical attention—is needed.

Medicine/Medical Care

As a matter of fact, Americans are well ahead on the use of medicine to stay healthy. As said, this is evident from the amount of human and material resources Americans devote to medicine. As noted above, Americans spend $1.6 trillion dollars for an estimated 70.5 million admissions annually in over 10,800 hospitals and medical centers with 1.7 million beds. An estimated 12.8 million personnel work in the healthcare industry to ensure the health and welfare of Americans. The number of healthcare personnel is expected to grow by 3,373,800, or 26%, by 2022.

Medical attention is a critical element in staying healthy. But for medical attention to make a difference, a person must have routine medical check-ups, such as physical exams, colonoscopies, prostate exams, breast exams, tests for HIV/AIDS and STDs, to name a few. My observation is that early detection is the key to fighting and winning the battle over these chronic diseases. Some of these diseases are genetically based, while others are acquired through risky behavior or due to age. Either way, it is important to seek treatment as soon as possible from the appropriate healthcare professional and facility.

It is also important to attend to acute medical incidents, such as falls, broken bones, concussions, sprains and bruises, a high fever, and a poisonous snake bite, to list a few. First aid treatment and a visit to the doctor and/or urgent care usually will mitigate the impact of these acute medical incidents while the body heals.

Although it helps to seek advice from family and friends regarding treatment for chronic and acute diseases, it certainly is very important to seek help for the right diagnosis, prescription, and treatment from a licensed and/or certified healthcare professional. As evident from the lists provided earlier, there are licensed or certified healthcare professionals in just about any area of medicine in America. In situations involving intrusive treatment or invasive surgery, it is always wise to seek a second opinion, just to be sure. However, a second opinion should not be construed as shopping for a healthcare professional who will tell you what you want to hear—and there are a lot of them out there, given the number of successful medical malpractice lawsuits in America every year.

Most healthcare professionals are conscientious and are there to assist you to reach your goals in developing and maintaining a healthy lifestyle. As a notable healthcare management organization puts it, healthcare professionals are there to help you thrive—that is, to the extent that you wish to thrive and are willing to play your part. Productive people are aware of this implied contractual agreement between them and their healthcare professional. Beyond awareness, they actually do develop and maintain a mindset to stay healthy, in addition to moving their muscles by doing exercise, controlling their mouth by watching what they eat and drink, and seeking medical care by keeping routine and urgent care appointments. Productive people do all this because they understand that staying healthy is a prelude to productivity, but also a precondition for and a part of having fun.

Having Fun in America

Americans love and enjoy the pursuit of happiness. The founders acknowledged the pursuit of happiness as among the inalienable rights of individuals, along with life and liberty. The law enforcement industries do a good job every day protecting the rights of life, among other responsibilities. In addition to other responsibilities, the free press also does an awesome job every day protecting the rights of liberty. Regarding the duties of the free press in a civilized society, a respected American journalist and anchorperson succinctly put it this way: "Silence is the end of freedom."

The right to the pursuit of happiness is the responsibility of everyone, including the free press and the law enforcement industries. The Happiness clause may be somewhat elusive to attain, but the Pursuit clause is alive and well. To many Americans, the logic appears to be: If you can't tame happiness, you might as well have fun pursuing it.

To reiterate, Americans are hardworking people. This is evident in their commitment to production, products, and services. They dutifully go to work every day, from morning until evening, five or six and sometimes seven days a week. They work in industries, offices, businesses, churches, and schools, to list a few. Meanwhile, Americans also know how to have fun.

As the saying goes, all work and no play makes Dick and Jane a dull couple. Nowhere is this assertion taken as seriously as it is in America. Recreation and leisure is part of the American social fabric. There are many ways that Americans have fun. The great amount of resources the nation devotes to recreation and leisure as well as the amount of money Americans spend on having fun is evidence in support of this observation. Take, for example, the hotel industry, which is one of the epicenters of recreation and leisure in America. Based on 2011 data, there are an estimated 51,214 hotels in the United States, with 4.8 million beds and 1.8 million personnel, and sales receipts in excess of $137.5 billion.

Consider the following sampling of material and personnel resources devoted to recreation and leisure in America (in no particular order; for details see Appendix 21 or visit or click on these links: http://www.bls.gov/ooh/, http://www.statista.com/, http://www.travelandleisure.com/).

Leisure, Recreation, Sports and Entertainment Facilities, and Output

	2011
Hotels	51,214
Guestrooms	4,874,837
Hotel personnel	1,800,000
Tourism and Travel/Multiplier personnel	7,500,000
Sales	$137,500,000,000
Top 20 Tourist Destinations annual visitors	342,931,530
Stadiums (football, baseball, soccer) (20,000 min. – 110,000 max seats)	221
Indoor Arenas (hockey, basketball, etc.)	24
Theaters (indoor and drive-in movie sites)	5,683
Movies screens	39,662
Cruises	21
RV's (Recreational Vehicle units)	9,000,000

Leisure, Recreation, Sports and Entertainment Personnel:

	2012	2022 Projections
Lodging Managers	50,400	51,100
Recreation Workers	345,400	394,400
Athletic Trainers and Exercise Physiologists	28,900	34,300
Fitness Trainers and Instructors	267,000	300,500
Meeting, Convention, and Event Planners	94,200	125,500
Actors	79,800	83,100
Athletes and Sports Competitors	14,900	15,900
Coaches and Scouts	243,900	280,100
Dancers and Choreographers	25,800	29200
Musicians and Singers	167,400	176,100

Producers and Directors	103,500	106,400
Umpires, Referees, and Other Sports Officials	17,500	18,800
Broadcast and Sound Engineering Technicians	121,400	131,400
Total	**1,560,100**	**1,872,300**

(Projected growth of 312,200 personnel, or 20%, by 2022)

There are many avenues for pursuing recreation and leisure as a way of having fun in America than can be listed and discussed here. The following are the most obvious:

> Movies and theaters
> Sports entertainment
> Musical entertainment and concerts
> Vacation and travel
> Holidays and celebrations
> Social and political events
> Time with family, friends, and faith

Movies and Theaters

According to the National Association of Theatre Owners, based on 2013 data, there are an estimated 39,622 screens in 5,317 sites and 366 movie theater sites in the country. Going to the movies is an all-American tradition. Americans of all ages and ethnicities go to the theater to watch all sorts of movies. Theaters serve many purposes, including socializing, education, entertainment, and just having fun. The major theater companies show all sorts of movies and serve anyone who can afford the ticket. Many smaller theaters target a particular segment of the population and show movies of specific genres that serve the interests of the target audience. By and large, large and small theaters as well as indoor and drive in screens have one thing in common: to entertain. The actors are keenly aware of this; hence, almost all movies have a sense of humor somewhere in the script to entertain the audience. Additionally, the theater owners or managers strive to make the theater environment as fun as possible. Assorted food, mostly snacks and beverages, are on display and in abundant supply. Some theaters have video game stands and others have well-lit sitting/chatting areas where customers wait for show time.

Sports Entertainment and Stadiums

Sports entertainment is a big industry in America. Americans love sports. The most prominent ones are football, baseball, basketball, hockey, and soccer, which are organized into the National Football League, Major League Baseball, National Basketball Association, Women's National Basketball Association, National Hockey League, and Major Soccer League, respectively. Others are tennis, golf, swimming, lacrosse, auto racing, wrestling, skiing, gymnastics, motorcycle racing, bicycling, chess, and running and marathons, to name a few. There are always sports events going on somewhere in America at any given time of the year.

The NFL usually play their regular season games in fall, with playoffs in January and the Super Bowl in late January or early February. The Super Bowl is a national championship game. It is usually played on Sunday by the two best teams— each team represented one of the two conferences in the league. Throughout the season, there are feverish sports talks, bravado, predictions, and forecasts in the airwaves, radios, cable, print media, social media, offices, and businesses, very much everywhere by everyone—radio and TV talk show hosts, players, fans, politicians, to name a few. The Super Bowl is as an unofficial holiday. Millions of Americans watch the game— more than any other game in America. Other sports have great fans and fanfare, though not as much as the NFL. Nevertheless, they are very entertaining and are talked about nationally.

MLB usually plays regular games for nearly 9 months and ends with a world series of seven championship games by the two best teams. NBA and WNBA also play regular games for nearly 9 months and end with a world series of seven games by the two best teams respectively. NHL also plays long season and ends with seven championship games by the two best teams. Soccer usually plays seasonal games and, much like NFL, ends with one championship game played by the best two teams.

In addition to the major professional sports, there are college and high school sports (football, baseball, basketball, hockey, soccer, etc.) which mirror, to some degree, the major professional sports in organizational structure, game rules, competition and championship events. Additionally, there are myriad other sports in communities across America.

All of these sports have several things in common: discipline, competition, rigor and, above all, having fun. There are 221 stadiums in the United States, with 20,000 to over 100,000 seats devoted to the major outdoor professional and college sports—NFL, MLB, MSL, etc. Then there are 24 indoor arenas for indoor major professional and college sports—NBA/ WNBA, NHL, AFL (Arena Football League), etc. There are about as many small to mid-sized stadiums and indoor arenas in about as many colleges and high schools in America. All of these resources are devoted to developing the mind and body of the players and fans. Somewhere in between, everyone is having fun playing, coaching, watching, and listening in person and/ or on television and the radio.

Additionally, there are international games that captivate Americans. Americans participate in these sports to compete and win, but also to watch, cheer, and just have fun. Among these sports are the summer Olympics (every four years), the winter Olympics (every four years), the Federation of International Football Association (FIFA, every four years). Somehow to the benefit of sports-loving Americans, these sports events are staggered so that they occur on different years and in the summer and winter months when there are no major sport events going on in America. These sports tend to sort of come just in time to fill the void in sports entertainment. There are also a variety of tennis opens (French, British, American, etc.) and golf opens (Augusta, etc.) every year. These tournaments are also staggered to the delight of American fans, players, and sponsors.

Admittedly, some of these sports can be "brutal" to attend – waiting in long lines, expensive tickets, traveling, hot or cold weather. Yet, the esprit de corps the fans exude during the games surpasses the long suffering. The tailgate parties before the games; the noise and the waves during the games; and the fans 20/20 hindsight "replays" and recollections of spectacular plays after the games are awesome! The agony of defeat can be quite humbling, but the joy of victory and the lingering effects are indescribable. The language used by the commentators to describe a spectacularly perfect score is intellectually stimulating to the roar of the crowd: Touchdown! Home Run! Slam Dunk!—in football, baseball, and basketball, respectively.

The food and beverages, especially at baseball games, are great, although not always as healthy as they should be. But I suppose the fans work it off by the time the games are over. Not only does a person needs to be healthy to participate as a fan or player, the games actually can and do contribute to staying healthy—the fun, the laughter, and the physical demands.

Musical Entertainment and Concerts

It's been said that music is the language of love. This observation is very much alive and well in America. Music and entertainment are integral part of the way Americans have fun on a daily basis and during special occasions. Next to food, music is present in almost any conceivable social event. As a commodity, music comes in all kinds of packages and genres: country music, folk music, hip hop, jazz, pop culture music, rap, reggae, rock-n-roll, gospel music, and spirituality and worship music, to name a few. Some are generational, while others are limited to a subculture or ethnic groups. There are well over 167,000 musicians and singers in America, based on 2012 data, not counting local groups, folks, church choirs, and school bands. Additionally, there are many small bands and individuals who operate outside of the research and census radar.

Americans consume music through a wide variety of avenues. Professional musicians provide a steady supply of music in concerts, social events, special occasions, and clubs all year round. These events are usually announced and tickets (if applicable) sold way ahead of time, making it possible for the audience to look forward to having fun.

Most Americans access music through radios, social media, Internet, YouTube, cable, broadcast TVs, and countless portable music gadgets. The ubiquitous nature of music is why it plays such a pervasive role in communicating popular messages to Americans in almost every nook and cranny across America.

It is hard to imagine a person who does not have access to at least a radio. Music is the primary product of the radio industry, followed by news and ads. So a steady supply of oldies, specialty, and contemporary music is in abundance anytime anywhere.

There are about as many themes in American music as there are different types of music and musicians. A common theme in almost all American music is love and romance. This theme is expressed in many different ways—directly or indirectly, explicitly or implied, celebrated or denounced, romanticized or caricaturized as ephemeral. As has already been said, music is truly the language of love used by Americans to communicate love, encouragement, spirituality, etc. to their fellow Americans.

At the end of the day, music is entertaining. It is both an expensive way (e.g., concerts, award ceremonies, etc.) and a cheap way (e.g., iPod, radio, karaoke, etc.) to have fun. A person can choose to have fun with a dose of music alone in the privacy of their car, home, and outdoors, or with others in a sleepover party, concert, major social events, and ceremonies, to list a few.

Vacation and Travel

America is a mobile society, especially during vacation season in the summer months. Americans visit everywhere in America and are present anywhere around the world for a variety of reasons, most notably vacationing, sightseeing, travel, adventure, and business, or a combination thereof. Name a cave or a mountain, a cruise, an airplane, a ship or a boat, and an American is there. Not that there's anything wrong with that. After all, traveling is a part of lifelong education. Experience is the best teacher, and knowledge is power. Besides, what a way to share the wealth of a nation with fellow Americans and with other nations! Education and sharing! What a way to have fun!

An estimated 7.5 million persons, in addition to the hotel statistics cited above, work in the tourism and travel industry. Although they serve many functions, a significant portion of their duties relate to providing services and products to vacationers and travelers. The 21 cruises in America (out of the total 55 cruises in the world) provide avenues for exclusively fun-filled vacations to millions of Americans each year. As Appendix 19 shows, some 342.9 million tourists visit the top 20 tourist destinations in America annually, not counting thousands of other tourist destinations with less than 8 million visitors. Many of these vacationers, travelers, and tourists spend time having fun in the 58 national parks located across the United States (for a list and additional information, visit the U.S. National Park Service website or clink on these links: http://www.nps.gov/faqs.htm, http://parks.mapquest.com/national-parks/).

To reach these and a host of other vacation and tourist destinations, Americans own and ride in well over 9 million recreational vehicles every year, not counting other means of transportation to these destinations, such as personal vehicles, airplanes, trains, travel buses, tour buses, boats, camels, and horses. High gasoline prices may slow but not stop the pursuit of fun and happiness on the road to places in America. Low gas prices mean busy times for recreation and leisure industries.

On average, most American families take at least one vacation a year, especially families with school age children. These vacations are usually taken in the summer months when schools are not in session. Children look forward to vacations. Adults look forward to them, too, but with cautious optimism given the stress associated with the planning, travel arrangements, activities to do, safety of everyone involved, and the costs. The stress is usually mitigated by going to same or similar destinations and by getting everyone involved in making some of the decisions. By democratizing aspects of the planning and decisions, everyone knows what to expect, their responsibilities, and the anticipated rewards associated with a well-planned vacation.

To control the cost, some families combine a business trip with a vacation. This requires careful planning and coordination, but is well worth the effort. Alternatively, others take a "staycation." This is taking time off from work or other work routines to vacation at home. Visits and travels are usually to local sightseeing destinations, attractive areas, and events. This alternative has become popular in recent years in the wake of the Great Recession in 2007 that affected millions of American families across all social economic statuses. Many have found staycations less stressful and quite rewarding, while controlling costs. Will children like it and will it become a permanent feature of American recreation and leisure culture? The jury is still out.

Vacation and travel also serve as coping mechanism by providing an avenue of escape for a stressful situation. As a musician put it, Americans love riding in their rodeos or in their cars with no particular place to go. When life as planned unraveled around him, an American country music legend noted that he'd get on the road again, visiting places he'd never visit again, and seeing things he'd never seen before. He is not alone. Vacation and travel are some of the ways many American cope with reality when life happens. To a degree, individuals go places to have fun. On this the jury is in.

Holidays and Celebrations

Holidays and celebrations are another way Americans spend their time having fun. There are holidays around the year. The major public holidays are:

New Year's Day – January 1st
Martin Luther King Jr. Day – 3rd Monday in January
Presidents Day – 3rd Monday in February
Memorial Day – last Monday in May
Independence Day – the 4th of July
Labor Day – 1st Monday in September
Columbus Day – 2nd Monday in October
Veterans Day – November 11th
Thanksgiving Day – last Thursday in November
Christmas Day – December 25th

Public offices and most businesses are closed in celebration of these public holidays. The employees who must work in businesses or offices for safety and security purposes are usually well compensated. Some are paid overtime, others are granted other days off in lieu of taking off on public holidays.

As evident from the list above, many of the holidays fall on Monday. The federal government planned these holidays this way to give families and individuals a three-day weekend for fun and relaxation. For employees who cannot afford vacations, these three-day holidays serve as "mini-vacations" for them and their families. Employees with school age children do not have to worry about child care on these days. Not paying for child care, which can be expensive, adds up very quickly in savings for these families. Additionally, when a holiday falls on a weekend, the holiday is taken either on the immediate Friday or the Monday. The point is to ensure family-friendly fun times for working Americans earning low wages who cannot afford time off for a vacation.

These holidays are filled with pomp and pageantry, food, entertainment, and fun. Some of the holidays are celebrated with special events, such as parades, political speeches, concerts, fireworks, and more. Others are marked by Americans flocking to the beaches, movie theaters, sports events, and just having a backyard barbecue cook-out.

There are many other holidays year round. These include the regional holidays (Freedom Day in Massachusetts, Emancipation Day in District of Columbia), religious holidays (Hanukkah, Easter, etc.), ethnically based holidays (St. Patrick, Kwanzaa, Cinco de Mayo), and social holidays (Valentine's Day, Mother's Day, Father's Day, etc.). Most public offices and businesses are not necessarily closed on these holidays, but the festivities and celebrations have just about as much pomp and pageantry as the traditional public holidays.

The period between November 25th and January 1st is generally considered the holiday season. More holidays are concentrated around this period than any other period of the year. The period beginning with Christmas and ending on January 1st is considered the core of the holiday season. This period includes Christmas Day, Hanukkah, Kwanzaa days, New Year's Eve, and New Year's Day. During the holiday season and especially the core period, there are parties and gift- giving everywhere—at the office, schools, businesses, neighborhoods, religious centers and places of worship, and shopping centers and malls, to list just a few. The frenzy of travel, shopping, decorating, and concerts are sometimes nearly to the point of insanity in some places, especially on the days leading up to Christmas Day. Except for die-hard Christians who go to church to begin the day with devotions, Christmas Day is awesomely quiet outside, with most people staying home. That is because people are busy unwrapping and admiring gifts, cooking and eating, and watching parades and sports. The frenzy returns the day after Christmas.

To many Americans, the stress and frenzy are well worth it. It's that time of the year after working hard all year long to pause to celebrate and express gratitude to loved ones, friends, co-workers, neighbors, long lost relatives, and well-wishers. For some, the holidays are an occasion to make up for lost time and mend fences in relationships. Places to go and things to do are always in abundant supply during these holiday seasons in America.

As evident from the foregoing, different holidays have different themes and purposes. Each holiday has its festive mood, songs, music, entertainments, special food and beverages, jokes, and even attire. However, they all have several things in common—most notably, having fun.

Social and Political Events

Social events are another way Americans pursue happiness and have fun. These events are many and well celebrated. Some examples of social events are winning team parades following a national championship game and a party following an Oscar award gala. The former is usually organized as a pop culture event designed to inspire the community/city, while the latter appeals to celebrities and high end culture. Many Americans identify themselves as a fan or an admirer of one celebrity icon or another. These celebrities may be a sport, music, or movie icon or a business mogul. People gather in bars, clubs, and other public places to watch their icon in major nationally televised social events, such as those listed above. Such gatherings provides fun-filled occasions for fellow fans and admirers of an icon to root for him or her to win or lose.

Americans also celebrate and have good times at political events. Examples of political events are swearing-in ceremonies of elected public officials and the inaugural balls that follow. These political events are usually designed to ensure a blend of attendees from all walks of life and social economic status. The primary goal is to celebrate and just have fun, especially following a lengthy campaign season or a hard win or both.

Time with Individuals, Family, Friends, and Faith

The most ubiquitous way Americans have fun is spending time with families and friends in the warmth and safety of their own homes. Americans take pride in their families. Family is considered the cornerstone of the American dream, next to having a house. Buying or building a house to house a family is central to the pursuit of happiness. A family and a house form the essence of a home—home sweet home. Dorothy, in the American movie classic "The Wizard of Oz" captured the sentiment of most Americans when she said: "There's no place like home." And as the saying goes, "A man's (and a woman's) home is his castle."

Americans spend time with friends and families around the dinner table or at the barbecue grill in the backyard having fun. They also spend time together in front of the TV watching a variety of programs, from news to movies, sports entertainment, comedy, and musical show with snacks, food, and beverages. Friends and sometimes relatives are invited over to these "happy hours." These gatherings are especially fun during major events such as national championship games, presidential inaugural ceremonies, national music awards, movie awards, parades, Olympics, etc. The major TV and cable networks usually broadcast these events nationwide. The ads themselves can be quite entertaining as well.

Families and friends also spend time having fun around special occasions, including birthdays, wedding anniversaries, picnics, potlucks, hiking, biking, and romantic celebrations. Many of these family and friends fun times occur in homes but also at the restaurants, local recreational parks, indoor recreational centers, community centers, campgrounds, trails, woods, mountains, beaches, libraries, and religious centers, to list just a few. Additionally, Americans also spend happy hours with fellow congregants within the faith community.

In fact, well over 90% of Americans identify themselves as religious or believing in higher power and over 70% identify themselves as Christians. According to Pew Charitable Trusts organization, 70 million Americans identify themselves as Evangelicals. The proliferation of churches and religious facilities in the United States attests to these figures. Fellowship, socializing, and happy hours are permanent features of the faith community in America, dating back to the earliest settlers in the 1600's.

At the other end of the spectrum are events and places where some Americans also spend time but which are commonly referred to as sin activities. Included in this category are drug and alcohol stores and facilities, gambling and betting facilities, strip clubs, dog fights, and cock fights, to name a few. They are labeled as sinful, given that they appear to offer no real or lasting fun activities that promote a healthy lifestyle. Nor do they offer real economic benefits to the participants, although they do contribute in some ways to the overall productivity economy from the point of tax base, employment, and the owners' profit margins.

Implications for Productivity

As noted throughout this book, Americans are among the hardest working people on earth. This is evident from the multi-dimensional nature of the nation's productivity complex. America is a nation that takes the health and welfare of its citizens very seriously. Additionally, Americans are also fun-loving people. A number of productivity implications flow from the discussions and data presented in this chapter. The following implications stand out.

First, the productivity outcomes of the healthcare industry with respect to jobs, businesses, and multiplier effects are impressively robust. As pointed out, an estimated 12.8 million personnel work in the healthcare industry. The core mission of these personnel is to ensure the health and welfare of the American people. If the healthcare industry in America were a country, it would be right behind the industrialized G8 nations (USA, Canada, Britain, France, Germany, Italy, Japan, and Russia).

Second, based on data from the U.S. Bureau of Labor Statistics (BLS), the healthcare workforce is expected to grow by 3,373,800, or 26%, by 2022. Two forces are at work here and account for this anticipated exponential growth: the Affordable Care Act of 2012 and the aging of the Baby Boomers. Given that the future outlooks for career and business opportunities in the healthcare industry are great, this can only be good for the economy, businesses, entrepreneurs, and individuals.

Third, the productivity outcomes of the travel, entertainment, and recreation and leisure industries with respect to jobs, businesses, and multiplier effects are quite astronomical. As noted, some 1.5 million Americans work in the travel, entertainment, and recreation and leisure industries.

The goal of these personnel is to ensure Americans are having fun if and whenever they want to, especially during the summers and holidays. Based on BLS projections, the entertainment industries are expected to grow by 312,200 personnel, or 20%, by 2022. If the travel, entertainment, and recreation and leisure industries in America were a country, it would rank among the most developed nations of the world.

Fourth, education seems to be the predominant determinant of great career opportunities in the healthcare industry and in the travel and recreation and leisure industries. Employees with college degrees and some graduate or professional degrees work in professional occupations with much higher pay grades. However, there are enough occupational jobs to go around for anyone who wants to work, especially in the travel, entertainment, and recreation and leisure industries. There is room in these industries for anyone with a degree and professional license/certification as well as anyone with a high school diploma or GED.

Fifth, the public sector plays a significant role in framing the broad policies, regulations, and safety and security guidelines of these industries. However, the programs, products, services, operations, businesses, and markets in these industries are overwhelming in the hands of the private and nonprofit sectors. Except for the national parks, the travel, entertainment, and recreation and leisure industries are virtually private and nonprofit sector affairs. This puts more money in the pockets of the people who, in turn, spend the money on goods and services, including healthcare, entertainment, and recreation and leisure. This is the essence and nature of a capitalist economy and the free markets at its best. The architectures of productivity don't get any better than this!

CHAPTER 13

RIGHTS, RULES, RESPONSIBILITIES, AND REWARDS

As the preacher put it, what is the conclusion of the whole matter? That American uniqueness is uniquely unique. My effort in this book was to submit evidence in support of this thesis. As such, my primary goal has been to identify and discuss the genius of American culture. The genius is the enduring ideals and values that have served to nurture and sustain a culture of unprecedented productivity in modern times. Given the founder's envisioned trajectory of social history and their faith in providence, people, and enduring principles, it would have been historically unprecedented if America did not turn out to be a super power. Super power in very much everything, including productivity and, yes, waste! Great nations are known for one or the other, but not for both at the same time. That is what is so uniquely unique about America's uniqueness. I hope my unique approach (a blend of quantitative and qualitative methods) in presenting the evidence has done justice to this uniqueness in a fair and balanced way in the chapters of this book.

In Chapters 2-5, we examined the human and economic elements that make America so productive—people, jobs and business. We noted that these elements constitute the means of productivity in American culture. In Chapters 6-9, we explored the ideas and values that make America tick: the quest for a more perfect Union; diversity; law and order; and the acceptance of life and productivity as not always being easy. We noted that these personified genres form the hardware of America culture. In Chapters 10-12, we reflected on the software that makes the culture of productivity runs rather smoothly albeit with bumps here and there: the role of gratitude to smooth relationships, the power of apology to de-escalate conflicts, and ways to live the American dream with cautious optimism by staying healthy and having fun. We noted that these themes exemplify the American culture mores and values that carry over and strengthen the culture of productivity. Theories, concepts, and models were presented to inform discussions.

We identified and discussed the ideas—inalienable rights of individuals, sovereign state, right monopoly of rights, etc.— that serve as engines that drive the American economy. We analyzed the infrastructures and structures that give meaning and reality to these ideas within the framework of primary and secondary cultures, forest-trees paradigm, and State-Society conceptual models of a more perfect Union. We identified and examined diversity in America and how the very strength of American diversity can also serve as source of challenge in law enforcement and social transformation. Further, we analyzed how cultural traits and manners such as gratitude and apology serve as software that make it possible to run and operate the various institutions, organizations, and associations where people from all walks of life gather to conduct business and make a living every day.

It would appear from the foregoing that there is a recipe for becoming well off in America. To some extent this observation is true. The operative term is "some extent." As discussed, life is not easy; neither is productivity. This is due in part to the reality that all things are never equal in life and in productivity. For example, social scientists have long observed that the three areas in society that tends to outpace inflation are health care, education, and housing. Interestingly, these are the three essential variables needed to be productive in America. Each of the variables is hard, if not impossible, to achieve alone without help in some fashion. It is not surprising that all three variables, among others, are subsidized by the government. Productivity is a joint enterprise.

The point is that it takes contractual complementary efforts on the part of the larger society and the individuals in that society to be productive. This contract between the citizens and its government has four essential principles at play: rights, rules, responsibilities, and rewards. There is a causal relationship between these principles. Although the state or governments are primarily tasked with the emergence and protection of the first two, society or citizens are primarily responsible for the actualization of the last two. The Declaration of Independence, the Constitution, and various statutes serve as the foundational sources of the principles, hence equal protection under the law.

What separates productive Americans from non-productive American is an accurate understanding of these principles. The level of engagement with these principles determines, by and large, where a person will end up on the food chain.

Rights

As a nation of laws, America is a nation of rights. These rights are well documented in the Declaration of Independence, the Constitution, the Statutes, and in various codes, ordinances, edicts, and executive orders, to name a few. There are rights of life and human dignity; to free religion, speech, and association; to pursue happiness, education, business, social interests, and property, to name a few. A primary function of government is to ensure that these rights are available to and accessible by all Americans. However, these rights are just that—rights—until an individual or group of individuals knows and exercises them. It is incredibly amazing how many citizens and immigrants alike do not know their rights, let alone exercise them. Productive individuals, businesses, and organizations know and exercise their rights.

Rules

For every right there are rules. To exercise a right, the rules associated with exercising the rights must be understood and followed. An individual serves himself well to know those rules and follow them. For example, an individual is free and has the right to pursue an education, seek employment, or start a business in a community. That is, an individual is free to pursue productivity or the means to productivity, provided that he or she, in exercising his or her right to education, a job, or business, knows and follows the rules associated with enrolling and going to school to acquire education; rules for seeking, gaining, and retaining employment; and rules for starting and operating a business. Many people know their rights, but fail to familiarize themselves with the rules associated with exercising those rights. Some know the rules but fail to follow them. It is not enough to know the rules if they are not followed. Others simply do not know the rules, let alone follow them in their effort to exercise their rights. Productive individuals, businesses, and organizations know and follow the rules in exercising their rights.

Responsibilities

For every right, there are rules. And for every rule, there are responsibilities. A primary function of rules is to assign responsibilities to parties involved—who will do what when, where, and how. Individuals serve themselves well to get acquainted with the responsibilities associated with rules. To follow a rule implies that an individual must not only understand and accept the responsibilities associated with the rule, but he or she must perform the responsibilities the rule assigns to him or her. This is where there is a breakdown in the exercising of rights. Many people appear to want to exercise their rights without accepting the corresponding rules and responsibilities that the exercising that right places on them—namely, to follow the rules and accept the responsibilities.

Admittedly, there are situations where the deck is stacked against individuals or a group of individuals in society. This is precisely why there are such provisions as peaceful protests, electoral processes, elections, and public officials. For example, if a system is educationally rigged, one approach is to stage a peaceful protest until the system is fixed. Another approach is for the individuals to exercise their voting rights to elect candidates who will address their concerns for fair and equitable rules. This will put them on a path to education, jobs, and business opportunities.

Productive individuals, businesses, and organizations not only know and follow commonly prescribed rules in exercising their rights, but they also assume their responsibilities and perform the tasks and assume the responsibilities assigned them. They also know how to organize in order to use the legitimate democratic process to correct a systemic dysfunction or to initiate an initiative in favor of their course. For productive people, inaction is not an option. There is nothing to gain from inaction and a lot to gain from active participation.

Rewards

For every right there are rules. For every rule, there are responsibilities. And for every responsibility, there are rewards. The European philosophers and the American founders got it right when they insisted that the inalienable rights of individuals are the foundations of a civil society—among them life, liberty, liberty, and the pursuit of happiness and property. At the end of the day, there is a reward to the acknowledgment and exercise of these constitutionally guaranteed rights. Three implications flow from this observation.

First, if there is a reward for exercising rights, most people will follow the rules and accept the responsibilities for exercising the rights. In this regard, the reward of, say, happiness and property serves both as an incentive and a trade-up for following the rules of law and accepting individual responsibilities.

Second, a civil society emerges as most people follow the rules and accept responsibilities.

Third, a wealthy society emerges as individuals are rewarded. That is, the cumulative effect of individual accumulation of wealth gives rise to the wealth of a nation. Productive individuals, businesses, and organizations exercise their rights, follow the rules, and accept their fair share of responsibilities the rules have assigned them. The reward is productivity and the accrued wealth thereof at the individual, business, and/or organizational levels. (See Appendix 22).

By and large, individuals fizzle and businesses and organizations falter when they compromise these principles. Individuals flourish and organizations prosper when their business philosophy and operations (modus operandi) are in congruence with these principles. The totality of the processes and the principles is at the heart of the culture of productivity in American culture, the subject of this book. An analysis of the interplay between the principles and the principal players, of which the American Experiment is a case in point, is beyond the scope of this book. As a matter of anticipation, such analysis begs a major literary work.

APPENDICES

APPENDIX 1

INDICATORS OF INTERNAL PRODUCTIVITY DYNAMICS

	GDP 2013	%GDP	World Pop.	%WP	Military Spending	%WMS	%GDP	WEC	%WEC 2013/14 MW.h/yr
World	$74,899,822,000,000		7,190,000,000		$1,747,000,000,000			19,320,360,620	24.2%
USA	16,800,000,000,000	22.4 %	318,804,000	4.43%	640,000,000,000	36.6%	3.8%	4,686,400,000	24.2%
China	9,240,270,000,000	12.3%	1,366,950,000	19%	188,000,000,000	10.76%	2.0%	5,322,300,000	27.5%
Japan	4,901,530,000,000	6.5%	127,040,000	1.77%	48,600,000,000	2.7%	1.0%	859,700,000	4.4%
Germa	3,634,823,000,000	4.8%	80,781,000	1.12%	48,800,000,000	2.7%	1.4%	607,000,000	3.1%
France	2,734,949,000,000	3.6%	65,991,000	0.92%	61,200,000,000	3.5%	2.2%	460,900,000	2.3%
UK	2,522,261,000,000	3.3%	64,105,654	0.89%	57,900,000,000	3.3%	2.3%	344,700,000	1.7%
Brazil	2,245,673,000,000	2.9%	203,202,000	2.83%	31,500,000,000	1.8%	1.4%	455,700,000	2.3%
Russia	2,096,777,000,000	2.7%	146,149,200	2.03%	87,700,000,000	5.0%	4.1%	1,016,500,000	5.2%
Italy	2,071,307,000,000	2.7%	60,780,377	0.85%	32,700,000,000	1.9%	1.6%	344,700,000	1.7%
India	1,876,797,000,000	2.5%	1,260,070,000	17.5%	47,400,000,000	2.7%	2.5%	1,051,375,000	5.4%

(Source: World Bank, Wikipedia World Population, World Energy Council, CIA World Factbook)
WGDP – World Growth Domestic Products; WP – World Population; WMS – World Military Spending;
WEC – World Electricity Consumption

APPENDIX 2

USA POPULATION/DEMOGRAPHIC QUICK FACTS
(www.quickfacts.census.gov)

Population, 2013 estimate	316,128,839
Population, 2010 (April 1) estimates base	308,747,716
Population, percent change, April 1, 2010 to July 1, 2013	2.4%
Population, 2010	308,745,538
Persons under 5 years, percent, 2013	6.3%
Persons under 18 years, percent, 2013	23.3%
Persons 65 years and over, percent, 2013	14.1%
Female persons, percent, 2013	50.8
White alone, percent, 2013 (a)	77.7%
Black or African American alone, percent, 2013 (a)	13.2%
American Indian and Alaska Native alone, percent, 2013 (a)	1.2%
Asian alone, percent, 2013 (a)	5.3%
Native Hawaiian and Other Pacific Islander alone, percent, 2013 (a)	0.2%
Two or More Races, percent, 2013	2.4%
Hispanic or Latino, percent, 2013 (b)	17.1%
White alone, not Hispanic or Latino, percent, 2013	62.6%
Living in same house 1 year & over, percent, 2008-2012	84.8%
Foreign born persons, percent, 2008-2012	12.9%

Language other than English spoken at home, percent age   20.5%
5+, 2008-2012

High school graduate or higher, percent of persons age   85.7%
25+, 2008-2012

Bachelor's degree or higher, percent of persons age 25+,   28.5%
2008-2012

Veterans, 2008-2012   21,853,912

Mean travel time to work (minutes), workers age 16+,   25.4
2008-2012

APPENDIX 3

EDUCATION IN USA – ELEMENTARY, POST-SECONDARY, BACCALAUREATE, AND GRADUATE
(US Department of Education, http://nces.ed.gov/)

Number of public school districts and public and private elementary and secondary schools: Selected years, 1998-99 through 2011-12

School Year	Total All Public School Districts	Total All Public and Private Schools	Total All Public Schools	Total All Private Schools
1998-1999	14,891	-	90,874	-
1999-2000	14,928	125,007	90,012	32,995
2009-2010	13,625	132,183	98,812	33,366
2010-2011	13,588	-	98,812	-
2011-2012	13,567	129,189	98,328	30,861

Enrollment, staff, and degrees/certificates conferred in degree-granting and non-degree-granting postsecondary institutions, by control and level of institution, sex of student, type of staff, and level of degree: Fall 2010, fall 2011, and 2011-12

Students, Staff, Diplomas	Total	Degree-granting Public	Degree-granting Private	Non-Degree Public	Non-Degree Private
Enrollments					
Fall 2010	21,588,124	15,152,809	5,873,317	137,461	434,534
4 year institutions	13,335,777	7,924,771	5,510,480	42	484
Males	5,779,795	3,568,544	2,211,141	15	95
Females	7,555,982	4,356,227	3,199,339	27	389
2 year institutions	7,847,996	7,218,038	462,837	66,575	100,546
Males	3,346,603	3,110,993	154,133	35,616	45,661
Females	4,501,393	4,107,045	308,704	30,959	54,685
Less than 2 yr. inst.	404,351	-	-	70,847	333,505
Males	113,722	-	-	29,720	84,002
Females	290,629	-	-	41,127	249,502
Staff					
Fall 2011	3,920,836	2,484,820	1,356,160	24,000	55,856
Professional Staff	2,986,568	1,865269	1,058,692	17,977	44,630
Administrative	248,982	112,473	126,245	1,430	8,834
Faculty	1,565,504	953,220	570,385	14,716	27,173
Graduate Assistants	355,916	285,905	70,011	-	-
Other Professionals	816,166	513,661	292,051	1,831	8,623
Nonprofessional Staff	934,268	619,551	297,468	6,023	11,226
Degrees/certificate Conferred					
2011-2012	4,720,590	2,780,118	1,590,875	66,276	283,321
Less than 1 yr. cert	987,715	458,131	180,043	66,255	283,286

Students, Staff, Diplomas	Total	Degree-granting Public	Degree-granting Private	Non-Degree Public	Non-Degree Private
4 year institutions	84,749	46,148	38,533	-	68
Males	33,574	21,800	11,762	-	12
Females	51,175	24,348	26,771	-	56
2 year institutions	638,990	411,983	141,510	32,020	53,477
Males	269,466	192,959	39,632	14,805	22,070
Females	369,524	219,024	101,878	17,215	31,407
Less than 2 yr inst.	263,976	-	-	34,235	229,741
Males	70,444	-	-	13,184	57,260
Females	193,532	-	-	21,051	172,481
Associate Degrees	1,017,538	756,063	261,419	21	35
4 year institutions	314,375	132,719	181,656	-	-
Males	118,927	52,866	66,061	-	-
Females	195,448	79,853	115,595	-	-
2 year institutions	703,128	623,344	79,763	21	-
Males	273,035	242,900	30,118	17	-
Females	430,093	380,444	49,645	4	-
Less than 2 yr inst.	35	-	-	-	35
Males	28	-	-	-	28
Females	7	-	-	-	7
Bachelor's degrees	1,791,046	1,131,886	659,160	-	-
Males	765,317	496,913	268,404	-	-
Females	1,025,729	634,973	390,756	-	-
Master's degrees	754,229	349,511	404,918	-	-
Males	302,191	142,656	159,535	-	-
Females	452,038	206,655	245,383	-	-
Doctor's degrees	170,062	84,727	85,335	-	-
Males	82,611	41,638	40,973	-	-
Females	87451	43,089	44,362	-	-

APPENDIX 4

U.S. EDUCATION FAST FACTS

(US Department of Education, http://nces.
ed.gov/fastfacts/display.asp?id=372)

Back to school statistics

Enrollment

In fall 2014, about 49.8 million students will attend public elementary and secondary schools. Of these, 35.1 million will be in prekindergarten through grade 8 and 14.7 million will be in grades 9 through 12. An additional 5.0 million students are expected to attend private schools (source). The fall 2014 public school enrollment is expected to remain near the record enrollment level of fall 2013.

Of the projected 49.8 million students attending public elementary and secondary schools in fall 2014, White students will account for 24.8 million. The remaining 25.0 million will be composed of 7.7 million Black students, 12.8 million Hispanic students, 2.6 million Asian/Pacific Islander students, 0.5 million American Indian/Alaska Native students, and 1.4 million students of two or more races (source). The national percentage of students who are White is projected to be less than 50 percent in 2014. The percentage of White students is expected to continue declining as the enrollments of Hispanics and Asians/Pacific Islanders increase through at least fall 2023, the last year for which projections are available (source).

About 1.3 million children are expected to attend public prekindergarten in fall 2014; enrollment in public kindergarten is projected to reach approximately 3.7 million students (source).

In fall 2014, about 4.1 million public school students are expected to enroll in 9ᵗʰ gradeï¿½the typical entry grade for many American high schools (source).

Teachers

Public school systems will employ about 3.1 million full-time-equivalent (FTE) teachers in fall 2014, such that the number of pupils per FTE teacherï¿½that is, the pupil/teacher ratioï¿½will be 16.0. This ratio is not measurably different from the 2000 ratio of 16.0. A projected 0.4 million FTE teachers will be working in private schools this fall, resulting in an estimated pupil/teacher ratio of 12.5, which is lower than the 2000 ratio of 14.5 (source).

Schools and Districts

In 2011ï¿½12, there were about 13,600 public school districts (source) with over 98,300 public schools, including about 5,700 charter schools (source). In fall 2011, there were about 30,900 private schools offering kindergarten or higher grades (source).

Expenditures

Current expenditures for public elementary and secondary schools are projected to be $619 billion for the 2014ï¿½15 school year. These expenditures include such items as salaries for school personnel, benefits, student transportation, school books and materials, and energy costs. The current expenditure per student is projected at $12,281 for the 2014ï¿½15 school year (source).

Attainment

About 3.3 million students are expected to graduate from high school in 2014ï¿½15, including 3.0 million students from public high schools and about 0.3 million students from private high schools (source).

The percentage of high school dropouts among 16- through 24-year-olds declined from 10.9 percent in 2000 to 6.6 percent in 2012 (source). Reflecting the overall decline in the dropout rate between 2000 and 2012, the rates also declined for Whites, Blacks, and Hispanics (source).

The percentage of students enrolling in college in the fall immediately following high school completion was 66.2 percent in 2012 (source). Females enrolled at a higher rate (71.3 percent) than males (61.3 percent) (source).

College and University Education

Enrollment

In fall 2014, some 21.0 million students are expected to attend American colleges and universities, constituting an increase of about 5.7 million since fall 2000 (source).

Females are expected to account for the majority of college students: about 12.0 million females will attend in fall 2014, compared with 9.0 million males. Also, more students are expected to attend full time than part time (an estimated 13.0 million, compared with about 8.0 million, respectively)(source).

About 7.3 million students will attend 2-year institutions and nearly 13.7 million will attend 4-year institutions. Some 18.0 million students are expected to enroll in undergraduate programs and about 3.0 million will enroll in post baccalaureate programs (source).

Increases in the traditional college-age population and rising enrollment rates have contributed to the increase in college enrollment. Between 2000 and 2012, the 18- to 24-year-old population rose from approximately 27.3 million to approximately 31.4 million (source). The percentage of 18- to 24-year-olds enrolled in college also was higher in 2012 (41.0 percent) than in 2000 (35.5 percent) (source).

In 2012, there were about 13 million students under age 25 and 8 million students 25 years old and over. Both the number of younger and older students increased between 2000 and 2012 (source).

Increasing numbers and percentages of Black and Hispanic students are attending college. Between 2000 and 2012, the percentage of college students who were Black rose from 11.7 to 14.9 percent, and the percentage of students who were Hispanic rose from 9.9 to 15.0 percent (source). Also, the percentage of Black 18- to 24-year-olds enrolled in college increased from 30.5 percent in 2000 to 36.4 percent in 2012, and the percentage of Hispanics enrolled increased from 21.7 to 37.5 percent (source).

Finance

For the 2012ï¿½13 academic year, the average annual price for undergraduate tuition, fees, room, and board was $15,022 at public institutions, $39,173 at private nonprofit institutions, and $23,158 at private for-profit institutions. Charges for tuition and required fees averaged $5,899 at public institutions, $28,569 at private nonprofit institutions, and $13,766 at private for-profit institutions (source).

Attainment

During the 2014ï¿½15 school year, colleges and universities are expected to award 1.0 million associateï¿½s degrees; 1.8 million bachelor's degrees; 821,000 master's degrees; and 177,500 doctor's degrees (source). In 2011ï¿½12, postsecondary institutions awarded 1.0 million certificates below the associateï¿½s degree level, 1.0 million associateï¿½s degrees, 1.8 million bachelorï¿½s degrees, 754,000 masterï¿½s degrees, and 170,100 doctorï¿½s degrees (source).

In 2012, about 73 percent of young adults ages 25ï¿½34 with a bachelor's or higher degree in the labor force had year-round, full-time jobs, compared with 65 percent of those with an associate's degree, 59 percent of those with some college education, 60 percent of high school completers, and 49 percent of those without a high school diploma or its equivalent (source). In 2013, a smaller percentage of young adults with a bachelor's degree or higher were unemployed than were their peers with lower levels of education (source).

In 2012, the median earnings for full-time year-round working young adults ages 25ï¿½34 with a bachelor's degree was $46,900, while the median was $22,900 for those without a high school diploma or its equivalent, $30,000 for those with a high school diploma or its equivalent, and $35,700 for those with an associate's degree. In other words, young adults with a bachelor's degree earned more than twice as much as those without a high school diploma or its equivalent (105 percent more) and 57 percent more than young adult high school completers. Additionally, in 2012 the median earnings for young adults with a master's degree or higher was $59,600, some 27 percent more than the median for young adults with a bachelor's degree (source).

APPENDIX 5

US EMPLOYMENT DATA

(U.S. Department of Labor, http://www.bls.
gov/news.release/empsit.toc.htm)

| Employment Data – USA | 2013,
2014 |

Bureau of Labor Statistics (BLS) - Economic News Release

HOUSEHOLD DATA - Employments
Summary table A. Household data, seasonally adjusted
[Numbers in thousands]

Category	Sept.2013	July2014	Aug.2014	Sept. 2014
Employment status				
Civilian non-institutional population	246,168	248,023	248,229	248,446
Civilian labor force	155,473	156,023	155,959	155,862
Participation rate	63.2	62.9	62.8	62.7
Employed	144,270	146,352	146,368	146,600
Employment-population ratio	58.6	59.0	59.0	59.0
Unemployed	11,203	9,671	9,591	9,262
Unemployment rate	7.2	6.2	6.1	5.9
Not in labor force	90,695	92,001	92,269	92,584
Unemployment rates				

Total, 16 years and over	7.2	6.2	6.1	5.9
Adult men (20 years and over)	7.0	5.7	5.7	5.3
Adult women (20 years and over)	6.2	5.7	5.7	5.5
Teenagers (16 to 19 years)	21.3	20.2	19.6	20.0
White	6.3	5.3	5.3	5.1
Black or African American	13.0	11.4	11.4	11.0
Asian (not seasonally adjusted)	5.3	4.5	4.5	4.3
Hispanic or Latino ethnicity	8.9	7.8	7.5	6.9
Total, 25 years and over	5.9	5.0	5.1	4.7
Less than a high school diploma	10.4	9.6	9.1	8.4
High school graduates, no college	7.5	6.1	6.2	5.3
Some college or associate degree	6.1	5.3	5.4	5.4
Bachelor's degree and higher	3.7	3.1	3.2	2.9

Reason for unemployment

Job losers/persons completed temp jobs 5,803	4,859	4,836	4,530	
Job leavers	984	862	860	829
Reentrants	3,165	2,848	2,845	2,809
New entrants	1,211	1,087	1,066	1,105
Duration of unemployment				
Less than 5 weeks	2,571	2,587	2,609	2,383
5 to 14 weeks	2,685	2,431	2,449	2,508
15 to 26 weeks	1,802	1,412	1,486	1,416
27 weeks and over	4,125	3,155	2,963	2,954

Employed persons at work part time

Part time for economic reasons	7,914	7,511	7,277	7,103
Slack work or business conditions	4,955	4,609	4,261	4,162
Could only find part-time work	2,548	2,519	2,587	2,562
Part time for noneconomic reasons	18,919	19,662	19,526	19,561

Persons not in the labor force (not seasonally adjusted)

Marginally attached to the labor force	2,302	2,178	2,141	2,226
Discouraged workers	852	741	775	698

- Over-the-month changes are not displayed for not seasonally adjusted data.
NOTE: Persons whose ethnicity is identified as Hispanic or Latino may be of any race.
Detail for the seasonally adjusted data shown in this table will not necessarily add to totals because of the independent seasonal adjustment of the various series. Updated population controls are introduced annually with the release of January data.

Employment Situation Summary Table B. Establishment data, seasonally adjusted

ESTABLISHMENT DATA
Summary table B. Establishment data, seasonally adjusted

Category	Sept2013	July2014	Aug2014(p)	Sept2014(p)
EMPLOYMENT BY SELECTED INDUSTRY				
(Over-the-month change, in thousands)				
Total nonfarm	164	243	180	248
Total private	153	239	175	236
Goods-producing	22	63	14	29
Mining and logging	6	9	2	9
Construction	13	30	16	16
Manufacturing	3	24	-4	4
Durable goods(1)	9	27	0	7
Motor vehicles and parts	2.9	13.7	-4.5	3.3
Nondurable goods	-6	-3	-4	-3
Private service-providing(1)	131	176	161	207
Wholesale trade	11.3	3.0	2.5	1.8
Retail trade	27.3	25.4	-4.7	35.3
Transportation and warehousing	23.1	21.1	8.5	1.9
Information	13	10	5	12
Financial activities	-1	15	12	12
Professional and business services(1)	37	50	63	81
Temporary help services	19.7	15.7	24.6	19.7
Education and health services(1)	9	37	42	32
Health care and social assistance	14.5	40.7	40.7	22.7
Leisure and hospitality	9	10	20	33
Other services	2	3	10	0
Government	11	4	5	12

WOMEN AND PRODUCTION AND NONSUPERVISORY EMPLOYEES (2) AS A PERCENT OF ALL EMPLOYEES

Total nonfarm women employees	49.5	49.4	49.4	49.3
Total private women employees	48.1	47.9	47.9	47.9
Total private production and nonsupervisory employees	82.6	82.6	82.6	82.6

HOURS AND EARNINGS
ALL EMPLOYEES

Total private

Average weekly hours	34.5	34.5	34.5	34.6
Average hourly earnings	$24.06	$24.46	$24.54	$24.53
Average weekly earnings	$830.07	$843.87	$846.63	$848.74
Index of aggregate weekly hours (2007=100)(3)	99.1	101.0	101.2	101.7
Over-the-month percent change	0.1	0.2	0.2	0.5
Index of aggregate weekly payrolls (2007=100)(4)	113.8	117.9	118.5	119.0
Over-the-month percent change	0.3	0.3	0.5	0.4

HOURS AND EARNINGS
PRODUCTION AND NONSUPERVISORY EMPLOYEES

Total private

Average weekly hours	33.6	33.7	33.8	33.7
Average hourly earnings	$20.21	$20.61	$20.67	$20.67
Average weekly earnings	$679.06	$694.56	$698.65	$696.58
Index of aggregate weekly hours (2002=100)(3)	106.3	108.7	109.2	109.1
Over-the-month percent change	-0.2	0.2	0.5	-0.1
Index of aggregate weekly payrolls (2002=100)(4)	143.5	149.7	150.8	150.6
Over-the-month percent change	0.0	0.3	0.7	-0.1

DIFFUSION INDEX(5)
(Over 1-month span)

Total private (264 industries)	59.8	67.8	62.7	57.8
Manufacturing (81 industries)	54.9	56.2	54.9	51.9

Footnotes

(1) Includes other industries, not shown separately.

(2) Data relate to production employees in mining and logging and manufacturing, construction employees in construction, and nonsupervisory employees in the service-providing industries.

(3) The indexes of aggregate weekly hours are calculated by dividing the current month's estimates of aggregate hours by the corresponding annual average aggregate hours.

(4) The indexes of aggregate weekly payrolls are calculated by dividing the current month's estimates of aggregate weekly payrolls by the corresponding annual average aggregate weekly payrolls.

(5) Figures are the percent of industries with employment increasing plus one-half of the industries with unchanged employment, where 50 percent indicates an equal balance between industries with increasing and decreasing employment.

(p) Preliminary

Table of Contents (http://www.bls.gov/news.release/, http://www.bls.gov/news.release/empsit.nr0.htm)

- Employment Situation Summary
- Employment Situation Summary Table A. Household data, seasonally adjusted
- Employment Situation Summary Table B. Establishment data, seasonally adjusted
- Employment Situation Frequently Asked Questions

301

- Table B-1. Employees on nonfarm payrolls by industry sector and selected industry detail
- Table B-2. Average weekly hours and overtime of all employees on private nonfarm payrolls by industry sector, seasonally adjusted
- Table B-3. Average hourly and weekly earnings of all employees on private nonfarm payrolls by industry sector, seasonally adjusted
- Table B-4. Indexes of aggregate weekly hours and payrolls for all employees on private nonfarm payrolls by industry sector, seasonally adjusted
- Table B-5. Employment of women on nonfarm payrolls by industry sector, seasonally adjusted
- Table B-6. Employment of production and nonsupervisory employees on private nonfarm payrolls by industry sector, seasonally adjusted(1)
- Table B-7. Average weekly hours and overtime of production and nonsupervisory employees on private nonfarm payrolls by industry sector, seasonally adjusted(1)
- Table B-8. Average hourly and weekly earnings of production and nonsupervisory employees on private nonfarm payrolls by industry sector, seasonally adjusted(1)
- Table B-9. Indexes of aggregate weekly hours and payrolls for production and nonsupervisory employees on private nonfarm payrolls by industry sector, seasonally adjusted(1)

- Access to historical data for the "A" tables of the Employment Situation Release
- Access to historical data for the "B" tables of the Employment Situation Release
- HTML version of the entire news release

The PDF version of the news release

APPENDIX 6

USA BUSINESS/PRODUCTIVITY QUICK FACTS

(US Census Bureau, http://www.census.gov/en.html#)

Private nonfarm establishments, 2012	7,431,808
Private nonfarm employment, 2012	115,938,468
Private nonfarm employment, percent change, 2011-2012	2.2%
Non-employer establishments, 2012	22,735,915
Total number of firms, 2007	27,092,908
Black-owned firms, percent, 2007	7.1%
American Indian- and Alaska Native-owned firms, percent, 2007	0.9%
Asian-owned firms, percent, 2007	5.7%
Native Hawaiian and Other Pacific Islander-owned firms, percent, 2007	0.1%
Hispanic-owned firms, percent, 2007	8.3%
Women-owned firms, percent, 2007	28.8%
Manufacturers shipments, 2007 ($1000)	5,319,456,312
Merchant wholesaler sales, 2007 ($1000)	4,174,286,516
Retail sales, 2007 ($1000)	3,917,663,456
Retail sales per capita, 2007	$12,990
Accommodation and food services sales, 2007 ($1000)	613,795,732
Building permits, 2012	829,658
Geography Quick Facts	USA:
Land area in square miles, 2010	3,531,905.43
Persons per square mile, 2010	87.4

APPENDIX 7

COMPARING PUBLIC AND PRIVATE ORGANIZATIONS

I. Organizational Forms and Structures

Org Type	Micro Orgs - Structure	Macro Orgs - Structure
Private Orgs	Manager	Senior Managers
	Supervisors	Middle Managers
	Staff	Admin support/Research and Development
		Operations -
		Managers and Supervisors
		Staff, Temps, Contractors
Public Orgs	Manager	Senior Managers
	Supervisors	Middle Managers
	Staff	Admin support/Research and Development
		Operations -
		Managers and Supervisors
		Staff, Temps, Contractors

Note: Private and Public Orgs are fundamentally alike in forms and structures

II. Organizational Operations and Functions

Org Type	Micro Orgs - Operations	Macro Orgs - Operations
Private Orgs	**Input bottom line:** Capitals and Investments resources **Core Technology:** Assembly, manufacturing, services	**Input bottom line:** Capitals and Investment resources **Core Technology:** Assembly, manufacturing, services
	Output bottom line: Profits, goods	**Output bottom line:** Profits, goods
Public Orgs	**Input bottom line:** Taxes, fees	**Input bottom line:** Taxes, fees
	Core Technology: Services, procurements	**Core Technology:** Services, procurements
	Output bottom line: Public good, safety	**Output bottom line:** Public good, safety

Note: Private and Public Orgs are fundamentally Un-like in functions, resources and goals

APPENDIX 8

STRATEGIC MANAGEMENT (SM)
(Inspiration from Robbins and Coulter, 2012, Michael Porter 1980, 1987)

Definitions -

Strategic Management is what managers do to develop the organization's strategies, including planning, organizing, leading, and controlling.

Corporate Strategy is an organizational strategy that determines what businesses a company is in, should be in, or wants to be in, and what it wants to do with those businesses.

Competitive Strategy – is specifically calculated plan or strategy for how the organization will compete and stay competitive with other organizations in the industry of choice in order to maintain competitive advantage or edge.

Business Model – is how a company is going to make money while meeting customers need (what customers need and whether company can make money meeting that need)

Strategic Management Process is a series of sequenced long range planning steps:

1. Identify organization's current mission, goals and strategy
2. Do internal analysis (the SW of SWOT)
3. Do external analysis (the OT of SWOT)
4. Formulate strategies
5. Implement strategies
6. Evaluate results

(Note: 1-3 = P; 4 = O; 5= L; 6 = C in **P**lanning, **O**rganizing, **L**eading and **C**ontrol mgmt. functions)

I. Types of Corporate Strategies (overall direction of organization)

1. Growth
   A. Concentration
   B. Vertical Integration
      1) Backward (supply, input control)
      2) Forward (outlet, output control)
   C. Horizontal integration
      1) Related (similar industry)
      2) Unrelated (different industry)
   D. Diversification
      1) Related (similar product lines);
      2) Unrelated (different product lines)
2. Stability – maintain current strategy or status quo
3. Renewal Strategy – revitalization; revive; revitalize to stop or reverse decline.
   Retrenchment (e.g. 6 Sigma, lay-off) or Turnaround (transformational) strategies

II. Types of Competitive Strategies (designed to gain competitive advantage/edge)

Strategy	Emphasis	Quality	Price	Likely Customers
1. Cost Leadership	Production	low	low	lower class
2. Quality Differential	Product	high	high	upper class
3. Cost/Price Focused`	Pricing	high	low	middle class

III. Functional Strategy (internal/dept. strategies to support competitive advantage)

1. Input/Supply Department strategy
2. Transformation/Manufacturing/Service Department strategy
3. Output/Marketing Department strategy

APPENDIX 9

STRATEGIC PLAN

<u>Aigbe Fictional Ice Company</u>

Vision: We will be the company of premium ice for the premium people of the metropolitan Washington, DC.

Motto (slogan): Premium Ice for Premium People

Mission Statement: Making and delivering quality ice for less price at all times.

Competitive advantage (slogan): Quality ice for less

Goal: Consistently sell the most (quantity) and best (quality) ice in the region.

Objectives:
1. Steady supply of quality spring water.
2. Quality and reliable production department.
3. Reliable delivery of 1,000,000 bags of ice a year to retail stores in the region

---

Strategic Goal: AIC will become a household word in the region in a decade.

Strategic Objectives:
1. Robust effective marketing department – products and services
2. Aggressive and reliable delivery services – AIC quality ice in all stores at all times
   NW Area 1
   NE Area II
   SW Area III
   SE Area IV

3. High profile public relations campaign
   Community involvement - donations
   Annual events – free ice in marathons and championship football games
   Scholarship and sponsorship of best and brightest kids

Notes/observations:
1. Values: quality and affordability, products and people
2. Management principles: TQM, EI
3. Beliefs: Philosophize or fossilize; produce or kaput
4. Strategy: market dominance; expansion into new frontiers (best defense is offensive defense)
5. Take away: Mission/goals, strategy and structural design must fit internally ...
   and externally must align with the environment.

APPENDIX 10

MANAGEMENT PRINCIPLES

Functions of Manager/Management POLE/C

P	Planning
O	Organizing
L	Leading
E/C	Evaluating/Controlling

Management
(Luther Gulick and Al Urwick, eds. Papers on the Science of PA, 1937)

P	Planning
O	Organizing
S	Staffing
D	Directing
Co	Coordinating
B	Budgeting
E	Evaluating

Management Control - GMAC
(Concept inspired by Draft 2010)

G	Goals
M	Metrics
A	Analysis
C	Correction

Organization Structural Components –SMART
(Concept inspired by Daft 2010)

S	Senior Management
M	Middle Management
A	Administration (Administrative Support)
R	Research/Development
T	Technical Core/Operations (Input-Transformation-Output)

Conflict/Crisis management/resolution

F	Find
A	Analyze
D	Develop
E	Execute/Evaluate

Policy Processes

I	Initiation
E	Estimation
S	Selection
I	Implementation
E	Evaluation
T	Termination

Inter-group/Systems Poor Functioning/Performance

D   Dissect
S   Sequence
A   Assign
N   Negotiate
E   Evaluate

Technology

D   Discover
D   Design
D   Develop
D   Deplore
D   Demonstrate

6 Ps of Managing Poor and Pitiful Performance
(Colby King, Washington Post columnist)

Proper Planning Prevents Poor and Pitiful Performance

4Ps of Going Entrepreneurial

P   Products - create product, goods and/or services
P   Presence - create presence, business infrastructure and marketing structure
P   Publicity - create publicity, launch out, roll out, make money
P   Providence - concede to providence; work hard, say a prayer and hope for the best prepare for the worst; luck, coincidence, OBE, timing, Murphy's law, etc.

314

Organizational Development Intervention Process: CoEDPIIE

(Adapted from Cummings and Worley, 2009)

Co	Contracting
E	Entrance
D	Diagnosis
P	Planning
I	Implementation
I	Institutionalization
E	Evaluation

Organizational Development Intervention Dimensions: PReSS

(Adapted from Cummings and Worley, 2009)

P	Process – Human Processes
Re	Resources – Human Resources
S	Structures – Techno-structures
S	Strategic – Strategic Changes

APPENDIX 11

WHITE COLLAR AND BLUE COLLAR OCCUPATIONS
(U.S. Office of Personnel Management, www.OPM.gov)

HANDBOOK OF OCCUPATIONAL
GROUPS AND FAMILIES MAY 2009

Handbook of Occupational Groups and Families May 2009 U.S. Office of Personnel Management **2**

(**Adapted from OPM's** <u>Handbook of Occupational Groups and Families</u> <u>May 2009</u> publication. For a detailed listing and definitions of jobs, refer to the Handbook at **http://www.opm.gov/policy-data-oversight/ classification-qualifications/classifying-general-schedule-positions/ occupationalhandbook.pdf**)

APPENDIX 12

SMART MODEL OF ORGANIZATIONS

(Inspired by Richard Daft, 2013; Henry Mintzberg, 1979, 1981)

S - Senior Management

M – Middle Management

A - Administrative Support   R- Research/Development

T - Technical Core/Operations Management

APPENDIX 13

KEY DIVERSITY AND INCLUSION STATUTES AND EXECUTIVE ORDERS

1865   The U.S. Constitution, 13th Amendment - Abolished slavery; passed by Congress January 31, 1865 and ratified December 6, 1865

1919   The U.S. Constitution, 19th Amendment - Women's Rights to Vote; passed by Congress June 4, 19919 and ratified August 18, 1920

1935   Wagner Act - Union recognition and rights to organize in workplace; inclusion in private sector

1961   President John F Kennedy EO #10925; 1965 President Lyndon Johnson EO #11246 -

1962   President John F Kennedy Executive Order (EO) 10988 - Union recognition and rights in public workplace, inclusion

| 1963 | Affirmative Action promoting including minorities and women in hiring, admissions and contracts |
| | Equal Pay Act - Equal pay for equal work regardless of gender and race, gender inclusion |

1963   Affirmative Action promoting including minorities and women in hiring, admissions and contracts

      Equal Pay Act - Equal pay for equal work regardless of gender and race, gender inclusion

1964   Civil Rights Act - Amended 1972; Title VII: No discrimination based on race, color, religion, national origin or gender

1965   Executive Order (EO) 11246 - Active recruitment, retention of minorities, women, persons with disabilities, covered veterans in workplace and employment

1967   Age Discrimination in Employment Act - Amended 1978; No employment discrimination based on age, 40 years and older

1978   Pregnancy Discrimination Act - No employment/ workplace discrimination against pregnant women, childrearing and associated medical needs

1978   Mandatory Retirement Act - No force retirement of employees, except in selected occupations due to physical demands

1990   Americans with Disabilities Act - No discrimination against individuals with physical disabilities and chronic illness; instead provide reason accommodation

1991   Civil Rights Act - Employee's rights to sue for damages and liabilities

1993   Family and Medical Leave Act - Medical leave to take care of family members up to 12 weeks; unpaid leave

2008   Genetic Nondiscrimination Act - No discrimination based genetic information regarding disease, disorder, heredity

2010   Patient Protection and Affordable Care Act - Health insurance for millions of uninsured Americans and Americans with pre-existing condition

VOTE, BY RACE AND IDEOLOGY, IN MID-TERM ELECTIONS, NOVEMBER 4, 2014

Vote, by race -

Race	Total %	Democrats %	Republicans %	Others %
White	75	38	60	2
African Americans	12	89	10	1
Latino	8	63	35	2
Asians	2	50	49	1
Others	3	50	46	4

Vote, by ideology –

	%	%	%	%
Conservatives	37	13	85	2
Moderates	40	53	44	3
Liberals/Progressive	23	87	11	2

APPENDIX 15

FEDERAL GOVERNMENT WORKFORCE

http://www.opm.gov/policy-data-oversight/data-analysis-documentation/
federal-employment-reports/employment-trends-data/2012/december/
graphic-presentation-of-federal-civilian-employment/

Distribution of Federal Civilian Employment by Branch for December 2012

Executive Branch (97.7%) - 2,118,000

Judicial Branch (1.2%) - 33,772

Legislative Branch (1.1%) - 29,848

Executive Branch Non Postal Service = 2,118,000

Postal Service = 595,783

Executive Branch Total = 2,713,783

Total Employment= 2,777,403

Total Government Employment Since 2000 (numbers in thousands)

Year	Executive branch civilians (thousands)	Uniformed military personnel (thousands)	Legislative/ Judicial personnel (thousands)	Total Federal personnel (thousands)
2000 (1)	2,639	1,426	63	4,129
2001 (1)	2,640	1,428	64	4,132
2002	2,630	1,456	66	4,152
2003	2,666	1,478	65	4,210
2004	2,650	1,473	64	4,187
2005	2,636	1,436	65	4,138
2006	2,637	1,432	63	4,133
2007	2,636	1,427	63	4,127
2008	2,692	1,450	64	4,206
2009	2,774	1,591	66	4,430
2010 4 (1)	2,776	1,602	64	4,443
2011	2,756	1,583	64	4,403
2012	2,697	1,551	64	4,312

Notes: [1]Includes temporary employees for the decennial census.

http://www.opm.gov/policy-data-oversight/data-analysis-documentation/federal-employment-reports/historical-tables/total-government-employment-since-1962/

APPENDIX 16

QUICK FACTS: LAW AND ORDER PERSONNEL IN USA – 2012 STATS

(US Dept. of Labor, Bureau of Labor Statistics, http://www.bls.gov/ooh/, http://www.bls.gov/ooh/legal/home.htm)

Quick Facts: Police and Detectives

2012 Median Pay	$56,980 per year; $27.40 per hour
Entry-Level Education	High school diploma or equivalent
Work Experience in a Related Occupation	See How to Become One
On-the-job Training	See How to Become One
Number of Jobs, 2012	780,000
Job Outlook, 2012-22	5% (Slower than average)
Employment Change, 2012-22	41,400

Quick Facts: Judges and Hearing Officers

2012 Median Pay	$102,980 per year; $49.51 per hour
Entry-Level Education	Doctoral or professional degree
Work Experience in a Related Occupation	See How to Become One
On-the-job Training	Short-term on-the-job training
Number of Jobs, 2012	43,200
Job Outlook, 2012-22	1% (Little or no change)
Employment Change, 2012-22	400

Quick Facts: Correctional Officers

2012 Median Pay	$38,970 per year; $18.74 per hour
Entry-Level Education	High school diploma or equivalent
Work Experience in a Related Occupation	None
On-the-job Training	Moderate-term on-the-job training
Number of Jobs, 2012	469,500
Job Outlook, 2012-22	5% (Slower than average)
Employment Change, 2012-22	23,000

Quick Facts: Probation Officers and Correctional Treatment Specialists

2012 Median Pay	$48,190 per year; $23.17 per hour
Entry-Level Education	Bachelor's degree
Work Experience in a Related Occupation	None
On-the-job Training	Short-term on-the-job training
Number of Jobs, 2012	90,300
Job Outlook, 2012-22	-1% (Little or no change)
Employment Change, 2012-22	-900

Quick Facts: Lawyers

2012 Median Pay	$113,530 per year; $54.58 per hour
Entry-Level Education	Doctoral or professional degree
Work Experience in a Related Occupation	None
On-the-job Training	None
Number of Jobs, 2012	759,800
Job Outlook, 2012-22	10% (As fast as average)
Employment Change, 2012-22	74,800

Quick Facts: Paralegals and Legal Assistants

2012 Median Pay	$46,990 per year; $22.59 per hour
Entry-Level Education	Associate's degree
Work Experience in a Related Occupation	None
On-the-job Training	None
Number of Jobs, 2012	277,000
Job Outlook, 2012-22	17% (Faster than average)
Employment Change, 2012-22	46,200

Quick Facts: Arbitrators, Mediators, and Conciliators

2012 Median Pay	$61,280 per year; $29.46 per hour
Entry-Level Education	Bachelor's degree
Work Experience in a Related Occupation	Less than 5 years
On-the-job Training	Moderate-term on-the-job training
Number of Jobs, 2012	8,400
Job Outlook, 2012-22	10% (As fast as average)
Employment Change, 2012-22	900

Quick Facts: Court Reporters

2012 Median Pay	$48,160 per year; $23.15 per hour
Entry-Level Education	Postsecondary non-degree award
Work Experience in a Related Occupation	None
On-the-job Training	Short-term on-the-job training
Number of Jobs, 2012	21,200
Job Outlook, 2012-22	10% (As fast as average)
Employment Change, 2012-22	2,000

APPENDIX 17

ARRESTS STATS IN USA 2011 AND 2013

13,211,110 arrest in USA in 2010 http://www.bjs.gov/content/pub/pdf/aus9010.pdf

11, 302,102 arrests in USA in 2013 http://www.fbi.gov/stats-services/crimestats

Estimated Number of Arrests - United States, 2013

Murder and non-negligent manslaughter	10,231
Rape	16,863
Robbery	94,406
Aggravated assault	358,860
Burglary	252,629
Larceny-theft	1,231,580
Motor vehicle theft	64,566
Arson	10,509
Violent crime	480,360
Property crime	1,559,284
Other assaults	1,097,741
Forgery and counterfeiting	60,969

Fraud	143,528
Embezzlement	15,730
Stolen property; buying, receiving, possessing	92,691
Vandalism	201,168
Weapons; carrying, possessing, etc.	137,779
Prostitution and commercialized vice	48,620
Sex offenses (except rape and prostitution)	57,925
Drug abuse violations	1,501,043
Gambling	6,024
Offenses against the family and children	101,247
Driving under the influence	1,166,824
Liquor laws	354,872
Drunkenness	443,527
Disorderly conduct	467,993
Vagrancy	25,755
All other offenses	3,282,651
Suspicion	1,096
Curfew and loitering law violations	56,371
Total	**11,302,202**

APPENDIX 18

BANKRUPTCIES FILED IN US 2006–2012

(Administrative Office of the Courts, http://news.uscourts.gov/)
http://www.angelfire.com/stars4/lists/bankruptcies.html

Business and Non-Business Filings - 2006-2012

Year	Total	Non-Business	Business
2012	1,221,091	1,181,016	40,075
2011	1,410,653	1,362,847	47,806
2010	1,593,081	1,536,799	56,282
2009	1,473,675	1,412,838	60,837
2008	1,117,641	1,074,108	43,533
2007	850,912	822,590	28,322
2006	617,660	597,965	19,695

APPENDIX 19

AMERICA'S 20 MOST VISITED TOURIST DESTINATIONS

(http://www.travelandleisure.com/articles/
americas-most-visited-tourist-attractions/2)

<u>Destination</u>	<u>Annual Visitors</u>
1. Times Square, New York City	**41,900,000**
2. Central Park, New York City	**40,000,000**
3. **Union Station, Washington, D.C.**	**36,500,000**
4. **Las Vegas Strip, Las Vegas**, NV	**29,500,000**
5. **Grand Central Terminal, New York City**, NY	**21,600,000**
6. **Magic Kingdom /Walt Disney World, Buena Vista, FL**	**17,142,000**
7. **Disneyland, Anaheim, CA**	**16,140,000**
8. **(tie) Golden Gate Bridge, San Francisco**, CA	**15,000,000**
9. **(tie) Faneuil Hall Marketplace, Boston**, MA	**15,000,000**
10. (tie) Golden Gate Park, San Francisco, CA	**13,000,000**
11. **(tie) Balboa Park, San Diego**, CA	**13,000,000**
12. **Epcot/Walt Disney World, Buena Vista, FL**	**10,825,000**
13. Pike Place Market, Seattle, WA	**10,000,000**

14.	Disney's Animal Kingdom, Buena Vista, FL	9,783,000
15.	Disney's Hollywood Studios, Buena Vista, FL	9,699,000
16.	Great Smoky Mountains National Park, TN and NC	9,008,830
17.	(tie) South Street Seaport, New York City, NY	9,000,000
18.	(tie) Mackinac Bridge, Mackinaw City, MI	9,000,000
19.	Navy Pier, Chicago, IL	8,700,000
20.	Pier 39, San Francisco, CA	8,133,700

Total Visits to 20 Top Tourist Destinations: 342,931,530

APPENDIX 20

HEALTHCARE WORKFORCE IN USA AS OF 2012

(US Bureau of Labor Statistics, http://www.bls.gov/ooh/healthcare/)

Quick Facts: Athletic Trainers and Exercise Physiologists

2012 Median Pay	$42,690 per year; $20.52 per hour
Entry-Level Education	Bachelor's degree
Work Experience in a Related Occupation	None
On-the-job Training	None
Number of Jobs, 2012	28,900
Job Outlook, 2012-22	19% (Faster than average)
Employment Change, 2012-22	5,400

Quick Facts: Audiologists

2012 Median Pay	$69,720 per year; $33.52 per hour
Entry-Level Education	Doctoral or professional degree
Work Experience in a Related Occupation	None
On-the-job Training	None
Number of Jobs, 2012	13,000
Job Outlook, 2012-22	34% (Much faster than average)
Employment Change, 2012-22	4,300

Quick Facts: Chiropractors

2012 Median Pay	$66,160 per year; $31.81 per hour
Entry-Level Education	Doctoral or professional degree
Work Experience in a Related Occupation	None
On-the-job Training	None
Number of Jobs, 2012	44,400
Job Outlook, 2012-22	15% (Faster than average)
Employment Change, 2012-22	6,500

Quick Facts: Dental Assistants

2012 Median Pay	$34,500 per year; $16.59 per hour
Entry-Level Education	Postsecondary non-degree award
Work Experience in a Related Occupation	None
On-the-job Training	None
Number of Jobs, 2012	303,200
Job Outlook, 2012-22	25% (Much faster than average)
Employment Change, 2012-22	74,400

Quick Facts: Dental Hygienists

2012 Median Pay	$70,210 per year; $33.75 per hour
Entry-Level Education	Associate's degree
Work Experience in a Related Occupation	None
On-the-job Training	None
Number of Jobs, 2012	192,800
Job Outlook, 2012-22	33% (Much faster than average)
Employment Change, 2012-22	64,200

Quick Facts: Dentists

2012 Median Pay	$149,310 per year; $71.79 per hour
Entry-Level Education	Doctoral or professional degree
Work Experience in a Related Occupation	None
On-the-job Training	See How to Become One
Number of Jobs, 2012	146,800
Job Outlook, 2012-22	16% (Faster than average)
Employment Change, 2012-22	23,300

Quick Facts: Diagnostic Medical Sonographers and Cardiovascular Technologists and Technicians, Including Vascular Technologists

2012 Median Pay	$60,350 per year; $29.02 per hour
Entry-Level Education	Associate's degree
Work Experience in a Related Occupation	None
On-the-job Training	None
Number of Jobs, 2012	110,400
Job Outlook, 2012-22	39% (Much faster than average)
Employment Change, 2012-22	42,700

Quick Facts: Dietitians and Nutritionists

2012 Median Pay	$55,240 per year; $26.56 per hour
Entry-Level Education	Bachelor's degree
Work Experience in a Related Occupation	None
On-the-job Training	Internship/residency
Number of Jobs, 2012	67,400
Job Outlook, 2012-22	21% (Faster than average)
Employment Change, 2012-22	14,200

Quick Facts: EMTs and Paramedics

2012 Median Pay	$31,020 per year; $14.91 per hour
Entry-Level Education	Postsecondary non-degree award
Work Experience in a Related Occupation	None
On-the-job Training	None
Number of Jobs, 2012	239,100
Job Outlook, 2012-22	23% (Much faster than average)
Employment Change, 2012-22	55,300

Quick Facts: Genetic Counselors

2012 Median Pay	$56,800 per year; $27.31 per hour
Entry-Level Education	Master's degree
Work Experience in a Related Occupation	None
On-the-job Training	None
Number of Jobs, 2012	2,100
Job Outlook, 2012-22	41% (Much faster than average)
Employment Change, 2012-22	900

Quick Facts: Home Health Aides

2012 Median Pay	$20,820 per year; $10.01 per hour
Entry-Level Education	Less than high school
Work Experience in a Related Occupation	None
On-the-job Training	Short-term on-the-job training
Number of Jobs, 2012	875,100
Job Outlook, 2012-22	48% (Much faster than average)
Employment Change, 2012-22	24,200

Quick Facts: Licensed Practical and Licensed Vocational Nurses

2012 Median Pay	$41,540 per year; $19.97 per hour
Entry-Level Education	Postsecondary non-degree award
Work Experience in a Related Occupation	None
On-the-job Training	None
Number of Jobs, 2012	738,400
Job Outlook, 2012-22	25% (Much faster than average)
Employment Change, 2012-22	182,900

Quick Facts: Massage Therapists

2012 Median Pay	$35,970 per year; $17.29 per hour
Entry-Level Education	Postsecondary non-degree award
Work Experience in a Related Occupation	None
On-the-job Training	None
Number of Jobs, 2012	132,800
Job Outlook, 2012-22	23% (Much faster than average)
Employment Change, 2012-22	30,000

Quick Facts: Medical and Clinical Laboratory Technologists and Technicians

2012 Median Pay	$47,820 per year; $22.99 per hour
Entry-Level Education	See How to Become One
Work Experience in a Related Occupation	None
On-the-job Training	None
Number of Jobs, 2012	325,800
Job Outlook, 2012-22	22% (Much faster than average)
Employment Change, 2012-22	70,600

Quick Facts: Medical Assistants

2012 Median Pay	$29,370 per year; $14.12 per hour
Entry-Level Education	Postsecondary non-degree award
Work Experience in a Related Occupation	None
On-the-job Training	None
Number of Jobs, 2012	560,800
Job Outlook, 2012-22	29% (Much faster than average)
Employment Change, 2012-22	162,900

Quick Facts: Medical Records and Health Information Technicians

2012 Median Pay	$34,160 per year; $16.42 per hour
Entry-Level Education	Postsecondary non-degree award
Work Experience in a Related Occupation	None
On-the-job Training	None
Number of Jobs, 2012	186,300
Job Outlook, 2012-22	22% (Much faster than average)
Employment Change, 2012-22	41,100

Quick Facts: Medical Transcriptionists

2012 Median Pay	$34,020 per year; $16.36 per hour
Entry-Level Education	Postsecondary non-degree award
Work Experience in a Related Occupation	None
On-the-job Training	None
Number of Jobs, 2012	84,100
Job Outlook, 2012-22	8% (As fast as average)
Employment Change, 2012-22	6,400

Quick Facts: Nuclear Medicine Technologists

2012 Median Pay	$70,180 per year; $33.74 per hour
Entry-Level Education	Associate's degree
Work Experience in a Related Occupation	None
On-the-job Training	None
Number of Jobs, 2012	20,900
Job Outlook, 2012-22	20% (Faster than average)
Employment Change, 2012-22	4,200

Quick Facts: Nurse Anesthetists, Nurse Midwives, and Nurse Practitioners

2012 Median Pay	$96,460 per year; $46.37 per hour
Entry-Level Education	Master's degree
Work Experience in a Related Occupation	None
On-the-job Training	None
Number of Jobs, 2012	151,400
Job Outlook, 2012-22	31% (Much faster than average)
Employment Change, 2012-22	47,600

Quick Facts: Nursing Assistants and Orderlies

2012 Median Pay	$24,400 per year; $11.73 per hour
Entry-Level Education	See How to Become One
Work Experience in a Related Occupation	None
On-the-job Training	See How to Become One
Number of Jobs, 2012	1,534,400
Job Outlook, 2012-22	21% (Faster than average)
Employment Change, 2012-22	321,200

Quick Facts: Occupational Health and Safety Specialists

2012 Median Pay	$66,790 per year; $32.11 per hour
Entry-Level Education	Bachelor's degree
Work Experience in a Related Occupation	None
On-the-job Training	Short-term on-the-job training
Number of Jobs, 2012	62,900
Job Outlook, 2012-22	7% (Slower than average)
Employment Change, 2012-22	4,200

Quick Facts: Occupational Health and Safety Technicians

2012 Median Pay	$47,440 per year; $22.81 per hour
Entry-Level Education	High school diploma or equivalent
Work Experience in a Related Occupation	None
On-the-job Training	Moderate-term on-the-job training
Number of Jobs, 2012	12,600
Job Outlook, 2012-22	11% (As fast as average)
Employment Change, 2012-22	1,400

Quick Facts: Occupational Therapists

2012 Median Pay	$75,400 per year; $36.25 per hour
Entry-Level Education	Master's degree
Work Experience in a Related Occupation	None
On-the-job Training	None
Number of Jobs, 2012	113,200
Job Outlook, 2012-22	29% (Much faster than average)
Employment Change, 2012-22	32,800

Quick Facts: Occupational Therapy Assistants and Aides

2012 Median Pay	$48,940 per year; $23.53 per hour
Entry-Level Education	See How to Become One
Work Experience in a Related Occupation	None
On-the-job Training	See How to Become One
Number of Jobs, 2012	38,600
Job Outlook, 2012-22	41% (Much faster than average)
Employment Change, 2012-22	15,900

Quick Facts: Dispensing Opticians

2012 Median Pay	$33,330 per year; $16.03 per hour
Entry-Level Education	High school diploma or equivalent
Work Experience in a Related Occupation	None
On-the-job Training	Long-term on-the-job training
Number of Jobs, 2012	67,600
Job Outlook, 2012-22	23% (Much faster than average)
Employment Change, 2012-22	15,800

Quick Facts: Optometrists

2012 Median Pay	$97,820 per year; $47.03 per hour
Entry-Level Education	Doctoral or professional degree
Work Experience in a Related Occupation	None
On-the-job Training	None
Number of Jobs, 2012	33,100
Job Outlook, 2012-22	24% (Much faster than average)
Employment Change, 2012-22	8,100

Quick Facts: Orthotists and Prosthetists

2012 Median Pay	$62,670 per year; $30.13 per hour
Entry-Level Education	Master's degree
Work Experience in a Related Occupation	None
On-the-job Training	Internship/residency
Number of Jobs, 2012	8,500
Job Outlook, 2012-22	36% (Much faster than average)
Employment Change, 2012-22	3,000

Quick Facts: Personal Care Aides

2012 Median Pay	$19,910 per year; $9.57 per hour
Entry-Level Education	Less than high school
Work Experience in a Related Occupation	None
On-the-job Training	Short-term on-the-job training
Number of Jobs, 2012	1,190,600
Job Outlook, 2012-22	49% (Much faster than average)
Employment Change, 2012-22	580,800

Quick Facts: Pharmacists

2012 Median Pay	$116,670 per year; $56.09 per hour
Entry-Level Education	Doctoral or professional degree
Work Experience in a Related Occupation	None
On-the-job Training	None
Number of Jobs, 2012	286,400
Job Outlook, 2012-22	14% (As fast as average)
Employment Change, 2012-22	41,400

Quick Facts: Pharmacy Technicians

2012 Median Pay	$29,320 per year; $14.10 per hour
Entry-Level Education	High school diploma or equivalent
Work Experience in a Related Occupation	None
On-the-job Training	Moderate-term on-the-job training
Number of Jobs, 2012	355,300
Job Outlook, 2012-22	20% (Faster than average)
Employment Change, 2012-22	70,700

Quick Facts: Phlebotomists

2012 Median Pay	$29,730 per year; $14.29 per hour
Entry-Level Education	Postsecondary non-degree award
Work Experience in a Related Occupation	None
On-the-job Training	None
Number of Jobs, 2012	101,300
Job Outlook, 2012-22	27% (Much faster than average)
Employment Change, 2012-22	27,100

Quick Facts: Physical Therapist Assistants and Aides

2012 Median Pay	$39,430 per year; $18.96 per hour
Entry-Level Education	See How to Become One
Work Experience in a Related Occupation	None
On-the-job Training	See How to Become One
Number of Jobs, 2012	121,400
Job Outlook, 2012-22	41% (Much faster than average)
Employment Change, 2012-22	49,400

Quick Facts: Physical Therapists

2012 Median Pay	$79,860 per year; $38.39 per hour
Entry-Level Education	Doctoral or professional degree
Work Experience in a Related Occupation	None
On-the-job Training	None
Number of Jobs, 2012	204,200
Job Outlook, 2012-22	36% (Much faster than average)
Employment Change, 2012-22	73,500

Quick Facts: Physician Assistants

2012 Median Pay	$90,930 per year; $43.72 per hour
Entry-Level Education	Master's degree
Work Experience in a Related Occupation	None
On-the-job Training	None
Number of Jobs, 2012	86,700
Job Outlook, 2012-22	38% (Much faster than average)
Employment Change, 2012-22	33,300

Quick Facts: Physicians and Surgeons

2012 Median Pay	≥ $187,200 per year or $90.00 per hour.
Entry-Level Education	Doctoral or professional degree
Work Experience in a Related Occupation	None
On-the-job Training	Internship/residency
Number of Jobs, 2012	691,400
Job Outlook, 2012-22	18% (Faster than average)
Employment Change, 2012-22	123,300

Quick Facts: Podiatrists

2012 Median Pay	$116,440 per year; $55.98 per hour
Entry-Level Education	Doctoral or professional degree
Work Experience in a Related Occupation	None
On-the-job Training	Internship/residency
Number of Jobs, 2012	10,700
Job Outlook, 2012-22	23% (Much faster than average)
Employment Change, 2012-22	2,400

Quick Facts: Psychiatric Technicians and Aides

2012 Median Pay	$27,440 per year; $13.19 per hour
Entry-Level Education	See How to Become One
Work Experience in a Related Occupation	None
On-the-job Training	Short-term on-the-job training
Number of Jobs, 2012	153,000
Job Outlook, 2012-22	5% (Slower than average)
Employment Change, 2012-22	7,600

Quick Facts: Radiation Therapists

2012 Median Pay	$77,560 per year; $37.29 per hour
Entry-Level Education	Associate's degree
Work Experience in a Related Occupation	None
On-the-job Training	None
Number of Jobs, 2012	19,100
Job Outlook, 2012-22	24% (Much faster than average)
Employment Change, 2012-22	4,500

Quick Facts: Radiologic and MRI Technologists

2012 Median Pay	$55,910 per year; $26.88 per hour
Entry-Level Education	Associate's degree
Work Experience in a Related Occupation	See How to Become One
On-the-job Training	None
Number of Jobs, 2012	229,300
Job Outlook, 2012-22	21% (Faster than average)
Employment Change, 2012-22	48,600

Quick Facts: Recreational Therapists

2012 Median Pay	$42,280 per year; $20.33 per hour
Entry-Level Education	Bachelor's degree
Work Experience in a Related Occupation	None
On-the-job Training	None
Number of Jobs, 2012	19,800
Job Outlook, 2012-22	13% (As fast as average)
Employment Change, 2012-22	2,700

Quick Facts: Registered Nurses

2012 Median Pay	$65,470 per year; $31.48 per hour
Entry-Level Education	Associate's degree
Work Experience in a Related Occupation	None
On-the-job Training	None
Number of Jobs, 2012	2,711,500
Job Outlook, 2012-22	19% (Faster than average)
Employment Change, 2012-22	526,800

Quick Facts: Respiratory Therapists

2012 Median Pay	$55,870 per year; $26.86 per hour
Entry-Level Education	Associate's degree
Work Experience in a Related Occupation	None
On-the-job Training	None
Number of Jobs, 2012	119,300
Job Outlook, 2012-22	19% (Faster than average)
Employment Change, 2012-22	22,700

Quick Facts: Speech-Language Pathologists

2012 Median Pay	$69,870 per year; $33.59 per hour
Entry-Level Education	Master's degree
Work Experience in a Related Occupation	None
On-the-job Training	None
Number of Jobs, 2012	134,100
Job Outlook, 2012-22	19% (Faster than average)
Employment Change, 2012-22	26,000

Quick Facts: Surgical Technologists

2012 Median Pay	$41,790 per year; $20.09 per hour
Entry-Level Education	Postsecondary non-degree award
Work Experience in a Related Occupation	None
On-the-job Training	None
Number of Jobs, 2012	98,500
Job Outlook, 2012-22	30% (Much faster than average)
Employment Change, 2012-22	29,300

Quick Facts: Veterinarians

2012 Median Pay	$84,460 per year; $40.61 per hour
Entry-Level Education	Doctoral or professional degree
Work Experience in a Related Occupation	None
On-the-job Training	None
Number of Jobs, 2012	70,300
Job Outlook, 2012-22	12% (As fast as average)
Employment Change, 2012-22	8,400

Quick Facts: Veterinary Assistants and Laboratory Animal Caretakers

2012 Median Pay	$23,130 per year; $11.12 per hour
Entry-Level Education	High school diploma or equivalent
Work Experience in a Related Occupation	None
On-the-job Training	Short-term on-the-job training
Number of Jobs, 2012	74,600
Job Outlook, 2012-22	10% (As fast as average)
Employment Change, 2012-22	7,100

Quick Facts: Veterinary Technologists and Technicians

2012 Median Pay	$30,290 per year; $14.56 per hour
Entry-Level Education	Associate's degree
Work Experience in a Related Occupation	None
On-the-job Training	None
Number of Jobs, 2012	84,800
Job Outlook, 2012-22	30% (Much faster than average)
Employment Change, 2012-22	25,000

APPENDIX 21

LEISURE, RECREATION, SPORTS AND ENTERTAINMENT WORKFORCE IN USA

(US Bureau of Labor Statistics, http://www.bls.gov/ooh/)

Quick Facts: Lodging Managers

2012 Median Pay	$46,810 per year; $22.50 per hour
Entry-Level Education	High school diploma or equivalent
Work Experience in a Related Occupation	Less than 5 years
On-the-job Training	None
Number of Jobs, 2012	50,400
Job Outlook, 2012-22	1% (Little or no change)
Employment Change, 2012-22	700

Quick Facts: Recreation Workers

2012 Median Pay	$22,240 per year; $10.69 per hour
Entry-Level Education	Bachelor's degree
Work Experience in a Related Occupation	None
On-the-job Training	None
Number of Jobs, 2012	345,400
Job Outlook, 2012-22	14% (As fast as average)
Employment Change, 2012-22	49,000

Quick Facts: Athletic Trainers and Exercise Physiologists

2012 Median Pay	$42,690 per year; $20.52 per hour
Entry-Level Education	Bachelor's degree
Work Experience in a Related Occupation	None
On-the-job Training	None
Number of Jobs, 2012	28,900
Job Outlook, 2012-22	19% (Faster than average)
Employment Change, 2012-22	5,400

Quick Facts: Fitness Trainers and Instructors

2012 Median Pay	$31,720 per year; $15.25 per hour
Entry-Level Education	High school diploma or equivalent
Work Experience in a Related Occupation	None
On-the-job Training	Short-term on-the-job training
Number of Jobs, 2012	267,000
Job Outlook, 2012-22	13% (As fast as average)
Employment Change, 2012-22	33,500

Quick Facts: Fitness Trainers and Instructors

2012 Median Pay	$31,720 per year; $15.25 per hour
Entry-Level Education	High school diploma or equivalent
Work Experience in a Related Occupation	None
On-the-job Training	Short-term on-the-job training
Number of Jobs, 2012	267,000
Job Outlook, 2012-22	13% (As fast as average)
Employment Change, 2012-22	33,500

Quick Facts: Meeting, Convention, and Event Planners

2012 Median Pay	$45,810 per year; $22.02 per hour
Entry-Level Education	Bachelor's degree
Work Experience in a Related Occupation	None
On-the-job Training	None
Number of Jobs, 2012	94,200
Job Outlook, 2012-22	33% (Much faster than average)
Employment Change, 2012-22	31,300

Quick Facts: Actors

2012 Median Pay	$20.26 per hour
Entry-Level Education	Some college, no degree
Work Experience in a Related Occupation	None
On-the-job Training	Long-term on-the-job training
Number of Jobs, 2012	79,800
Job Outlook, 2012-22	4% (Slower than average)
Employment Change, 2012-22	3,300

Quick Facts: Athletes and Sports Competitors

2012 Median Pay	$40,060 per year
Entry-Level Education	High school diploma or equivalent
Work Experience in a Related Occupation	None
On-the-job Training	Long-term on-the-job training
Number of Jobs, 2012	14,900
Job Outlook, 2012-22	7% (Slower than average)
Employment Change, 2012-22	1,000

Quick Facts: Coaches and Scouts

2012 Median Pay	$28,360 per year
Entry-Level Education	Bachelor's degree
Work Experience in a Related Occupation	None
On-the-job Training	None
Number of Jobs, 2012	243,900
Job Outlook, 2012-22	15% (Faster than average)
Employment Change, 2012-22	36,200

Quick Facts: Dancers and Choreographers

2012 Median Pay	$15.87 per hour
Entry-Level Education	High school diploma or equivalent
Work Experience in a Related Occupation	See How to Become One
On-the-job Training	Long-term on-the-job training
Number of Jobs, 2012	25,800
Job Outlook, 2012-22	13% (As fast as average)
Employment Change, 2012-22	3,400

Quick Facts: Musicians and Singers

2012 Median Pay	$23.50 per hour
Entry-Level Education	High school diploma or equivalent
Work Experience in a Related Occupation	None
On-the-job Training	Long-term on-the-job training
Number of Jobs, 2012	167,400
Job Outlook, 2012-22	5% (Slower than average)
Employment Change, 2012-22	8,700

Quick Facts: Producers and Directors

2012 Median Pay	$71,350 per year; $34.31 per hour
Entry-Level Education	Bachelor's degree
Work Experience in a Related Occupation	Less than 5 years
On-the-job Training	None
Number of Jobs, 2012	103,500
Job Outlook, 2012-22	3% (Slower than average)
Employment Change, 2012-22	2,900

Quick Facts: Umpires, Referees, and Other Sports Officials

2012 Median Pay	$23,290 per year
Entry-Level Education	High school diploma or equivalent
Work Experience in a Related Occupation	None
On-the-job Training	Moderate-term on-the-job training
Number of Jobs, 2012	17,500
Job Outlook, 2012-22	8% (As fast as average)
Employment Change, 2012-22	1,300

Quick Facts: Broadcast and Sound Engineering Technicians

2012 Median Pay	$41,200 per year; $19.81 per hour
Entry-Level Education	See How to Become One
Work Experience in a Related Occupation	None
On-the-job Training	Short-term on-the-job training
Number of Jobs, 2012	121,400
Job Outlook, 2012-22	9% (As fast as average)
Employment Change, 2012-22	10,600

Links:

http://www.bls.gov/ooh/

http://www.bls.gov/ooh/management/lodging-managers.htm#TB_inline?height=325&width=325&inlineId=qf-wage

http://www.bls.gov/ooh/personal-care-and-service/recreation-workers.htm

http://www.bls.gov/ooh/business-and-financial/meeting-convention-and-event-planners.htm

http://www.bls.gov/ooh/entertainment-and-sports/

http://www.bls.gov/ooh/media-and-communication/print/broadcast-and-sound-engineering-technicians.htm

APPENDIX 22

USA 2014 GROSS DOMESTIC PRODUCT (BUREAU OF ECONOMIC ANALYSIS)

(Table 1.1.5, http://www.bea.gov/iTable/iTable.
cfm?ReqID=9&step=1#reqid=9&step=1&isuri=1)

[Millions of dollars] Seasonally adjusted at annual
rates - Revised on: February 27, 2015

		2014 Q1	2014 Q2	2014 Q3	2014 Q4
1.	**Gross domestic product**	**17,043,989**	**17,328,241**	**17,599,753**	**17,701,267**
2.	**Personal consumption expenditure**	**11,728,451**	**11,870,703**	**12,001,960**	**12,113,212**
3.	Goods	3,890,605	3,964,522	4,011,536	4,006,123
4.	Durable goods	1,262,254	1,298,415	1,320,225	1,328,750
5.	Nondurable goods	2,628,351	2,666,107	2,691,311	2,677,373
6.	Services	7,837,846	7,906,181	7,990,424	8,107,089

7.	**Gross private domestic Investment**	**2,714,401**	**2,843,632**	**2,905,060**	**2,952,098**

8.	Fixed investment	2,674,291	2,743,369	2,810,610	2,849,586
9.	Nonresidential	2,134,558	2,191,175	2,244,251	2,272,245
10.	Structures	487,892	504,378	513,344	521,082
11.	Equipment	979,470	1,008,635	1,038,162	1,043,230
12.	Intellectual properties Products	667,196	678,162	692,745	707,933
13.	Residential	539,733	552,194	566,359	577,341
14.	Change in private Inventories	40,110	100,263	94,450	102,512
15.	**Net exports of goods and Services**	**-537,968**	**-549,219**	**-516,536**	**-555,606**
16.	Exports	2,284,709	2,344,327	2,366,473	2,344,962
17.	Goods	1,575,255	1,623,264	1,645,039	1,614,680
18.	Services	709,454	721,063	721,434	730,282
19.	Imports	2,822,677	2,893,546	2,883,009	2,900,568
20.	Goods	2,341,479	2,405,622	2,393,699	2,404,568
21.	Services	481,198	487,924	489,310	496,000
22.	**Government consumption expenditures and gross investment**	**3,139,105**	**3,163,125**	**3,209,269**	**3,191,563**
23.	Federal	1,208,132	1,210,488	1,241,292	1,216,324
24.	National defense	749,896	754,624	784,036	757,148
25.	Nondefense	458,236	455,864	457,256	459,176
26.	State and Local	1,930,973	1,952,637	1,967,977	1,975,239

Printed in the United States
By Bookmasters